FREEZE FRESH MEAL PREP

FREEZE FRESH MEAL PREP

160 MEAL STARTERS
and Make-Ahead Dishes for the Freezer

CRYSTAL SCHMIDT

Storey Publishing

The mission of Storey Publishing is to serve our customers by publishing practical information that encourages personal independence in harmony with the environment.

EDITED BY Carleen Madigan and Sarah Guare Slattery
ART DIRECTION BY Carolyn Eckert
BOOK DESIGN BY Erin Dawson
TEXT PRODUCTION BY Jennifer Jepson Smith

COVER PHOTOGRAPHY BY
© Crystal L. Schmidt, back
© Ryan Dyer, front, IFC, IBC
INTERIOR PHOTOGRAPHY BY
© Crystal L. Schmidt, 8, 19, 25, 33, 36, 39, 41, 43, 44, 47, 49, 51, 53, 54, 57, 63, 65, 66, 69, 71, 73, 75, 77, 79, 80, 86, 88–102, 105, 107, 108, 115, 117, 119, 120, 125, 127, 131, 133, 135, 137, 143–153, 156, 159–162, 165, 168–172, 178, 181–198, 204–206, 209–216, 219–223, 231–234, 237–245, 258–262, 265–274, 277–291, 299–306, 309–312
© Ryan Dyer, 1–6, 10, 15–17, 20–24, 26–31, 58–62, 82–84, 110–113, 138–142, 174–177, 200–203, 224–226, 229, 252–257, 292–294, 297, 320
Food styling of Ryan Dyer's photographs by Madeline Fitzgerald

Storey Publishing
210 MASS MoCA Way
North Adams, MA 01247
storey.com

Storey Publishing is an imprint of Workman Publishing, a division of Hachette Book Group, Inc., 1290 Avenue of the Americas, New York, NY 10104. The Storey Publishing name and logo are registered trademarks of Hachette Book Group, Inc.

ISBNs: 978-1-63586-843-2 (paperback);
978-1-63586-844-9 (ebook)

Printed in China by R. R. Donnelley on paper from responsible sources
10 9 8 7 6 5 4 3 2 1

APS

Library of Congress Cataloging-in-Publication Data on file

CONTENTS

Welcome

I thought I knew a lot about freezing produce when I wrote my first book, *Freeze Fresh*. And I did: Freezing has always been my preferred way to put up fruits and veggies. It was through developing that guidebook—testing countless freezer recipes and eating a tremendous amount of extraordinary frozen food—that I realized we had only scratched the surface. And hearing all your wonderful feedback gave me the confidence to expand the boundaries of how produce could be frozen.

This isn't your typical "freezer meals" book. The focus of these recipes is on freezing what's in season and available now, with an eye to having prepared or partially prepared dishes for later. It's right at the intersection of where preserving meets convenience food! This is a sweet spot for me as a gardener and lover of fresh foods. Being able to grab something homemade from the freezer and turn it into a quick and tasty dinner feels like having a treasure chest full of gold.

In this book you'll find recipes for prepared baked goods, soups, sauces, vegetable side dishes, cooked fruits, pie fillings, jams, and frozen treats. You'll also find recipes for "starters," which is one of my most beloved categories to freeze. A starter is typically the vegetable and herb portion of a recipe cooked together and frozen. There are soup starters, meal starters, and even dip starters! It's a way to preserve the fresh ingredients you have now but not take up more freezer space than necessary. Making the dish is as simple as thawing the starter and adding pantry staples or refrigerated ingredients to complete it. It's the ultimate meal prep and the perfect balance of home-cooked and convenient!

Whether you grow the fruits and vegetables yourself or get them from a local farm, farmers' market, or grocery store, you'll be able to take advantage of seasonality while freezing an amazing selection of diverse foods that help you get dinner on the table with little effort.

The thing about food, though, is that it's personal. We all have different likes, different produce in season where we live, and different regional dishes, familial dishes, and cultural dishes we want to make. So besides providing a cookbook with lots of recipes to glean inspiration from, my goal is to teach you the ins and outs of freezing the foods *you* love to eat. I want you to be able to understand what works in the freezer and why, and to adapt your favorite meals to the freezer successfully.

As a reminder, when freezing it's important to manage your expectations. Frozen food is remarkably good when done right, but it's not the same as fresh. Although freezing is an exceptional preservation tool, most fruits and vegetables will change in the freezer, and it's helpful to recognize this. What we can do is be smart about what we freeze and learn to use frozen food in ways that highlight its best qualities.

There is a lot of satisfaction in taking beautiful produce and transforming it into fresh frozen meals that your family enjoys. I hope the ideas in this book inspire you and serve as a jumping-off point for you to try freezing foods in new ways!

Crystal

PRESERVING AT A GLANCE FROM A TO Z

STRAWBERRIES

SWEET POTATOES

TOMATILLOS

TOMATOES

WINTER SQUASH & PUMPKIN

ZUCCHINI & OTHER SUMMER SQUASHES

FREEZING BASICS & BEST PRACTICES

Successful freezing is all in the details! While freezing fruits and vegetables is certainly not difficult, following these trusted techniques will ensure your frozen produce turns out exceptional. The quality of your food can be impacted by things like how quickly the food is cooled, what container it's stored in, and even how the food is thawed.

Cool It!

It's a universal rule that cooked or heated food will need to be cooled to room temperature before being frozen, no matter what it is. Putting warm food in the freezer is not only bad for the food's quality, but it will raise the temperature inside the freezer and affect the surrounding items.

Good-quality freezer containers help prevent freezer burn and increase the shelf life of your frozen foods.

In some cases the dish might even benefit from chilling in the refrigerator overnight to allow the flavors to meld. You know how soup or chili often tastes better the day after it was made? This is the same for many types of blended sauces and salsas, too.

Dishes that are raw, like Shredded Beet Salad (page 146), should be frozen immediately after being made (unless the recipe states otherwise).

Freezer Containers

The type of freezer container you choose makes all the difference in how long food keeps and how it tastes once thawed. Use containers designed for freezing, like thick freezer bags or rigid plastic freezer containers. The importance of having the right tool for the job is one of those life lessons I learn over and over. It's true for so many things, including freezer containers! They're a critical preserving tool.

Plastic freezer bags are best for holding foods that are bulky, like Parmesan Ranch Green Beans & Broccoli (page 148) or Almond Cookie Crumble Baked Peaches (page 190). Large pieces of food will have air space between them, but luckily most of that air can easily be squished out of a bag. One thing I appreciate about freezer bags is that you can overstuff them; you can fit more in a quart-size freezer bag than in a quart-size rigid container. You get what you pay for with freezer bags, so I prefer a quality brand like Ziploc.

Rigid containers are ideal for foods that will go from the freezer to the fridge and, once thawed, may be used multiple times over the span of a week, like

Blueberry Lemon Jam (page 205). I prefer rigid containers for thicker sauces or foods frozen in smaller quantities so that I don't lose any of the product sticking to the inside of the bag. Dishes with small soft pieces that can pack together without air gaps, like Coconut Cauliflower Rice (page 155), will also freeze well in rigid containers. My favorite brand is Reditainer Extreme Freeze. These containers are affordable, reusable for years, and available in 1-cup, 1½-cup, 2-cup, and 4-cup sizes.

If freezing in glass, choose brands that are freezer-safe, and use straight-sided jars without shoulders. Make sure to leave headspace at the top for expansion, and chill the food and jar in the refrigerator before freezing. Even if you do everything perfectly, glass containers can still crack in the freezer. I use glass for jams and for oil-based sauces like pesto that I like to freeze in small quantities. Personally, I don't use glass for freezing many other things.

REMOVING AIR

Say it with me now: "Air is the enemy of frozen food!" Exposure to oxygen will degrade the quality of frozen food over time, so it's important to remove as much air from your containers as possible. This will keep the food tasting just as fresh as the day it was frozen.

Plastic Freezer Bags

For recipes that are saucy or have a lot of liquid, start by turning the very top of the bag inside out, so that food doesn't get in the seal. Set the bag in a large cup to help stabilize it, or enlist a helper to hold it. Fill the bag, then turn the top of the bag right-side out again. With the bag standing up, close the seal all the way, except for the very corner. Use your hands to slowly push the liquid in the bag upward toward the

Don't spill! To fill freezer bags with liquids or saucy recipes, turn the top of the bag inside out and place it in a large cup to prop it up.

seal (but not into the seal!), which will push out any air. Once the liquid is near the top of the bag, quickly close the seal the rest of the way.

For freezing food that isn't saucy or messy, the process is much easier. Disperse the food so that the entire bag has a uniform thickness. Set the bag flat on the counter and close the seal all the way, except for the very corner. Use your hand to push air out of the bag and quickly close the seal the rest of the way.

Rigid Containers

Rigid containers should be filled to the top, with only a small amount of headspace left for expansion. A container that is only half full of food is half full of air, and it will get freezer burn much quicker than a completely full container. I keep a variety of sizes on hand so I can always choose the one that fits best.

LABELING

I label my frozen goods with the date and contents—that's a given. Some of the recipes in this book require a cooking step after the frozen portion is thawed, which is a helpful fact to indicate on the package. I like to note if the recipe is a "starter" or "complete" recipe so that there's no confusion with what to do once it's thawed. For these freeze-now-and-finish-later recipes, I recommend including the book's page number as well. This way you'll know right where to go when you want to complete the dish.

When using freezer bags, I write directly on the bag with a permanent marker. For containers I prefer good old masking tape. A name-brand masking tape like Scotch sticks better in the freezer than generic; blue painter's tape works as well.

What Quantity to Freeze In

Most frozen foods will be at their best quality immediately after being thawed, so it's best to freeze in whatever quantity your family will use for one meal. Recipes like meal starters, baked fruits, and vegetable side dishes can be adapted to your household size.

Acidic sauces, like Sweet Pepper Relish (page 92), will keep a week or more in the refrigerator once thawed. We often use these types of foods over multiple meals, which I take into consideration when choosing a container size.

Sweet condiments, like jam, will keep for up to a month. I freeze these in 8-ounce jars since that's what my family will use before the food goes bad.

PREVENTING FREEZER BURN

I think we've all felt the disappointment of pulling a container of food out of the freezer to find it discolored, dried out, and smelling a little funky. Freezer burn happens when food is damaged by dehydration and oxidation; the food is still safe to eat, but it won't taste good.

To prevent this, use proper packaging and be mindful to remove air from your containers. Use a dedicated freezer, which is colder than the freezer attached to your fridge. This is notably important for anything that will be stored longer than a month. Don't open the door more than you need to, and be as quick as you can when looking for things. Freezer burn is more likely to happen the longer an item is stored, so rotate your inventory and use older foods first.

Fully cooked dishes, like prepared soups, will keep with good quality for several days in the refrigerator. I like to package these in single-serving portions, since they're often a quick grab-and-go lunch item for me.

Baked goods like muffins, pancakes, tortillas, and breakfast sandwiches can be frozen individually or together in larger quantities. Loaf cakes are something you'll undoubtedly find in my freezer, but with a household size of two, we can never finish a full one. I've started freezing them in halves, which works well for us.

Small quantities, or recipes that only one person likes (that's anything with beets in my house!), work well in molds like silicone muffin pans and plastic ice cube trays. My favorite brand of silicone mold is Souper Cubes. To freeze in molds, follow the recipe prep instructions, fill the mold, and place it in the freezer until completely frozen. To store, pop out the frozen blocks and transfer them to a freezer bag.

Keep in mind that food frozen in small blocks and stored loosely in a freezer bag won't keep quite as long. It's that pesky air again. There's more surface area and more airflow around these smaller portions than there is around food packaged tightly in a freezer bag or rigid container.

Flash freeze fruit for blending up into sorbet or ice pops that have a creamy texture.

Flash Freezing

For the home preserver, flash freezing is the technique of freezing individual pieces of food separately, rather than packing fresh food together in a container and then freezing it. Flash-frozen food won't be stuck together in a clump, so it's easier to use in small quantities. I use this technique for foods that I might want an individual serving of, like Onion Cheddar Hash Brown Casserole Squares (page 164), and when freezing fruit for making sorbet or ice pops.

To flash freeze, put the prepared items on a parchment paper–lined pan with the pieces barely touching or not touching at all. Place the entire pan in the freezer until the food is completely frozen, at least 4 hours or up to overnight. Remove the food from the pan and pack it into freezer containers for storage. In most cases, flash-frozen foods will pack best in freezer bags.

Thawing Prepared Foods

According to the USDA, there are three safe ways to thaw frozen foods: in the refrigerator, in a bowl of cold water, or in the microwave.

Option 1: In the refrigerator. Thawing food overnight in the refrigerator is usually my preferred method. Make sure to place the frozen containers on a tray or in a bowl to catch condensation and leaks. Even better, unpackage items in freezer bags while they're still frozen. Peel away the bag and place the frozen block of food in a container to thaw. This works well for saucy dishes, as thawed sauce likes to stick to the inside of the bag.

It takes a teeny bit of planning ahead, but thawing in the refrigerator gives the best quality. I've gotten into a good rhythm of consulting my weekly meal plan in the evening and taking out what I need for the next day. If I forget, there are always the faster-thaw methods to fall back on.

Option 2: In a bowl of cold water. To thaw prepared foods with cold water, place the bag or container in a bowl of very cold tap water, and change the water every 30 minutes until the dish is just thawed. Use the food immediately after thawing.

Option 3: In the microwave. If you need to thaw something *right now*, microwave it on 50 percent power, or use the defrost setting to heat it gently without overcooking. Heat until the food is just thawed and still has a few ice crystals left. Not every food will thaw well in this manner, and foods thawed with heat should be used immediately. This is typically my last resort, and I only use this technique when I'm in a true hurry.

Foods that are meant to be eaten cold or raw, or foods frozen in glass, should not be thawed in a microwave or with any form of heat.

Remove the plastic freezer bag while the food is still frozen. This prevents saucy items like pie filling or marinara sauce from sticking to the inside of the bag.

HELPFUL TOOLS, SUPPLIES & INGREDIENTS

A well-supplied kitchen makes a big difference in the ease and enjoyment of putting up food! The following items are very helpful for freezing and are frequently used in my kitchen.

Kitchen Tools

Blender. I rely heavily on my blender when preserving, especially for puréeing sauces. An immersion blender can also be used, but in most cases I prefer a countertop model because it's more powerful.

Fine-mesh sieve. A metal mesh sieve is useful for tasks such as removing seeds from raspberry purée or straining the mint leaves for making Herbal Mint Chip Ice Cream (page 300).

Sheet pans and baking pans. While many of the recipes in this book can be adapted to whatever size rimmed sheet pans or baking pans you have, there are a few that require a specific size to get the recipe just right, and it's necessary to use the correct size.

Sharp knives. Having a good, sharp knife makes all the difference when you are prepping a lot of fruits and veggies. A dull knife not only makes cooking feel like a chore, but it can tear and bruise produce, which will affect its quality.

Tape measure or ruler. It helps to keep a small tape measure handy in the kitchen. For most recipes the dicing or chopping size has a little wiggle room, but for some the size is specific and being accurate is important.

Ingredients & Consumable Supplies

All-purpose and gluten-free flours. These recipes were developed using organic all-purpose flour or a gluten-free flour blend. If using gluten-free, it's important to select a blend that is made to be used as a 1:1 substitute for all-purpose flour. My preferred brands are Pamela's Gluten-Free 1:1 All-Purpose Flour and Bob's Red Mill Gluten-Free 1-to-1 Baking Flour.

Avocado oil. For baking I prefer avocado oil for its clean flavor, but you can substitute any other neutral-tasting vegetable oil for the baking recipes in this book.

Baking cups. I like using baking cups for muffins intended for the freezer because it gives them an extra layer of protection against freezer burn. I greatly prefer the If You Care brand liners because baked goods don't stick to them, unlike more traditional paper liners.

Butter. You'll only find salted butter in my kitchen because it's the most universal. I used salted butter to test and develop these recipes, but you can adapt them to use unsalted if that's what you have.

Extra-virgin olive oil. I use this oil in most of my cooking because it's healthy and I like the flavor it adds. You can substitute avocado oil or another neutral-tasting oil if you need to.

Lemon and lime juice. Citrus juice is used for flavor and not for food safety in freezing recipes. Freshly squeezed is suggested in recipes where the flavor is important, but fresh or bottled works for recipes where it's the acidity that is needed.

Parchment paper. Parchment paper prevents food from adhering to the pan when roasting or flash freezing, and it prevents loaf cakes from sticking to the bottom of the pan.

Sea salt. I prefer the delicate flavor and the extra dose of minerals that come from using sea salt instead of iodized table salt or kosher salt. Salt is for taste and is not an integral part of preservation by freezing, so feel free to adjust the seasoning to your preference.

RECIPE NOTES

Doubling and tripling recipes. To maximize this book's usefulness for those who want to preserve larger batches or make multiple batches, I've indicated which recipes are suitable for doubling or tripling. Make sure to consider pot or pan size and cooking times when doubling. Since the recipes are written for single batches, follow the recipe cues, like "cook until tender," instead of the cooking times when increasing the batch size.

Recipe format. There are many different types of recipes in this book and several different formats to go along with them. Some recipes are straightforward—once the dish is thawed, you'll intuitively know how to use it, like jam or prepared soup. Other recipes include a simple heating or serving suggestion in case you need it, like for vegetable side dishes or pie fillings. Recipes that require more guidance to get just right, like those that include freezing a starter and then thawing it to finish the dish, have more detailed instructions so that you know exactly how to prepare them.

Making recipes gluten-free. For my gluten-free friends, you'll find that most of the recipes in this book that call for all-purpose flour can be made with a "cup for cup" gluten-free flour blend. This is indicated in the recipe ingredient list. There are only a few recipes that don't turn out well gluten-free, and those do *not* have a gluten-free flour option in the ingredient list. I follow a mostly gluten-free diet myself, so I have tested all the recipes with gluten-free flour. When working with gluten-free flour, make sure to fluff up the flour with a spoon and then spoon it into the measuring cup to get the most accurate measurement.

GIFTING FROZEN MEALS

Frozen meals are particularly well suited for gifting to others. Bringing someone a meal doesn't just feed them; it shows them that you care. Whether it's an elderly family member, a friend with a new baby, or someone dealing with a hard life moment, a homemade meal is a warm way to say, "I'm thinking of you."

Gifting a frozen meal instead of a fresh one provides a lot of flexibility and allows the recipient to prepare it whenever they need. It still only requires minimal effort, but they aren't obligated to eat it immediately. The meal can be thawed and made right away, saved for a later time when it may be more helpful, or eaten when that particular meal sounds more appetizing.

Or consider planning ahead for your own needs! Prepping and freezing meals and meal starters can be profoundly helpful for postpartum recovery, a scheduled surgery, or a busy season of life.

Frozen homemade soup is a perfect meal for gifting. Because it's frozen, the recipient can thaw and heat it whenever it's most useful or most appetizing to them.

Tips for Gifting Frozen Meals

Find out their preferences. If you don't know the recipient's food preferences, ask them about food allergies and if there are any meals or foods they don't care for. This ensures you bring something they'll enjoy. Pick recipes that are simple and straightforward to prepare once thawed. The goal is to provide a meal that doesn't take much thought or energy.

Make it a well-balanced meal. Aim for a protein, starch, and vegetable. This can be a welcome deviation from the pasta-centered dishes and casseroles that are commonly gifted. Because this book focuses on fruits and vegetables, coupling these recipes with a frozen cooked meat of your choosing will provide a complete meal. (By the way, cooked meats of all types freeze very well.)

For a hearty breakfast, I would combine Sweet Potato, Apple & Bacon Hash (page 171) and Green Smoothie Muffins (page 275) with cooked breakfast sausage links or patties. For a filling dinner, try Savory Seasoned Broccoli (page 147) and Onion Cheddar Hash Brown Casserole Squares (page 164) with a slow-cooked shredded beef roast.

Frozen baked goods, like a loaf of Fresh Peach Streusel Bread (page 280), make a lovely gift.

A prepared frozen soup, like Hamburger & Tater Soup (page 68) or Swiss Chard & Lentil Soup (page 76), is also perfect for gifting. It feels like giving a warm hug, and it travels easily. Pair it with a loaf of good crusty bread and butter, homemade biscuits, or garlic bread.

Don't choose dishes that require additional refrigerated ingredients. But do consider add-on items that can be held in the freezer or pantry and will support the meal. For example, I might pair Smothered Green Beans (page 160) and Cinnamon Breakfast Apples (page 179) with slow cooker pulled pork. Providing hamburger buns, which can be frozen, and a bottle of barbecue sauce, which can sit in the pantry, will complete the meal.

Include the heating instructions. Remember to write any prep or heating instructions on the package, and keep them brief but complete. Also include instructions if the item is meant to be eaten cold, just so there's no confusion. I prefer masking tape and black permanent marker for this because they hold up well in the freezer.

Consider a special treat instead of a meal. A frozen loaf of Fresh Peach Streusel Bread (page 280) or a package of ready-to-bake Sweet Cherry Almond Scone Dough (page 272) will also bring joy and comfort.

CHAPTER 1

SOUP STARTERS

A soup starter is simply the vegetable and herb portion of a soup, cooked together and frozen. It's a space-saving way to preserve seasonal ingredients while ensuring that everyone's beloved comfort food is almost ready to go! To make a nourishing soup, just thaw the starter and add broth, cooked protein, and pantry staples like beans, rice, or noodles to complete it.

From Starter to Soup

Naturally, soup is cooked until all the ingredients are tender, which means that soup starters freeze very well. The expectation is already set that the veggies will be soft, so their texture doesn't suffer in the freezer. Because the veggie portion is already cooked, the soup heats quickly but tastes like it's been simmering away all day.

A soup starter can be as simple or as elaborate as you want it to be, depending on the produce you have available. Most of the soup starters in this chapter include all the vegetables that the soup calls for. For example, the starter for Zucchini Corn Chowder (page 55) combines fresh onion, jalapeño, garlic, sweet corn, zucchini, potatoes, herbs, and spices. To make the soup, you combine the thawed starter with broth and cream, heat, and serve. Homemade soup in less than 10 minutes!

In Cabbage & Vegetable Soup (page 32), the starter combines fresh cabbage and tomatoes, and that's it. These are two veggies I constantly find myself needing to preserve, and throwing them together takes very little effort during the busy season. When it comes time to make the soup, I start with fresh onion, celery, and carrots. The frozen starter with cabbage and tomatoes, along with broth and a few pantry ingredients, completes the soup. Even though this starter only contains two ingredients and the finished soup takes a little more work to make, it's still incredibly useful.

Crafting Your Own Soup Starter

I'm convinced that you can turn just about any soup into a soup starter. Soups that are vegetable-heavy or puréed are the best candidates. From French Onion Soup (page 40) to Quick & Easy Oven-Roasted Chili Base (page 46), you'll find a lot of veggie-loaded recipes in this chapter.

Soups that are thickened with a significant amount of flour or contain a lot of dairy may be more difficult to make a starter for, though not impossible. Sausage, Potato & Kale Soup (page 38) is a lightly creamy soup that this method works well for. The onions, potatoes, and kale are frozen together, and the cream and Parmesan cheese are added when the soup is put together and heated for serving.

Most great soups start by sautéing onions, celery, and garlic in olive oil or butter; great soup starters begin this way, too! Cook each vegetable the way you want it done in the final soup. Make sure onions and celery are translucent and soft, and root vegetables like carrots, beets, and potatoes are cooked all the way through. If you want veggies like green beans to have some bite to them, add them toward the end, but do make sure they are tender before freezing.

Soup starters are cooked similarly to how the whole soup would be cooked, just in a slightly disjointed way. For example, the traditional version of Chicken Tortilla Soup (page 50) starts with sautéing aromatics like onions, garlic, and bell peppers. Then canned tomatoes, broth, and spices are added to simmer and soften the veggies. Finally, cooked chicken, frozen or canned corn, and black beans make up the body of the soup and are added toward the end of cooking. It's a very classic soup using a very standard "soup method" to build it.

Here's how I transfer that method to a soup starter, with the goal being to preserve the fresh vegetables available now. I start the same way: by sautéing the onions, garlic, and bell peppers. I'll add fresh tomatoes because they're in season, plus they provide liquid for the veggies to simmer and soften in. I won't add the broth at this point, but I will add the

Making Chicken Tortilla Soup (page 50) is as easy as thawing a bag of soup starter and adding leftover cooked chicken, plus fridge and pantry items like cheese, broth, beans, and tortilla chips.

spices so their flavors can develop. Fresh corn is the last to go in and will simmer until just tender. This flavorful veggie mixture is frozen as the starter. When it's time to make the soup, I thaw the starter and add cooked chicken, broth, and a can of beans from the pantry. It's still a typical soup, just made with a different method that takes advantage of seasonality.

Does a Soup Starter Contain Liquid?

Yes, a liquid component is what softens the veggies and gives the finished soup that slow-cooked, homemade taste. My goal is to use enough liquid to keep the vegetables submerged while they cook but to end up with very little liquid in the finished starter.

This is so the starter takes up less room in the freezer and the water doesn't dilute the broth in the finished soup. You can always add more liquid during the cooking process if it seems dry, so start with a modest amount. I typically use water because it's a relatively small amount and easiest, but you can certainly use broth instead. Either way it turns out great.

Soup with a tomato-based broth is especially well suited for a starter because the fresh tomatoes provide a liquid for the veggies to cook in. Plus this is a top-notch way to preserve in-season tomatoes!

If you want to make tomato-based soup starters but don't have fresh tomatoes, there are two good options for adapting the recipes. The first is to use canned tomatoes in the starter. One 14.5-ounce can of diced tomatoes is equivalent to about 4 cups of diced fresh tomatoes. The other option is to use a small amount of water in the starter instead of fresh tomatoes, and add canned tomatoes when you are ready to make the soup. Soup (and soup starter!) is such an easygoing and adaptable food.

Making Blended Soup Starters

Soup that will be blended smooth freezes extremely well as a starter. You cook the vegetables in a small amount of water, but instead of adding broth and blending, you freeze the veggies. Once thawed, the vegetables are combined with the broth and puréed. All that's left is to heat the soup for serving.

It may seem easier to just blend the finished soup and freeze it like that, but the texture will be better when it's blended after thawing. Many blended soups, particularly those with high-water-content vegetables, will separate once thawed. It's worth noting that all it takes to bring them back together is a short whirl in the blender, but I prefer to use (and clean!) the blender only one time.

The downside to this approach is that you must freeze the entire recipe instead of individual servings. If you prefer single servings, any of the blended soup recipes in this chapter that don't contain a lot of dairy, like Sunny Carrot Soup (page 37) and Roasted Cauliflower Soup (page 35), can be frozen in their blended, finished form instead. Just remember to give them a spin in the blender again once thawed!

Some blended soups do come out of the freezer without separating. Curried Acorn Squash Soup (page 78) is a good example, and this is why you'll find it in the Soups chapter instead of the Soup Starters chapter. The thickness and low water content of the squash allow it to freeze exceptionally well.

Freezing Soup Starters

With potatoes. Potatoes can develop a grainy texture once frozen and thawed, which seems to be accentuated in soup. To minimize this, use waxy varieties; many red-skinned and fingerling types are waxy. All-purpose varieties, like Yukon Gold, can work if you don't mind a little more graininess. Starchy potatoes like russets are not recommended for soups.

The larger the pieces, the more obvious the texture change, so cut them smaller. Graininess is harder to detect in potatoes that are shredded, puréed, diced very small, or thinly sliced. Just be careful with thinly sliced potatoes, as they can be fragile. Stir them gently when making the starter and heating the final soup.

With dairy. Dairy ingredients like milk, cream, and cheese tend to become separated once thawed, so don't add them to the starter. Instead, save them for when the soup is thawed and heated for serving. Fortunately, just about any soup can be adapted to adding dairy at the end.

When freezing potatoes in soup starters, use waxy types and cut them into thin slices or small pieces for the best texture.

If using shredded cheese, buy it in block form and shred it yourself. Preshredded cheese has been treated with anticaking agents that can make it more resistant to melt or create a grainy texture.

Thawing & Heating Soup Starters

A soup starter will be best when thawed overnight in the refrigerator or with the cold-water method (see page 21). If your starter is partially thawed but still a little icy come dinnertime, just add it to the pot with the warm broth, and it will thaw the rest of the way quickly. Avoid heating a completely frozen block of starter in boiling broth, as the ingredients on the outside can overcook before the ingredients in the middle even thaw.

Keep in mind that the starter is already cooked and nearly ready to serve, so heat it gently. Do allow it to simmer with the broth and other ingredients until warmed through, usually 5 to 10 minutes, but don't overcook it. Ingredients like potatoes and squash are more sensitive and can break apart or turn to mush if reheated too long.

Add dairy ingredients at the very end. Turn off the heat and stir in items like cream and cheese; the residual heat will melt the cheese just fine. This ensures they don't curdle from being cooked too hot or too long.

If the soup will have noodles added to it when heated for serving, I prefer to cook them separately and then add them to the soup, instead of letting them cook in the broth. This ensures they are cooked just right! Gluten-free noodles should always be cooked separately from soup because they release a lot of starch into the cooking water.

Cabbage & Vegetable Soup

This is a shining example of how simple a soup starter can be. It's only cabbage and tomatoes: two veggies I always find myself needing to preserve at the end of summer, and two veggies that happen to make a great base for future soup. Once you have this combo in your freezer, turn it into a classic vegetable soup with fresh onion, celery, carrots, and potatoes.

YIELD: 1 BATCH OF STARTER, MAKES 4 SERVINGS

This recipe can be doubled or tripled to make additional batches.

MAKING & FREEZING THE STARTER

- 4 cups diced paste tomatoes or other meaty tomatoes, in ½-inch pieces
- 4 cups chopped green cabbage, in 1-inch pieces (about ½ medium head)

1. Place the tomatoes in a large pot over medium heat. Bring to a boil, then simmer until they've released some of their liquid, about 5 minutes. Stir in the cabbage, then cover the pot and simmer until it is just wilted and tender, about 10 minutes.
2. **TO FREEZE:** Cool completely before freezing. This starter packs well in a freezer bag or rigid container. The recipe fits in a 1-quart freezer bag.

MAKING THE SOUP

- 2 tablespoons butter or extra-virgin olive oil
- 1 large yellow onion, diced
- 2 celery stalks, diced
- 2 garlic cloves, minced
- 4 cups chicken or vegetable broth
- 2 cups peeled, diced waxy potatoes
- 2 medium carrots, thinly sliced
- 2 tablespoons tomato paste
- 1 teaspoon dried basil
- 1 teaspoon dried oregano
- 1 teaspoon sea salt, plus more as needed
- ¼ teaspoon freshly ground black pepper
- 1 recipe frozen Cabbage & Vegetable Soup starter, thawed
- 1 tablespoon finely chopped fresh parsley

1. Melt the butter in a large pot over medium heat. Add the onion and celery, and sauté until tender, about 7 minutes. Add the garlic and cook for 3 minutes longer.
2. Stir in the broth, potatoes, carrots, tomato paste, basil, oregano, salt, and pepper. Bring to a boil, then simmer until the potatoes and carrots are tender, about 15 minutes.
3. Stir in the starter and simmer for 5 minutes. Turn off the heat and stir in the parsley. Because some broths are saltier than others, taste the soup and add more salt if necessary.

Creamy Asparagus Soup

I'm an advocate of stuffing oneself with as much fresh asparagus as possible in springtime, but I also think it's worthwhile to have enticing ways to put it up when you have too much. Asparagus is difficult to preserve because it turns very soft after being frozen or canned. Luckily we can use this to our advantage. Freezing asparagus as a soup starter means you can preserve the delicate flavor of this fleeting veggie, and the soft texture is welcomed.

YIELD: 1 BATCH OF STARTER, MAKES 4 SERVINGS

This recipe can be doubled or tripled to make additional batches.

MAKING & FREEZING THE STARTER

- 1 tablespoon butter or extra-virgin olive oil
- ½ small yellow onion, diced
- 1 garlic clove, minced
- 1½ cups water
- 5 cups chopped asparagus, in 1-inch pieces (about 1½ pounds)
- 1 teaspoon sea salt
- ¼ teaspoon freshly ground black pepper

1. Melt the butter in a medium saucepan over medium heat. Add the onion and sauté until just tender, about 5 minutes. Add the garlic and cook for 3 minutes longer.
2. Stir in the water, asparagus, salt, and pepper. Bring to a boil, then simmer, stirring occasionally, until the asparagus is just tender all the way through. Do not overcook; it should still retain a vibrant green color. This will take about 12 minutes for thick pieces, 8 to 10 minutes for medium, and 6 to 8 minutes for thin pieces. If you have a mix of different sizes, put the larger pieces in a few minutes before the smaller. Remove the pan from the stove to cool.
3. **TO FREEZE:** Cool completely before freezing. This starter packs well in a freezer bag or rigid container. The recipe fits in a 1-quart freezer bag.

MAKING THE SOUP

- 2 cups chicken or vegetable broth
- 1 recipe frozen Creamy Asparagus Soup starter, thawed
- ⅓ cup heavy whipping cream
- Sea salt

1. Combine the broth and starter in a blender and blend on high until smooth, about 1 minute. Pour the mixture into a large pot over medium-low heat. Bring to a gentle boil, then simmer, stirring occasionally, until heated through, about 5 minutes.
2. Turn off the heat and stir in the cream. Because some broths are saltier than others, taste the soup and add salt if necessary.

Roasted Cauliflower Soup

With its short ingredient list, this soup gets its flavor from roasting the cauliflower. It gives this otherwise plain vegetable a lot of character. An abundance of garlic and plenty of good olive oil and butter play an important supporting role. Serve as is, or add cream and Parmesan cheese once thawed and heated for serving.

YIELD: 1 BATCH OF STARTER, MAKES 4 SERVINGS

This recipe can be doubled or tripled to make additional batches.

MAKING & FREEZING THE STARTER

- 1 whole head of garlic
- 2 tablespoons plus 1 teaspoon extra-virgin olive oil
- 8 cups cauliflower florets (about 1 large head)
- 2 tablespoons butter
- 1 medium yellow onion, diced
- 1 cup water
- 2 teaspoons chopped fresh thyme
- ½ teaspoon sea salt
- ¼ teaspoon freshly ground black pepper

1. Preheat the oven to 400°F (200°C).
2. Cut off the top of the garlic head to just expose the cloves. Cut an 8-inch square of aluminum foil and cradle the garlic bulb in it. Drizzle the exposed garlic cloves with 1 teaspoon of the oil, then wrap the garlic in the foil.
3. Place the cauliflower florets on a large sheet pan. Toss with the remaining 2 tablespoons oil, then spread in a single layer. Put the foil-wrapped garlic on the pan off to the side.
4. Bake for 30 to 35 minutes, until the cauliflower is turning golden brown on the bottom.
5. Melt the butter in a large pot over medium heat. Add the onion and sauté until tender, about 7 minutes.
6. Stir in the water, along with the roasted cauliflower, thyme, salt, and pepper. Unwrap the garlic and squeeze out the softened cloves. Add about a third of the cloves to the pot; save the rest for a different use. Bring to a boil, then cover and simmer gently until the cauliflower is tender and easily mashed, about 15 minutes.
7. **TO FREEZE:** Cool completely before freezing. This starter packs well in a freezer bag or rigid container. The recipe fits in a 1-quart freezer bag.

MAKING THE SOUP

- 4 cups chicken or vegetable broth
- 1 recipe frozen Roasted Cauliflower Soup starter, thawed
- Sea salt

1. Combine the broth and starter in a blender and blend on high until smooth, about 45 seconds.
2. Pour the mixture into a large pot over medium heat. Bring to a boil, then simmer, stirring occasionally, until heated through, about 5 minutes. Because some broths are saltier than others, taste the soup and add salt if necessary.

Sunny Carrot Soup

We gardeners are always looking for ways to preserve the carrot harvest, and this soup starter is a remarkably good way to do it! The ginger and coriander give this soup a lot of depth without overpowering the sweet and earthy flavor of the carrots. Like most blended soups, this one wants to have a crunchy topping—try it with croutons or crispy fried onions.

YIELD: 1 BATCH OF STARTER, MAKES 4 SERVINGS

This recipe can be doubled or tripled to make additional batches.

MAKING & FREEZING THE STARTER

- 2 tablespoons butter
- 1 tablespoon extra-virgin olive oil
- 1 medium yellow onion, diced
- 2 garlic cloves, minced
- ½ teaspoon sea salt
- ¼ teaspoon ground coriander
- ¼ teaspoon ground cumin
- ¼ teaspoon ground ginger
- ¼ teaspoon freshly ground black pepper
- ⅛ teaspoon crushed red pepper
- 1½ cups water
- 5 cups sliced carrots, in ½-inch-thick rounds (about 2 pounds)

1. Melt the butter and oil together in a large pot over medium heat. Add the onion and sauté until tender, about 7 minutes. Add the garlic, salt, coriander, cumin, ginger, black pepper, and red pepper, and cook for 3 minutes longer.
2. Stir in the water and carrots. Bring to a boil, then cover and simmer gently, stirring occasionally, until the carrots are very soft, about 15 minutes.
3. **TO FREEZE:** Cool completely before freezing. This starter packs well in a freezer bag or rigid container. The recipe fits in a 1-quart freezer bag.

MAKING THE SOUP

- 4 cups vegetable broth
- 1 recipe frozen Sunny Carrot Soup starter, thawed
- Sea salt

1. Combine the broth and starter in a blender and blend on high until smooth, about 1 minute.
2. Pour the mixture into a large pot over medium heat. Bring to a boil, then simmer, stirring occasionally, until heated through, about 5 minutes. Because some broths are saltier than others, taste the soup and add salt if necessary.

Sausage, Potato & Kale Soup

My homemade version of this popular restaurant soup doesn't skimp on the sausage, potatoes, or kale. It's absolutely jam-packed with them! To get the potatoes just right for freezing, use a waxy variety so they hold their shape and have the best texture, and stir them gently while heating so they don't fall apart.

YIELD: 1 BATCH OF STARTER, MAKES 6 SERVINGS

This recipe can be doubled or tripled to make additional batches.

MAKING & FREEZING THE STARTER

- 1 tablespoon extra-virgin olive oil
- 1 large yellow onion, diced
- 3 celery stalks, diced
- 2 garlic cloves, minced
- 2 cups water
- 4 cups peeled, sliced waxy potatoes, ¼ inch thick
- 1 teaspoon dried oregano
- 1 teaspoon sea salt
- ½ teaspoon dried basil
- ¼ teaspoon crushed red pepper
- ¼ teaspoon freshly ground black pepper
- 4 cups roughly chopped kale (see Note)

1. Heat the oil in a large pot over medium heat. Add the onion and celery, and sauté until tender, about 7 minutes. Add the garlic and cook for 3 minutes longer.
2. Stir in the water, potatoes, oregano, salt, basil, red pepper, and black pepper. Bring to a boil, then cover and simmer gently, stirring occasionally, until the potatoes are just cooked through, about 10 minutes. Fold in the kale and turn off the heat.
3. **TO FREEZE:** Cool completely before freezing. This starter packs well in a freezer bag or rigid container. The recipe fits in a 1-quart freezer bag.

NOTE: *To prepare and measure the kale, remove the center rib from the leaves and cut them into bite-size pieces. Pack the kale pieces lightly in the measuring cup to make 4 cups.*

MAKING THE SOUP

- 4 cups chicken broth
- 1 recipe frozen Sausage, Potato & Kale Soup starter, thawed
- 2 pounds mild Italian sausage, cooked, crumbled, and drained
- ⅓ cup heavy whipping cream
- Sea salt
- Grated Parmesan cheese

1. Combine the broth, starter, and sausage in a large pot over medium heat. Bring to a boil, then simmer, stirring occasionally, until heated through, about 10 minutes.
2. Turn off the heat and stir in the cream. Because some broths are saltier than others, taste the soup and add salt if necessary.
3. Ladle into bowls and top with a sprinkle of Parmesan.

STAUB

French Onion Soup

If you need a way to turn a lot of onions into something useful that doesn't take up much freezer space, this is definitely it. Besides making French onion soup much more approachable, this starter is adaptable to many other dishes. Turn it into an oniony beef and noodle soup, use it in casseroles and slow cooker meals, or try the French Onion Soup Baked Rice on page 41.

YIELD: 1 BATCH OF STARTER, MAKES 4 SERVINGS

Do not double. To increase yield, make consecutive batches.

MAKING & FREEZING THE STARTER

- 3 tablespoons butter or extra-virgin olive oil
- 6 cups sliced yellow onions (about 3 large; see Note)
- 2 teaspoons chopped fresh thyme
- 1 teaspoon sugar
- 1 bay leaf
- ½ teaspoon sea salt
- ¼ teaspoon freshly ground black pepper
- 2 garlic cloves, grated
- ½ cup water
- 1 teaspoon balsamic vinegar

1. Melt the butter in a large skillet over medium heat. Add the onions and sauté, stirring every few minutes, until they have softened and turned translucent, about 15 minutes.
2. Stir in the thyme, sugar, bay leaf, salt, and pepper, and reduce the heat to low. Continue cooking, stirring occasionally, until the onions have turned golden brown, about 45 minutes. Make sure to scrape the bottom of the pan when stirring so that the onions don't stick and burn.
3. Stir in the garlic, water, and vinegar, and scrape any brown bits from the bottom and sides of the pan. Turn off the heat and remove and discard the bay leaf.
4. **TO FREEZE:** Cool completely before freezing. Because it cooks down into a relatively small amount, this starter packs best in a rigid container. The recipe fits in a 1½-cup container.

MAKING THE SOUP

- 4 slices toasted French bread, about 1 inch thick
- 1 tablespoon extra-virgin olive oil
- ½ cup shredded Swiss or white cheddar cheese
- ½ cup shredded mozzarella cheese
- 4 cups beef broth
- 1 recipe frozen French Onion Soup starter, thawed
- Sea salt

1. Position an oven rack in the middle of the oven and preheat the broiler. Place the bread on a baking sheet and brush each slice evenly with the oil. Divide all the cheese among the bread, then broil until it is just browning, about 4 minutes.
2. Combine the broth and starter in a large pot over medium heat. Bring to a boil, then simmer, stirring occasionally, until heated through, about 5 minutes. Because some broths are saltier than others, taste the soup and add salt if necessary.
3. Ladle the soup into bowls and top each one with a slice of the toasted cheesy bread.

NOTE: *To slice the onions, start by cutting off the very top of the onion and the root. Cut the onion in half from top to bottom, and lay each half cut-side down on the cutting board. Cut ¼-inch-thick slices from the top of the onion to the bottom of the onion so they form petal-shaped slices and not half-moon-shaped segmented slices.*

BONUS USE FOR STARTER

French Onion Soup Baked Rice

This might seem a little out of place in the soup section, but it's an extraordinary way to use French Onion Soup starter. This rice is rich and buttery, full of flavor from the caramelized onions and beef broth. Make this for dinner and enjoy the leftovers for days to come!

YIELD: 8–10 SERVINGS

- 1 recipe frozen French Onion Soup starter (page 40), thawed
- 4 cups beef broth
- 1 cup water
- 4 tablespoons butter
- Sea salt
- Cooking spray, for greasing the pan
- 2 cups long-grain white rice

1. Preheat the oven to 425°F (220°C).
2. Roughly chop the starter to cut the onions into smaller pieces. Combine the starter, broth, water, and butter in a medium saucepan over medium heat. Warm, stirring frequently, until the butter is melted and the onions separate from each other, about 5 minutes. Because some broths are saltier than others, taste the onion and broth mixture; it should be noticeably but pleasantly salty. Add more salt if necessary (remember, the onion and broth mixture will season the rice, too; I typically add 1 teaspoon of salt).
3. Spray a 13- by 9-inch baking pan with cooking spray and spread the rice on the bottom. Pour the broth mixture over the top, and then lightly stir to combine. Cover the baking dish tightly with aluminum foil.
4. Bake for 30 minutes. Remove the foil and bake for 20 to 25 minutes longer, until the rice is tender but not drying out. Fluff the rice with a fork to stir in the onions.

TIP Have leftovers? This rice dish also freezes well!

Minestrone Soup

With this starter in my freezer, I can throw together a filling minestrone soup anytime with very little planning ahead. It's full of fresh-frozen veggies like green beans and zucchini and pantry staples like kidney beans and pasta. I like to reserve some of the fresh tomatoes for adding at the end of making the starter, which gives the soup both a cooked and fresh tomato flavor.

YIELD: 1 BATCH OF STARTER, MAKES 6 SERVINGS

This recipe can be doubled or tripled to make additional batches.

MAKING & FREEZING THE STARTER

- 1 tablespoon butter
- 1 tablespoon extra-virgin olive oil
- 1 medium yellow onion, diced
- 2 celery stalks, diced
- 2 garlic cloves, minced
- 4 cups diced paste tomatoes or other meaty tomatoes, in ½-inch pieces, or 1 (14.5-ounce) can diced tomatoes
- 2 tablespoons tomato paste
- 1 teaspoon dried basil
- 1 teaspoon dried oregano
- 1 teaspoon sea salt
- ¼ teaspoon freshly ground black pepper
- 1 large carrot, thinly sliced
- 1 cup diced green beans, in ½-inch pieces
- 1 cup diced zucchini, in ½-inch pieces

1. Melt the butter and oil together in a large pot over medium heat. Add the onion and celery, and sauté until tender, about 7 minutes. Add the garlic and cook for 3 minutes longer.
2. Stir in 3 cups of the tomatoes (if using canned tomatoes, add them all), along with the tomato paste, basil, oregano, salt, and pepper. Bring to a boil, then simmer, stirring occasionally, until the tomatoes are juicy and have reduced slightly, about 10 minutes.
3. Stir in the carrot, green beans, and zucchini. Continue cooking until the vegetables have softened slightly but are still crisp, about 10 minutes. Turn off the heat and stir in the remaining 1 cup tomatoes. The vegetables will continue to soften as they cool.
4. **TO FREEZE:** Cool completely before freezing. This starter packs well in a freezer bag or rigid container. The recipe fits in a 1-quart freezer bag.

MAKING THE SOUP

- 4 cups vegetable broth
- 1 recipe frozen Minestrone Soup starter, thawed
- 1 (16-ounce) can red kidney beans, drained and rinsed
- 8 ounces small shell or macaroni pasta, cooked and drained
- Sea salt
- Grated Parmesan cheese

1. Combine the broth, starter, and beans in a large pot over medium heat. Bring to a boil, then simmer, stirring occasionally, until heated through, about 10 minutes.
2. Turn off the heat and stir in the pasta. Because some broths are saltier than others, taste the soup and add salt if necessary.
3. Ladle into bowls and top with a sprinkle of Parmesan.

Roasted Red Pepper
Tomato Soup starter

Roasted Red Pepper Tomato Soup

I love a recipe that roasts in the oven with very little effort on my part. Besides being easy, roasting the vegetables adds an extra layer of caramelized flavor. I prefer to blend the veggies into soup once they're thawed for serving, so I shovel them right into freezer bags after they've roasted and cooled. This soup does freeze well in its blended form, too (though without the cream), if that's more convenient for you.

YIELD: 1 BATCH OF STARTER, MAKES 4 SERVINGS

This recipe can be doubled but requires an additional pan.

MAKING & FREEZING THE STARTER

- 12 cups chopped paste tomatoes or other meaty tomatoes, in 2-inch pieces (about 4 pounds whole)
- 1 large red bell pepper, cut into 2-inch pieces
- 1 small yellow onion, quartered
- 2 garlic cloves, peeled
- 1 tablespoon chopped fresh thyme
- 2 tablespoons extra-virgin olive oil
- 1 teaspoon sea salt
- ¼ teaspoon freshly ground black pepper

1. Preheat the oven to 425°F (220°C).
2. Combine the tomatoes, bell pepper, onion, garlic, and thyme on an 18- by 13-inch rimmed sheet pan. Toss with the oil, salt, and black pepper, then spread the vegetables in a single layer.
3. Bake for 55 to 60 minutes, until the vegetables are tender and starting to brown in places.
4. **TO FREEZE:** Cool completely before freezing. This starter packs well in a freezer bag or rigid container. The recipe fits in a 1-quart freezer bag.

MAKING THE SOUP

- 1 recipe frozen Roasted Red Pepper Tomato Soup starter, thawed
- ¼ cup heavy whipping cream or water

1. Place the starter in a blender and blend on high until smooth. Pour the mixture into a large pot over medium heat. Bring to a boil, then simmer, stirring occasionally, until heated through, about 5 minutes.
2. Turn off the heat and stir in the cream.

Quick & Easy Oven-Roasted Chili Base

I've made a lot of different chili starters and chili bases over the years, and this one is my undisputed favorite. Here's why: It uses up a lot of peppers and tomatoes when my harvest baskets are overflowing. All the veggies are cut into big, chunky pieces so the hands-on time is short. And because the spices roast with the veggies, making a pot of chili takes no time, yet the dish tastes like it simmered all day.

YIELD: 1 BATCH OF STARTER, MAKES 6 SERVINGS

This recipe can be doubled but requires an additional pan.

MAKING & FREEZING THE STARTER

- 8 cups chopped paste tomatoes or other meaty tomatoes, in 2-inch pieces (about 3 pounds whole)
- 1 medium yellow onion, cut into 6 pieces
- 1 large green bell pepper, cut into 2-inch pieces
- 3 jalapeños, deseeded and cut into 2-inch pieces
- 1 celery stalk, cut into 2-inch pieces
- 2 garlic cloves, peeled
- 2 tablespoons extra-virgin olive oil or avocado oil
- 3 tablespoons mild chili powder
- 1 teaspoon sea salt
- ½ cup water

1. Preheat the oven to 400°F (200°C).
2. Combine the tomatoes, onion, bell pepper, jalapeños, celery, and garlic on an 18- by 13-inch rimmed sheet pan. Toss with the oil, chili powder, and salt, then spread in an even layer. Gently pour the water into the pan (without washing all the seasoning off the vegetables).
3. Bake for 45 to 50 minutes, until the vegetables are tender and starting to brown.
4. Cool to a safe handling temperature, then transfer the vegetables to a food processor, including any liquid from the pan. Pulse until broken up into a chunky sauce, about 15 seconds; don't overprocess into a smooth purée.
5. **TO FREEZE:** Cool completely before freezing. This starter packs well in a freezer bag or rigid container. The recipe fits in a 1-quart freezer bag.

MAKING THE CHILI

- 1 cup water, plus more as needed
- 1 recipe frozen Quick & Easy Oven-Roasted Chili Base starter, thawed
- 2 pounds lean ground beef, cooked, crumbled, and drained
- 1 (16-ounce) can red kidney beans, drained and rinsed
- 1 teaspoon sea salt
- Shredded cheddar cheese
- Sour cream

1. Combine the water, starter, ground beef, beans, and salt in a large pot over medium heat. Bring to a boil, then simmer, stirring occasionally, until heated through, about 10 minutes. Add additional water to thin the chili if it is too thick.
2. Ladle into bowls and top with a sprinkle of cheese and a dollop of sour cream.

White Chicken Chili

This chili falls a little out of bounds from the traditional style. There are no tomatoes, and it uses chicken meat and broth, which pushes it somewhere between chili and soup. It's warm and cozy on a cool evening, and I love that it highlights our fresh garden peppers and sweet corn.

YIELD: 1 BATCH OF STARTER, MAKES 4 SERVINGS

This recipe can be doubled or tripled to make additional batches.

MAKING & FREEZING THE STARTER

- 1 tablespoon extra-virgin olive oil or avocado oil
- 1 large yellow onion, diced
- 1 large poblano pepper, diced
- 2 jalapeños, deseeded and finely diced
- 2 garlic cloves, minced
- 1 cup water
- 2 cups fresh sweet corn kernels (about 2 large ears)
- 2 teaspoons ground cumin
- 1 teaspoon chili powder
- 1 teaspoon dried oregano
- ½ teaspoon sea salt
- ¼ teaspoon smoked paprika

1. Heat the oil in a large pot over medium heat. Add the onion, poblano, and jalapeños, and sauté until tender, about 7 minutes. Add the garlic and cook for 3 minutes longer.
2. Stir in the water, corn, cumin, chili powder, oregano, salt, and paprika. Bring to a boil, then cover and simmer gently, stirring occasionally, until the corn is tender and the flavors have melded, about 15 minutes.
3. **TO FREEZE:** Cool completely before freezing. This starter packs well in a freezer bag or rigid container. The recipe fits in a 1-quart freezer bag.

MAKING THE SOUP

- 4 cups chicken broth
- 1 recipe frozen White Chicken Chili starter, thawed
- 3–4 cups cooked, diced chicken breasts
- 1 (16-ounce) can pinto beans, rinsed and drained
- ½ cup sour cream
- Sea salt
- Shredded Monterey Jack cheese

1. Combine the broth, starter, chicken, and beans in a large pot over medium heat. Bring to a boil, then simmer, stirring occasionally, until heated through, about 10 minutes.
2. Turn off the heat and ladle about ½ cup of the warm broth from the pot into a small bowl. Stir the sour cream into this broth, then stir this mixture back into the soup. Because some broths are saltier than others, taste the soup and add salt if necessary.
3. Ladle into bowls and top each with a sprinkle of cheese.

Stuffed Pepper Soup

Turning this classic (and time-consuming!) dish into a filling soup with the same flavors is more sensible for my busy kitchen. I use two pounds of ground beef, but it works just as well with less.

YIELD: 1 BATCH OF STARTER, MAKES 4–6 SERVINGS

This recipe can be doubled or tripled to make additional batches.

MAKING & FREEZING THE STARTER

- 2 tablespoons butter or extra-virgin olive oil
- 1 medium yellow onion, diced
- 2 celery stalks, diced
- 1 large green bell pepper, diced
- 1 large red bell pepper, diced
- 2 garlic cloves, minced
- 4 cups diced paste tomatoes or other meaty tomatoes, in ½-inch pieces, or 1 (14.5-ounce) can diced tomatoes
- ¼ cup tomato paste
- 1 teaspoon dried basil
- 1 teaspoon dried oregano
- 1 teaspoon sea salt
- 1 teaspoon Worcestershire sauce
- ¼ teaspoon freshly ground black pepper
- 2 tablespoons finely chopped fresh parsley

1. Melt the butter in a large pot over medium heat. Add the onion, celery, and bell peppers, and sauté until tender, about 10 minutes. Add the garlic and cook for 3 minutes longer.
2. Stir in the tomatoes, tomato paste, basil, oregano, salt, Worcestershire, and black pepper. Bring to a boil, then simmer, stirring occasionally, until the tomatoes are juicy and the flavors have melded, about 10 minutes. Turn off the heat and stir in the parsley.
3. **TO FREEZE:** Cool completely before freezing. This starter packs well in a freezer bag or rigid container. The recipe fits in a 1-quart freezer bag.

MAKING THE SOUP

- 4 cups chicken broth
- 1 recipe frozen Stuffed Pepper Soup starter, thawed
- 1–2 pounds lean ground beef, cooked, crumbled, and drained
- ½ teaspoon sea salt, plus more as needed
- ¾ cup long-grain white rice
- Shredded cheddar cheese

1. Combine the broth, starter, ground beef, and salt in a large pot over medium heat. Bring to a boil, then stir in the rice and simmer until the rice is just tender, about 15 minutes. Because some broths are saltier than others, taste the soup and add salt if necessary.
2. Ladle into bowls and top with a sprinkle of cheese.

Chicken Tortilla Soup

This is the new number one favorite, queen of all soups in my house, and it's on our monthly meal rotation all year. So naturally this starter is one of the most important things I keep in the freezer. When the tomatoes and peppers begin producing, it's only a matter of waiting for the sweet corn to ripen. Once it does, I get busy squirreling this away!

YIELD: 1 BATCH OF STARTER, MAKES 4–6 SERVINGS

This recipe can be doubled or tripled to make additional batches.

MAKING & FREEZING THE STARTER

- 1 tablespoon extra-virgin olive oil or avocado oil
- 1 medium yellow onion, diced
- 1 large red or orange bell pepper, diced
- 1 poblano or green bell pepper, diced
- 1 jalapeño, deseeded and finely diced
- 2 garlic cloves, minced
- 4 cups diced paste tomatoes or other meaty tomatoes, in ½-inch pieces, or 1 (14.5-ounce) can diced tomatoes
- 2 tablespoons tomato paste
- 1 tablespoon taco seasoning
- 1 teaspoon dried oregano
- ½ teaspoon sea salt
- 1 cup sweet corn kernels, fresh or frozen

1. Heat the oil in a large pot over medium heat. Add the onion, bell pepper, poblano, and jalapeño, and sauté until tender, about 10 minutes. Add the garlic and cook for 3 minutes longer.
2. Stir in the tomatoes, tomato paste, taco seasoning, oregano, and salt. Bring to a boil, then simmer, stirring occasionally, until the tomatoes are juicy, about 10 minutes. Stir in the corn and continue cooking until the corn is tender, about 10 minutes.
3. **TO FREEZE:** Cool completely before freezing. This starter packs well in a freezer bag or rigid container. The recipe fits in a 1-quart freezer bag.

MAKING THE SOUP

- 4 cups chicken broth
- 1 recipe frozen Chicken Tortilla Soup starter, thawed
- 3–4 cups cooked, chopped chicken breasts
- 1 (15-ounce) can black beans, drained and rinsed
- Sea salt
- Tortilla chips
- Shredded cheddar cheese
- Sour cream

1. Combine the broth, starter, chicken, and beans in a large pot over medium heat. Bring to a boil, then simmer, stirring occasionally, until heated through, about 10 minutes. Because some broths are saltier than others, taste the soup and add salt if necessary.
2. Place crushed tortilla chips in the bottom of each bowl and ladle the soup over them. Top with a sprinkle of cheese and a dollop of sour cream.

Creamy Zucchini Soup

This starter comes together lightning fast, which is good news when you're stuck dealing with the consequences of planting too many zucchini plants. If you're a fan of broccoli cheese soup, you'll enjoy this one, too; the green zucchini and Parmesan cheese give it similar flavor notes. Medium zucchini are best for this recipe, but if you've only got the big-big ones, scrape out the spongy, seedy center part first.

YIELD: 1 BATCH OF STARTER, MAKES 4 SERVINGS

This recipe can be doubled or tripled to make additional batches.

MAKING & FREEZING THE STARTER

2 tablespoons butter or extra-virgin olive oil
1 medium yellow onion, diced
2 garlic cloves, minced
1 cup water
8 cups chopped zucchini, in 1-inch pieces (about 3 medium)
1 teaspoon chopped fresh thyme
½ teaspoon sea salt
¼ teaspoon freshly ground black pepper

1. Melt the butter in a large pot over medium heat. Add the onion and sauté until tender, about 7 minutes. Stir in the garlic and cook for 3 minutes longer.
2. Add the water, zucchini, thyme, salt, and pepper. Bring to a boil, then cover and simmer gently, stirring occasionally, until the zucchini is tender, about 15 minutes.
3. **TO FREEZE:** Cool completely before freezing. This starter packs well in a freezer bag or rigid container. The recipe fits in a 1-quart freezer bag.

MAKING THE SOUP

2 cups chicken broth, plus more as needed
1 recipe frozen Creamy Zucchini Soup starter, thawed
⅓ cup grated Parmesan cheese
Sea salt

1. Combine the broth and starter in a blender and blend on high until smooth, about 45 seconds. Pour the mixture into a large pot over medium heat. If it is too thick, thin the soup with additional broth as needed. Bring to a boil, then simmer, stirring occasionally, until heated through, about 5 minutes.
2. Turn off the heat and stir in the Parmesan until it's melted into the soup. Because some broths are saltier than others, taste the soup and add salt if necessary.

Zucchini Corn Chowder

Smoky bacon, flavorful sweet corn, tender potatoes, and fresh zucchini are some of the best ingredients of summer, if you ask me! This chowder has an extra creamy texture, thanks to one of my favorite soup-making techniques: I remove and purée a small portion of the cooked veggies, then add them back in to thicken the broth.

YIELD: 1 BATCH OF STARTER, MAKES 4 SERVINGS

This recipe can be doubled or tripled to make additional batches.

MAKING & FREEZING THE STARTER

- 1 teaspoon extra-virgin olive oil or avocado oil
- 4 ounces bacon, diced
- 1 medium yellow onion, diced
- 1 jalapeño, deseeded and finely diced
- 2 garlic cloves, minced
- 1½ cups water
- 2 cups peeled, diced waxy potatoes, in ½-inch pieces
- ½ teaspoon dried parsley
- ½ teaspoon dried thyme
- ½ teaspoon sea salt
- ¼ teaspoon sweet paprika
- ¼ teaspoon freshly ground black pepper
- 2 cups diced zucchini, in ½-inch pieces
- 2 cups fresh sweet corn kernels (about 2 large ears)

1. Heat the oil in a large pot over medium heat. Add the bacon and sauté until brown and crispy, about 10 minutes. Use a slotted spoon to transfer the bacon to a plate.
2. To the pot with the warm bacon grease add the onion and jalapeño, and sauté until tender, about 7 minutes. Add the garlic and cook for 3 minutes longer.
3. Stir in the water, potatoes, parsley, thyme, salt, paprika, and pepper. Bring to a boil, then simmer gently for 5 minutes to give the potatoes a head start cooking. Stir in the zucchini and corn. Return to a boil, then cover and simmer gently, stirring occasionally, until the vegetables are just tender, about 10 minutes.
4. Cool to a safe handling temperature, then measure out 1 cup of the soup mixture and place it in a blender. Blend on high until smooth, about 1 minute. Stir the blended soup back into the pot along with the bacon.
5. **TO FREEZE:** Cool completely before freezing. This starter packs well in a freezer bag or rigid container. The recipe fits in a 1-quart freezer bag.

MAKING THE SOUP

- 2 cups chicken broth
- 1 recipe frozen Zucchini Corn Chowder starter, thawed
- ¼ cup heavy whipping cream (optional)
- Sea salt

1. Combine the broth and starter in a large pot over medium heat. Bring to a boil, then simmer, stirring occasionally, until heated through, about 10 minutes.
2. Turn off the heat and stir in the cream, if using. Because some broths are saltier than others, taste the soup and add salt if necessary.

Classic Chicken Soup

When I was growing up, my mom would whip out the soup pot and have a whole chicken bubbling away on the stove at the first sign of a cough or sniffle. With a base of carrot, celery, onion, and herbs, the starter for this iconic soup is very versatile. Make it into a standard chicken soup as done below, or tailor it however you prefer (I recommend the Chicken Wild Rice Soup on page 57). To keep it simple and adaptable, this recipe calls for adding cooked rice, noodles, or potatoes, but you can certainly modify it to cook those ingredients right in the broth.

YIELD: 1 BATCH OF STARTER, MAKES 4 SERVINGS

This recipe can be doubled or tripled to make additional batches.

MAKING & FREEZING THE STARTER

- 1 tablespoon butter or extra-virgin olive oil
- 1 large yellow onion, diced
- 4 celery stalks, diced
- 2 garlic cloves, minced
- 1 cup water
- 2 large carrots, thinly sliced
- ½ teaspoon dried rosemary
- ½ teaspoon dried sage
- ½ teaspoon dried thyme
- ½ teaspoon sea salt
- ¼ teaspoon freshly ground black pepper
- 2 teaspoons finely chopped fresh parsley

1. Melt the butter in a large pot over medium heat. Add the onion and celery, and sauté until tender, about 7 minutes. Add the garlic and cook for 3 minutes longer.
2. Stir in the water, carrots, rosemary, sage, thyme, salt, and pepper. Bring to a boil, then cover and simmer gently, stirring occasionally, until the carrots are tender, about 12 minutes. The vegetables will barely be covered with liquid, which is okay. Turn off the heat and stir in the parsley.
3. **TO FREEZE:** Cool completely before freezing. This starter packs well in a freezer bag or rigid container. The recipe fits in a 1-quart freezer bag.

MAKING THE SOUP

- 4 cups chicken broth
- 1 recipe frozen Classic Chicken Soup starter, thawed
- 2–3 cups cooked, chopped chicken
- Cooked rice, cooked noodles, or cooked potatoes (optional)
- Sea salt

Combine the broth, starter, and chicken in a large pot over medium heat. Bring to a boil, then simmer, stirring occasionally, until heated through, about 10 minutes. Stir in the rice, if using, and cook 3 minutes longer. Because some broths are saltier than others, taste the soup and add salt if necessary.

BONUS USE FOR STARTER

Chicken Wild Rice Soup

If I'm making a chicken soup, chances are good it's this one! This is my go-to bowl of comfort, and it comes together easily, thanks to the starter. The chewy texture and nutty flavor of wild rice gives this soup a lot of personality. Just make sure to cook the wild rice separately and then add it to the soup; otherwise it can discolor the broth.

YIELD: 4–6 SERVINGS

- 3 tablespoons butter
- 3 tablespoons all-purpose flour or gluten-free flour blend
- 4 cups chicken broth
- 1 recipe frozen Classic Chicken Soup starter (page 56), thawed
- 3 cups cooked, chopped chicken
- 3 cups cooked wild rice (about ⅔ cup dry)
- ¼ teaspoon freshly ground black pepper
- ⅓ cup heavy whipping cream
- Sea salt

1. Melt the butter in a large pot over medium heat. Add the flour and cook, stirring frequently, until cooked through but not browning, about 3 minutes.
2. Slowly stream in the broth while whisking so that the flour doesn't clump. Stir in the starter, chicken, wild rice, and pepper. Bring to a boil, then simmer, stirring occasionally, until heated through, about 5 minutes.
3. Turn off the heat and stir in the cream. Because some broths are saltier than others, taste the soup and add salt if necessary.

CHAPTER 2

READY-MADE SOUPS FOR THE FREEZER

There are many good reasons to keep a stockpile of ready-made soups in the freezer! I like to make big batches and freeze them in individual servings for lunches or use them when I have zero time or energy left to cook a filling dinner. They become most valuable when illness hits—there's nothing more healing than a bowl of homemade soup, especially when it's already prepared for you.

How to Build a Great Soup for the Freezer

Whether the soup is destined for fresh eating or the freezer, I usually use a classic soup-building method to make it. This technique allows each ingredient to be cooked according to its needs, it builds flavor as you go, and it results in an exceptional finished soup.

Step 1: Cook the aromatics. To build a soup, start by sautéing aromatic vegetables like onions, celery, peppers, and garlic, which will soften them and develop their flavors. I prefer extra-virgin olive oil or butter for added flavor, but you can use other fats or oils.

Step 2: Add flour, if using. If the soup is thickened with flour, now is the time to stir that in and let it cook with the vegetables for several minutes. All-purpose flour or a gluten-free flour blend should be incorporated once the aromatic veggies are tender but before adding the broth.

Step 3: Stir in the broth. Homemade is best, if you have it! This is also the optimal time to add ingredients like tomato paste, canned or fresh tomatoes, and dried herbs and seasonings, so that their flavors can start to blossom.

Step 4: Add meat, if using. If the soup calls for things like diced chicken, ground beef, sausage, or ground pork, I prefer to cook it separately, which allows me to drain away any excess fat before adding the meat to the soup.

If the meat needs to tenderize in the soup, like in Beef Stew over Mashed Potatoes (page 74), sear the meat in a pan, then transfer it to the soup. Allow it to fully tenderize before adding any other vegetables; otherwise, they will overcook before the meat becomes tender.

Step 5: Stir in the vegetables. Once the broth comes to a boil, add vegetables that take the longest time to cook, like squash, potatoes, and carrots. When those are tender, add the quicker-cooking vegetables like sweet corn, peas, broccoli, green beans, cabbage, and spinach, and simmer until just tender. Cooked dried beans or canned beans can also be stirred in now.

Step 6: Don't overcook. The process of freezing and reheating soup softens the ingredients and helps the flavors meld, so I err on the side of not overcooking soups meant for the freezer. The vegetables should be tender, but not boiled to mush.

Step 7: Use fresh herbs. I love the dimension fresh herbs give to soup, and incorporating them toward the end of cooking ensures the freshest flavor. Tougher herbs like rosemary, thyme, and sage can go in during the last 10 minutes of cooking. More tender herbs like parsley, dill, and basil are best added once the soup is off the heat.

Step 8: Add dairy, if using. If the recipe calls for milk, cream, or cheese, turn off the heat before adding it; otherwise it can curdle. Remember to use only a modest amount of dairy for freezer soups, and consider including it when the soup is thawed and heated for serving instead. If using shredded cheese, buy it in block form and shred it yourself. Preshredded cheeses have anticaking agents that can make them more resistant to melting or give the soup a grainy texture.

What Types of Soups Freeze Best?

The nature of soup makes it very freezer friendly. Soups are intentionally slow cooked and soft, which means they survive the freezer well. In fact, many vegetable-heavy soups thrive in the freezer!

It's probably easier to talk about the soups that *don't* freeze well, as the list of those is much shorter than the ones that do. Any recipe that contains a lot of flour or dairy is liable to separate once thawed, so try them as starters instead. Soups that have just a small amount of flour or dairy, like Creamy Chipotle Butternut Squash Stew (page 79), generally freeze just fine.

Soup that is heavy with noodles or rice is also a poor candidate for the freezer. Pasta and other grains need to be cooked and reheated *just right* to turn out well. Soups with these ingredients can be frozen with success, but it's best if they are a smaller component of the dish.

FREEZING SOUP WITH PASTA OR RICE

Soup with pasta or rice can be frozen successfully if you take a little extra care when freezing and reheating it. I have the best results from cooking these ingredients separately and slightly underdone, then stirring them into the soup after it has cooled. Pasta and rice will still be on the softer side once frozen, thawed, and reheated, but this technique prevents them from becoming mush.

Another option is to ladle the cooled soup into freezer containers and place the pasta or rice on top, so they're not mixed in. This is the best option for gluten-free or other specialty noodles that can be delicate and fickle.

You may choose to forgo adding these ingredients to your frozen soup and instead cook them fresh when the soup is heated for serving. This is also a wise way to save freezer space. Of course, this isn't as practical if you're freezing individual portions of soup.

FREEZING SOUP WITH POTATOES

Once frozen and thawed, potatoes can develop a grainy texture, which seems to be accentuated in soup. To minimize this, use waxy varieties; many red-skinned and fingerling types are waxy. All-purpose varieties, like Yukon Gold, can work if you don't mind a little more graininess. Starchy potatoes like russets are not recommended for soups.

The larger the pieces, the more obvious the texture change, so cut them smaller. Graininess is hard to detect in potatoes that are shredded, diced very small, or thinly sliced.

Creamy Chipotle Butternut Squash Stew (page 79) is a lightly creamy soup that freezes beautifully. These 2-cup containers make the perfect serving size for one person.

Drain and rinse canned beans before adding them to soup to prevent them from discoloring the broth.

FREEZING SOUP WITH LEGUMES

Ingredients like beans and lentils hold their shape and flavor very well in the freezer. If using dried beans, cook them separately until tender, and then add them to the soup. Unless it is a distinctly bean-based soup, drain away any of the cooking or canning liquid and rinse the beans before adding them so they don't muddy the broth.

Lentils are moderately quick cooking, and most types (especially the green and orange varieties) do well when cooked directly in the broth, like in Swiss Chard & Lentil Soup (page 76). They can also be cooked separately and added to the soup toward the end of cooking.

Thawing & Heating Frozen Soups

Frozen soup will do best when thawed overnight in the refrigerator or with the cold-water method (see page 21). Freezer bags with a lot of liquid can leak when thawing, so make sure to place them in a tray or bowl in the refrigerator. I often go one step further, cutting the bag away from the frozen block of soup and placing the block in a covered soup pot in the fridge to thaw, which makes one fewer dirty dish.

Remember that soup is already cooked and ready to serve, so be gentle when heating it. Do allow it to simmer, but don't overcook it. Ingredients like potatoes and squash are more sensitive and can break apart or turn into mush if reheated too long or stirred too vigorously. Soups with dairy can curdle if heated too hot.

Puréed soups can appear separated when thawed, which doesn't affect their taste but does make them look less appealing. They are completely edible this way, but a 15-second whirl in the blender will bring back their silky smoothness.

I tend to make my freezer soups a little on the thick side. If you prefer them thinner, you can add a splash of water, broth, or cream when heating.

FREEZING SOUP WITH SEAFOOD?

Seafood broth freezes fine, but avoid freezing soup with pieces of seafood. Ingredients like fish and shrimp will suffer after being cooked, frozen, and reheated.

Borscht

As I am the only beet lover in my household, this is the ideal soup for freezing in single-serve portions just for me. There are many different cultural variations of borscht, but this vegetarian version freezes well. Feel free to add meat, though, if that's how you like it. And don't forget to serve it topped with a dollop of sour cream!

YIELD: 5 SERVINGS

This recipe can be doubled or tripled.

- 2 tablespoons butter or extra-virgin olive oil
- 1 medium yellow onion, diced
- 2 celery stalks, diced
- 2 garlic cloves, minced
- 4 cups vegetable broth
- 2 tablespoons tomato paste
- 1 tablespoon distilled white vinegar
- 2 bay leaves
- 1 teaspoon sea salt, plus more as needed
- ¼ teaspoon freshly ground black pepper
- 3 cups peeled, shredded beets (about 2 medium)
- 3 cups chopped green cabbage, in 1-inch pieces (about ½ small head)
- 2 cups peeled, diced waxy potatoes, in ½-inch pieces
- 2 medium carrots, thinly sliced
- 2 tablespoons chopped fresh dill
- 1 tablespoon freshly squeezed lemon juice

1. Melt the butter in a large pot over medium heat. Add the onion and celery, and sauté until tender, about 7 minutes. Add the garlic and cook for 3 minutes longer.
2. Stir in the broth, tomato paste, vinegar, bay leaves, salt, and pepper. Bring to a boil, then add the beets, cabbage, potatoes, and carrots. Return to a simmer and cook, stirring occasionally, until the vegetables are tender, about 18 minutes.
3. Turn off the heat and stir in the dill and lemon juice. Because some broths are saltier than others, taste the soup and add more salt if necessary.
4. **TO FREEZE:** Remove and discard the bay leaves, and cool the soup completely before freezing. This soup packs well in freezer bags or rigid containers.

Summer Harvest Soup

At the height of the growing season when fresh produce is rolling in faster than I know what to do with, I make *this* soup. Then when the winter doldrums set in, diving into a bowl reminds me of the warmer months ahead. I always serve this with a generous sprinkle of Parmesan cheese—it really complements the fresh tomatoes and basil.

YIELD: 5 SERVINGS

This recipe can be doubled or tripled.

- 2 tablespoons butter or extra-virgin olive oil
- 1 medium yellow onion, diced
- 2 celery stalks, diced
- 2 garlic cloves, minced
- 4 cups chicken or vegetable broth
- 2 cups peeled, diced waxy potatoes, in ½-inch pieces
- 1 teaspoon dried basil
- 1 teaspoon dried oregano
- ½ teaspoon dried thyme
- ½ teaspoon sea salt, plus more as needed
- ¼ teaspoon freshly ground black pepper
- 2 cups diced green beans, in ½-inch pieces
- 2 cups diced zucchini, in ½-inch pieces
- 1 cup fresh sweet corn kernels (about 1 large ear)
- 1 cup diced paste tomatoes or other meaty tomatoes, in ½-inch pieces
- 1 tablespoon chopped fresh basil
- 1 tablespoon finely chopped fresh parsley

1. Melt the butter in a large pot over medium heat. Add the onion and celery, and sauté until tender, about 7 minutes. Add the garlic and cook for 3 minutes longer.
2. Stir in the broth, potatoes, dried basil, oregano, thyme, salt, and pepper. Bring to a boil, then simmer gently for 5 minutes to give the potatoes a head start cooking. Add the green beans, zucchini, and corn. Return to a simmer and cook until all the vegetables are tender, about 10 minutes.
3. Turn off the heat and stir in the tomatoes, fresh basil, and parsley. Because some broths are saltier than others, taste the soup and add more salt if necessary.
4. **TO FREEZE:** Cool completely before freezing. This soup packs well in freezer bags or rigid containers.

Cheesy Bratwurst Stew

Bratwursts, potatoes, and cheese . . . all of this Wisconsin gal's favorite food groups! This soup uses leftover bratwursts, but if those are hard to come by in your house, you can cook some up just for this recipe. Grill, roast, or panfry—just make sure that they're golden brown on the outside and some of the fat is rendered out.

YIELD: 4 SERVINGS

This recipe can be doubled or tripled.

- 1 tablespoon extra-virgin olive oil or avocado oil
- 1 medium yellow onion, diced
- 2 celery stalks, diced
- 1 large red bell pepper, diced
- 3 garlic cloves, minced
- 1 tablespoon all-purpose flour or gluten-free flour blend
- 4 cups chicken broth
- 1 pound cooked bratwursts, sliced into thin rounds (see Note)
- 4 cups peeled, sliced waxy potatoes, ¼ inch thick
- 1 teaspoon dried oregano
- ½ teaspoon sea salt, plus more as needed
- ¼ teaspoon crushed red pepper
- ¼ teaspoon freshly ground black pepper
- 4 ounces medium-sharp cheddar cheese, shredded
- 1 tablespoon finely chopped fresh parsley

1. Heat the oil in a large pot over medium heat. Add the onion, celery, and bell pepper, and sauté until tender, about 10 minutes. Add the garlic and flour, and cook for 3 minutes longer.
2. Whisk in the broth, then add the bratwursts, potatoes, oregano, salt, red pepper, and black pepper. Bring to a boil, then simmer gently until the potatoes are tender, about 15 minutes.
3. Turn off the heat and stir in the cheese and parsley. Because some broths and bratwursts are saltier than others, taste the stew and add more salt if necessary.
4. **TO FREEZE:** Cool completely before freezing. This stew packs well in freezer bags or rigid containers.

NOTE: *You can use any brand of bratwursts you like, but just make sure they are cooked (grilled, roasted, or panfried) and browned. Properly cooking the bratwursts also helps make sure that some of the fat is rendered from them so the stew doesn't end up too oily.*

Hamburger & Tater Soup

This is the soup form of a popular casserole that's made with cream soup and ground beef and baked with crispy potato tots on top. Using shredded potatoes mimics the texture of a tot, and it prevents the potatoes from becoming mealy once thawed. As someone who comes from the "hot dish" region of the United States where this type of casserole is homey and nostalgic, this soup always hits the spot!

YIELD: 4–5 SERVINGS

This recipe can be doubled or tripled.

- 2 tablespoons extra-virgin olive oil or butter
- 1 pound lean ground beef
- 1 medium yellow onion, diced
- 1 celery stalk, finely diced
- 2 garlic cloves, minced
- 2 tablespoons all-purpose flour or gluten-free flour blend
- 4 cups chicken broth
- 1½ cups water or additional chicken broth
- 3 cups peeled, shredded waxy potatoes (see Note)
- 1 large carrot, finely diced
- 1 cup sweet corn kernels, fresh or frozen
- 1 teaspoon dried basil
- 1 teaspoon sea salt, plus more as needed
- ½ teaspoon dried oregano
- ½ teaspoon granulated garlic
- ¼ teaspoon freshly ground black pepper
- ⅛ teaspoon crushed red pepper
- ⅓ cup heavy whipping cream or half-and-half (optional)
- 2 tablespoons finely chopped fresh parsley

1. Heat 1 tablespoon of the oil in a large skillet over medium heat. Add the beef and cook, stirring and chopping it into small pieces, until browned, about 10 minutes. Drain any excess fat and set the meat aside.
2. Heat the remaining 1 tablespoon oil in a large pot over medium heat. Add the onion and celery, and sauté until tender, about 7 minutes. Stir in the garlic and flour, and cook for 3 minutes longer.
3. Stir in the broth, water, potatoes, carrot, corn, basil, salt, oregano, granulated garlic, black pepper, and red pepper, along with the cooked ground beef. Return to a simmer and cook, stirring occasionally, until the vegetables are tender, about 15 minutes.
4. Turn off the heat and stir in the cream, if using, and parsley. Because some broths are saltier than others, taste the soup and add more salt if necessary.
5. **TO FREEZE:** Cool completely before freezing. This soup packs well in freezer bags or rigid containers.

NOTE: *Shred the potatoes immediately before adding them to the soup so they don't have a chance to turn brown.*

Italian Beef & Veggie Stew

This "everything but the kitchen sink" stew is a wonderful way to use up the veggie odds and ends you have hanging around. It's got a ton of vegetables, and I just love how they seem to soak up the rich beef broth.

YIELD: 6 SERVINGS

This recipe can be doubled or tripled.

- 2 tablespoons extra-virgin olive oil
- 2 pounds lean ground beef
- 1 small yellow onion, diced
- 2 celery stalks, diced
- 3 garlic cloves, minced
- 4 cups beef broth
- 4 cups diced paste tomatoes or other meaty tomatoes, in ½-inch pieces, or 1 (14.5-ounce) can diced tomatoes
- 2 tablespoons tomato paste
- 2 medium carrots, thinly sliced in half-moons
- 1½ cups diced zucchini, in ½-inch pieces
- 1 cup diced green beans, in ½-inch pieces
- 1 teaspoon dried basil
- 1 teaspoon dried oregano
- 1 teaspoon dried rosemary
- 1 teaspoon sea salt, plus more as needed
- ¼ teaspoon freshly ground black pepper
- 1 (16-ounce) can kidney beans, drained and rinsed

1. Heat 1 tablespoon of the oil in a large skillet over medium heat. Add the beef and cook, stirring and chopping it into small pieces, until browned, about 10 minutes. Drain any excess fat and set the meat aside.
2. Heat the remaining 1 tablespoon oil in a large pot over medium heat. Add the onion and celery, and sauté until tender, about 7 minutes. Stir in the garlic and cook for 3 minutes longer.
3. Stir in the broth, tomatoes, tomato paste, carrots, zucchini, green beans, basil, oregano, rosemary, salt, and pepper, along with the cooked ground beef. Bring to a boil, then simmer gently until the carrots are tender, about 15 minutes.
4. Turn off the heat and add the kidney beans. Because some broths are saltier than others, taste the stew and add salt if necessary.
5. **TO FREEZE:** Cool completely before freezing. This stew packs well in freezer bags or rigid containers.

Roasted Carrot & Tomato Soup with Lentils

Roasting the veggies is a small extra step that gives this soup big flavor. The carrots caramelize nicely, the tomatoes deepen in flavor, and the garlic turns from pungent to nutty. And by the way, your house is about to smell amazing!

YIELD: 4–6 SERVINGS

This recipe can be doubled or tripled.

- 1 whole head of garlic
- 2 tablespoons plus 1 teaspoon extra-virgin olive oil
- 4 large carrots, cut into 1-inch pieces
- 4 cups chopped paste tomatoes or other meaty tomatoes, in 2-inch pieces
- 2 cups water
- 1 tablespoon butter
- ½ medium yellow onion, finely diced
- 1 celery stalk, finely diced
- 4 cups vegetable broth
- 1½ cups dry French green lentils
- 1 teaspoon dried thyme
- 1 teaspoon sea salt, plus more as needed
- ¼ teaspoon freshly ground black pepper
- 1 tablespoon finely chopped fresh parsley

1. Preheat the oven to 425°F (220°C). Cut off the top of the garlic head to just expose the cloves. Cut an 8-inch square of aluminum foil and cradle the garlic bulb in it. Drizzle the exposed garlic cloves with 1 teaspoon of the oil, then wrap the garlic in the foil.
2. Place the carrots and tomatoes on a large sheet pan and toss with the remaining 2 tablespoons oil. Put the foil-wrapped garlic on the pan off to the side.
3. Bake for 45 to 50 minutes, until the carrots are tender and starting to brown.
4. Cool to a safe handling temperature, then transfer the carrots and tomatoes to a blender, including any liquid from the pan. Unwrap the garlic and squeeze out the softened cloves. Add about half of the cloves to the blender; save the rest for a different use. Add the water and blend on high until very smooth, about 1 minute.
5. Melt the butter in a large pot over medium heat. Add the onion and celery, and sauté until tender, about 7 minutes.
6. Stir in the broth, lentils, thyme, salt, and pepper, along with the puréed carrot and tomato mixture. Bring to a boil, then cover and simmer gently, stirring occasionally, until the lentils are tender, about 35 minutes.
7. Turn off the heat and stir in the parsley. Because some broths are saltier than others, taste the soup and add more salt if necessary.
8. **TO FREEZE:** Cool completely before freezing. This soup packs well in freezer bags or rigid containers.

TIP Turn this recipe into a soup starter! Roast the tomatoes, carrots, and garlic following steps 1 through 3, then unwrap the garlic as instructed in step 4 and freeze the ingredients. After thawing, blend with 2 cups water and proceed to step 5.

STAUB
STAUB

Beef Stew over Mashed Potatoes

Traditional beef stew with hearty chunks of potato will always hold a place in my heart, but it's hard to beat the combination of buttery mashed potatoes with a rich gravy. Once you try it, I think you'll be hooked! And because mashed potatoes freeze quite well, this is an excellent way to preserve beef stew.

YIELD: 6 SERVINGS

This recipe can be doubled or tripled.

FOR THE STEW

- 3 tablespoons extra-virgin olive oil
- 2 pounds beef stew meat, cut into 1-inch cubes
- ½ cup water
- 1 large yellow onion, diced
- 2 celery stalks, diced
- 3 garlic cloves, minced
- 2 tablespoons all-purpose flour or gluten-free flour blend
- 4 cups beef broth
- 1 teaspoon dried rosemary
- 1 teaspoon dried thyme
- ½ teaspoon sea salt, plus more as needed
- ¼ teaspoon freshly ground black pepper
- 3 large carrots, diced
- 1 cup frozen peas
- 2 tablespoons finely chopped fresh parsley

FOR THE MASHED POTATOES

- 3 pounds starchy or all-purpose potatoes (like russets or Yukon Golds)
- 4 tablespoons butter, cut into small pieces
- 1 teaspoon sea salt
- ¾ cup half-and-half or whole milk

1. To make the stew, heat 1 tablespoon of the oil in a large skillet over medium heat. Dry the stew meat with a paper towel if it is moist, then place half of it in the pan in a single layer. Sear the meat on one side until it is brown, about 5 minutes. Toss the meat around and cook for 2 minutes longer, then remove it from the pan and set aside. Repeat with 1 more tablespoon of oil and the remaining meat. Pour the water into the hot pan and use a spatula to scrape up any brown bits from the bottom. Set the skillet with the pan juices aside.
2. Heat the remaining 1 tablespoon oil in a large pot over medium heat. Add the onion and celery, and sauté until tender, about 7 minutes. Stir in the garlic and flour, and cook for 3 minutes longer.
3. Add the broth, rosemary, thyme, salt, and pepper, along with the seared meat and the pan juices. Bring to a boil, then simmer gently until the meat is tender, about 1 hour.
4. Stir in the carrots and continue cooking until tender, about 15 minutes. Stir in the peas and cook for 3 minutes longer.
5. Turn off the heat and stir in the parsley. Because some broths are saltier than others, taste the stew and add salt if necessary.

6. Meanwhile, make the mashed potatoes. Scrub and peel the potatoes, then cut them into 2-inch pieces. Place them in a large pot and fill it with cold water to about 2 inches above the potatoes. Bring to a boil, then simmer gently until the potatoes are tender, about 20 minutes. When the potatoes can be pierced with a fork, they're done.
7. Drain the potatoes and immediately return them to the pot. Add the butter and salt, and use a handheld masher to mash the potatoes until almost smooth. Use a whisk to incorporate the half-and-half while giving the potatoes a light final whipping.
8. **TO FREEZE:** Cool completely before freezing. For individual servings, ladle the stew into rigid containers, then spoon the mashed potatoes on top. Alternatively, freeze the stew and mashed potatoes in separate containers; they pack well separately in freezer bags or rigid containers.

Swiss Chard & Lentil Soup

This is the soup I want to eat when I'm feeling under the weather. With sausage, lentils, and lots of greens in a rich chicken broth, it may just have the power to cure whatever ails you. Kidding, of course . . . but that's what it feels like. This soup goes into the freezer thick, so feel free to thin it with extra broth or water when thawed for serving.

YIELD: 5 SERVINGS

This recipe can be doubled or tripled.

- 2 tablespoons extra-virgin olive oil
- 1 pound mild Italian pork sausage
- 1 medium yellow onion, diced
- 2 celery stalks, diced
- 2 garlic cloves, minced
- 4 cups chicken broth
- 1 cup water
- 1 cup dry French green lentils
- 2 medium carrots, thinly sliced
- 1 cup diced paste tomatoes or other meaty tomatoes, in ½-inch pieces
- 1 bay leaf
- 1 teaspoon dried oregano
- ½ teaspoon dried thyme
- ½ teaspoon sea salt, plus more as needed
- ¼ teaspoon freshly ground black pepper
- 2 cups firmly packed chopped Swiss chard leaves (see Note)

1. Heat 1 tablespoon of the oil in a large skillet over medium heat. If the sausage is in link form, remove it from the casings. Add the sausage and cook, stirring and chopping it into small pieces, until browned, about 10 minutes. Drain any excess fat and set the meat aside.
2. Heat the remaining 1 tablespoon oil in a large pot over medium heat. Add the onion and celery, and sauté until tender, about 7 minutes. Add the garlic and cook for 3 minutes longer.
3. Stir in the broth, water, lentils, carrots, tomatoes, bay leaf, oregano, thyme, salt, and pepper, along with the cooked sausage. Bring to a boil, then simmer until the lentils are just tender, about 25 minutes.
4. Turn off the heat and immediately add the Swiss chard, stirring it into the soup until it is slightly wilted, about 3 minutes. Because some broths are saltier than others, taste the soup and add more salt if necessary.
5. **TO FREEZE:** Cool completely before freezing. This soup packs well in freezer bags or rigid containers.

NOTE: *To prepare and measure the Swiss chard, tear the leaves from the center rib, then chop the leaves into 2- to 3-inch pieces. Pack them firmly into the measuring cup until you have 2 cups.*

Swiss Chard & Lentil Soup and Curried Acorn Squash Soup (page 78) ready for the freezer

Curried Acorn Squash Soup

I'd usually recommend using whatever type of winter squash you have on hand for a soup like this, but it really is superior with acorn. Squash that is vibrant orange and richer will overpower the warm curry spice. I like to swirl a spoonful of cream into my bowl after the soup is heated, and top it with butter-fried pepitas (pumpkin seeds).

YIELD: 4 SERVINGS

This recipe can be doubled or tripled.

- 2 medium acorn squash
- 2 tablespoons butter or extra-virgin olive oil
- 1 medium yellow onion, diced
- 1 large carrot, diced
- 2 garlic cloves, minced
- 2 teaspoons curry powder
- 4 cups vegetable broth
- ½ teaspoon sea salt, plus more as needed
- ¼ teaspoon freshly ground black pepper

1. Preheat the oven to 400°F (200°C). Line a large sheet pan with parchment paper.
2. Remove the squash stems, then cut each squash in half from top to bottom. Place the halves cut-side down on the prepared pan.
3. Bake for 55 to 60 minutes, until the squash is tender and starting to caramelize on the bottom.
4. Cool to a safe handling temperature, then use a spoon to scrape out and discard the squash seeds. Scoop out the flesh, measure out 3 cups, and set it aside.
5. Melt the butter in a large pot over medium heat. Add the onion and carrot, and sauté until tender, about 10 minutes. Stir in the garlic and curry powder, and cook for 3 minutes longer.
6. Add the broth, salt, and pepper, along with the cooked squash. Bring to a boil, then simmer gently until the carrots are very tender and the flavors have melded, about 15 minutes.
7. Cool to a safe handling temperature, then use an immersion blender or transfer to a countertop blender and blend on high until smooth, about 30 seconds. Because some broths are saltier than others, taste the soup and add more salt if necessary.
8. **TO FREEZE:** Cool completely before freezing. This soup packs well in freezer bags or rigid containers.

TIP Turn this recipe into a soup starter! Roast the acorn squash following steps 1 through 4, then freeze it. To make the soup, thaw the squash and proceed with step 5.

Creamy Chipotle Butternut Squash Stew

Growing squash always feels like capturing sunshine, and I love adding that brightness to soups. Thanks to the fiber-rich squash, beans, and corn, this vegetarian stew is a hearty one! There's a bit of heat from the chipotle peppers, but the sweet squash has a delightful way of mellowing it out.

YIELD: 5 SERVINGS

This recipe can be doubled or tripled.

- 1 tablespoon extra-virgin olive oil or avocado oil
- 1 medium yellow onion, diced
- 1 large red bell pepper, diced
- 2 jalapeños, deseeded and finely diced
- 2 garlic cloves, minced
- 4 cups vegetable broth
- 2 cups diced paste tomatoes or other meaty tomatoes, in ½-inch pieces
- 2 tablespoons tomato paste
- 1 chipotle pepper in adobo sauce (canned), finely chopped
- 2 teaspoons taco seasoning
- ½ teaspoon sea salt, plus more as needed
- 3 cups peeled, diced butternut squash, in ½-inch pieces
- 1 cup sweet corn kernels, fresh or frozen
- 1 (15-ounce) can black beans, drained and rinsed
- ⅓ cup heavy whipping cream

1. Heat the oil in a large pot over medium heat. Add the onion, bell pepper, and jalapeños, and sauté until tender, about 10 minutes. Add the garlic and cook for 3 minutes longer.
2. Stir in the broth, tomatoes, tomato paste, chipotle pepper, taco seasoning, and salt. Bring to a boil, then add the squash and corn. Return to a simmer and cook, stirring occasionally, until the squash is tender, about 15 minutes.
3. Turn off the heat and stir in the beans and cream. Because some broths are saltier than others, taste the stew and add more salt if necessary.
4. **TO FREEZE:** Cool completely before freezing. This stew packs well in freezer bags or rigid containers.

Autumn Pumpkin & Sausage Soup

This soup is loveliest during fall when those cold-weather foods seem to hit just right. There's no flour or dairy in this soup. Instead the broth is slightly thickened by puréeing some of the squash, which means it holds up very well in the freezer.

YIELD: 4 SERVINGS

This recipe can be doubled or tripled.

- 2 tablespoons extra-virgin olive oil or avocado oil
- 1 pound mild Italian pork sausage
- 1 medium yellow onion, diced
- 2 celery stalks, diced
- 3 garlic cloves, minced
- 4 cups chicken broth
- 1 medium carrot, diced
- 3 cups peeled, diced butternut or other winter squash, in ½-inch pieces
- 2 teaspoons dried sage
- ½ teaspoon dried rosemary
- ½ teaspoon dried thyme
- ½ teaspoon sea salt, plus more as needed
- ¼ teaspoon crushed red pepper
- ¼ teaspoon freshly ground black pepper
- 1 (15-ounce) can cannellini beans, drained and rinsed
- 2 cups firmly packed chopped spinach or Swiss chard leaves (see Note)

1. Heat 1 tablespoon of the oil in a large skillet over medium heat. If the sausage is in link form, remove it from the casings. Add the sausage and cook, stirring and chopping it into small pieces, until browned, about 10 minutes. Drain any excess fat and set the meat aside.
2. Heat the remaining 1 tablespoon oil in a large pot over medium heat. Add the onion and celery, and sauté until tender, about 7 minutes. Add the garlic and cook for 3 minutes longer.
3. Stir in the broth, carrot, 1 cup of the squash, and the sage, rosemary, thyme, salt, red pepper, and black pepper. Bring to a boil, then cover and simmer gently until the carrot and squash are tender, about 15 minutes.
4. Allow the soup to cool to a safe handling temperature, then use an immersion blender or transfer to a countertop blender and blend on high until smooth, about 30 seconds. Pour the purée back into the pot if you used a countertop blender. Return the pot to the stove and bring to a simmer.
5. Stir in the remaining 2 cups squash, along with the cooked sausage. Simmer uncovered, stirring occasionally, until the squash is tender, about 15 minutes.
6. Add the beans and spinach, and cook until the spinach is wilted, about 3 minutes. Because some broths are saltier than others, taste the soup and add more salt if necessary.
7. **TO FREEZE:** Cool completely before freezing. This soup packs well in freezer bags or rigid containers.

NOTE: *To prepare and measure the spinach or Swiss chard, tear the leaves from the center rib, then chop the leaves into 2- to 3-inch pieces. No need to remove the ribs if using baby greens. Pack them firmly into the measuring cup until you have 2 cups.*

CHAPTER 3

DRINK STARTERS, SAUCES & DIPS

During the growing season, there's no shortage of sensational flavors to be preserved. Fruity beverages add brightness to our days, flavorful sauces add depth to our meals, and homemade dips are a joy to serve to company. Being able to pull a container of garden-fresh salsa, marinara sauce, or pesto from the freezer is a feeling I'll never tire of!

Freezing Drink Starters

Freezing fresh fruit juice or purée as a drink starter is a fun way to preserve the flavor of in-season fruit. Having drink starters on hand will liven up sparkling water, cocktails, or smoothies. Turning cranberries into Cranberry Juice Cubes (page 86) will give you a refreshing glass of cranberry juice whenever you want!

Peach Iced Tea (page 88) will turn ripe fruit into a high-value freezer item. Juicy ripe peaches are blended, strained, sweetened, and frozen. To make a spectacular peach iced tea any time of year, brew up some black tea and stir in a container of starter. This technique can be applied to other fruits like raspberries and drinks such as lemonade.

Freezing Salsas, Sauces & Pestos

Most vegetable-based sauces and salsas do incredibly well in the freezer, which hinges on the fact that they're usually cooked until tender, and sometimes blended. A good rule of thumb is that if the dish is cooked and the texture is meant to be soft, it will likely freeze well. Garden Veggie Marinara Sauce (page 97) is a prime example of this. Vegetables like zucchini, green beans, and bell peppers are roasted in the oven with tomatoes, then blended into a smooth sauce. When tossed with pasta or served over meatballs, it's a flavorful way to enjoy these frozen veggies. Vegetables do better in the freezer when cooked or blanched first, so raw veggie-based sauces should

Blanching kale before turning it into pesto will give it a vibrant color as well as a clean flavor that keeps well in the freezer.

be avoided. In Rustic Kale Pesto (page 91), the kale is blanched, which helps it retain a bright color and avoid a skunky flavor in the freezer. Because herbs freeze well raw, herb-based pestos and sauces don't require blanching or cooking.

Herbs also freeze well as blended sauces, especially when paired with citrus juice, like in Cilantro Lime Sauce (page 89). The citrus provides a liquid to help the herbs blend down into a purée and gives the mixture a punch of flavor. There's a huge variety of herb and citrus combinations you can put together for flavoring everything from tacos to roasted potatoes. Hot peppers (in small quantities) are also a welcome addition to blended sauces.

Tomatoes are the most talented members of the freezing world—they seem to work in just about everything! Cooked tomato sauces of all kinds freeze splendidly, so you can have confidence in experimenting with them. My frozen pantry is perpetually stocked with unique tomato-based staples like Roasted Butternut Squash Tomato Sauce (page 98) and Fire-Roasted Tomato, Corn & Black Bean Salsa (page 94).

Freezing Dips & Dip Starters

Dipping foods into other foods always delights me! And between completed dips and dip starters, there are some absolute gems in this chapter.

Most cooked vegetables do well in the freezer, and that also translates to dips. Spicy Roasted Carrot Dip (page 100) is an unconventional dip that uses carrots roasted with harissa, and it comes out of the freezer just as it went in. Dips that are based in raw vegetables are not good candidates for the freezer, as their taste and texture are likely to suffer. However, dips with a small amount of finely chopped, raw aromatics like jalapeño, onion, garlic, or herbs will do just fine.

Raw fruits fare much better in the freezer. Cranberry Salsa & Cream Cheese Dip (page 103) is a fruit-based dip that will make you want to stock up on cranberries every fall! The chopped cranberries are combined with a little sugar, ginger, onion, jalapeño, and lime before being frozen. This fruity, crowd-pleasing salsa is spooned over cream cheese and served with crackers. Its brilliant red color makes it perfect for stashing away for wintertime parties.

Cheesy and creamy dishes will often turn crumbly or separate once thawed, so most dairy-heavy dips are not recommended for freezing. This is where crafting a dip starter is helpful! We'll freeze the portion of the recipe that uses fresh ingredients and needs preserving, then add the dairy once it's thawed. In Eggplant Yogurt Dip (page 104), the eggplant is roasted, mixed with garlic and spices, then frozen. To make the dip, the thawed eggplant mixture is stirred into yogurt for an instant appetizer. One exception is that if the dip will be baked and the base is predominately cream cheese, it will come out of the freezer just fine. This is the case for Creamy Baked Swiss Chard Dip (page 106).

Thawing Drink Starters, Sauces & Dips

When thawing foods with raw ingredients like fruit or herbs, use the refrigerator or the cold-water method (see page 21); do not thaw with heat. Similarly, anything that will be served cold, like some drink starters and dips, should not be thawed with heat. Sauces and salsa that were cooked and will be served warm can be thawed with any of the recommended methods, including in the microwave if needed.

Cranberry Juice Cubes

Enjoy a single serving of of cranberry juice whenever you want! Add these frozen cubes to a glass of still or sparkling water for instant cranberry juice, or use them in smoothies or vodka cocktails. I freeze these unsweetened (otherwise they can get sticky) and sweeten my drink to taste with honey or maple syrup once the cubes have thawed.

YIELD: NINE 1½-INCH CUBES
This recipe can be doubled or tripled.

- 3 cups cranberries
- 2 cups water

1. Combine the cranberries and water in a blender. Blend on low until the cranberries are broken up to between the size of peas and rice, about 5 seconds; do not completely purée them.
2. Pour the cranberry mixture into a medium saucepan over medium heat. Bring to a boil, then simmer gently for 10 minutes. Turn off the heat, cover the pan, and let the cranberries steep for 10 minutes.
3. Set a fine-mesh sieve over a heatproof bowl and pour the cranberry mixture into the sieve. Let the cranberries drain for 20 minutes, stirring and folding them around occasionally to help them drain. Use the back of a spoon to gently press any remaining liquid out of the cranberries. Discard the leftover cranberry purée from the sieve. (It can be used for another purpose, though it will have lost a lot of its flavor.)
4. **TO FREEZE:** Pour the mixture into an ice cube mold (or similar). Freeze overnight until the cubes are frozen solid, then transfer the cubes to a freezer bag for storage.

Cranberry Juice and Lemon Ginger Tea

Lemon Ginger Tea Cubes

A cube of sour lemon and spicy ginger melted into a mug of hot water is a surefire way to get me going in the morning! I like that these are blended instead of juiced, so they contain the fiber, though you could adapt this idea to juicing instead. In addition to making a tea, these cubes can also flavor drinks like sparkling water or kombucha.

YIELD: EIGHT 2-INCH CUBES

This recipe can be doubled or tripled.

- 1 cup peeled, deseeded, roughly chopped lemons (about 4 medium; see Note)
- ⅓ cup chopped fresh ginger, in ½-inch pieces
- ¼ cup water

1. Combine the lemons, ginger (no need to peel), and water in a high-speed blender. Blend on high until it forms a smooth purée, about 30 seconds.
2. **TO FREEZE:** Pour the mixture into an ice cube mold (or similar). Freeze overnight until the cubes are frozen solid, then transfer the cubes to a freezer bag for storage.

NOTE: *To peel a lemon, cut a small slice from the top and bottom so it sits flat. Cut the rind and white pith away from the flesh, then remove the seeds and cut into chunks.*

Honey Lemonade

Every year our local beekeepers club has a booth at the county fair selling lemonade made with locally produced honey. The lemonade is always a big hit, and it's a fantastic opportunity to educate the public about honey bees. Just thaw this starter and mix with water for lemonade in an instant—it's very restorative on a hot day.

YIELD: 1 BATCH OF CONCENTRATE, MAKES 5 CUPS OF LEMONADE

This recipe can be doubled or tripled to make additional batches.

MAKING & FREEZING THE STARTER

- 1¼ cups freshly squeezed lemon or lime juice
- ⅔ cup raw honey
- Pinch of sea salt
- 1 (3-inch) strip lemon zest

1. Whisk together the lemon juice, honey, and salt in a mixing bowl until the honey is completely dissolved, which may take several minutes. Stir in the lemon zest.
2. **TO FREEZE:** Because it is liquid, this starter packs best in a rigid container. The recipe fits in a 2-cup freezer container.

MAKING THE LEMONADE

- 1 recipe frozen Honey Lemonade starter, thawed
- 3 cups cold water
- Ice

Remove the lemon zest from the starter and discard it. Stir together the starter and water, then pour over ice and serve.

Peach Iced Tea

Fresh peaches can fill a room with their perfumed scent, and this method captures that essence perfectly! To enjoy a pitcher of peach iced tea anytime, brew up a pot of black tea and add a container of this concentrate. This starter conveniently fits in a 2-cup container and makes 2 quarts of lightly sweetened tea. If you're highly particular about your tea, feel free to adapt the recipe to your preferences.

YIELD: 1 BATCH OF CONCENTRATE, MAKES 2 QUARTS OF TEA

This recipe can be doubled or tripled to make additional batches.

MAKING & FREEZING THE STARTER

- 4 cups chopped peaches, in 1-inch pieces (about 3 large)
- 1 cup water
- ⅓ cup sugar

1. Combine the peaches and water in a blender. Blend on medium until the peaches are broken up to the size of peas, about 3 seconds; do not completely purée them.
2. Pour the peach mixture into a medium pan over medium heat. Bring to a boil, then simmer gently for 5 minutes. Turn off the heat, cover the pan, and let the peaches steep for 10 minutes.
3. Set a fine-mesh sieve over a heatproof bowl. Place the sugar in the bowl underneath, and pour the peach mixture into the sieve on top. Let the peaches drain for 20 minutes, stirring and folding them around occasionally to help them drain. Use the back of a spoon to gently press any remaining liquid out of the peaches.
4. As the juice and sugar cool, stir the mixture in the bowl occasionally to help the sugar dissolve. Discard the leftover peach purée from the sieve. (It can be used for another purpose, though it will have lost a lot of its flavor and sweetness.)
5. **TO FREEZE:** Cool completely before freezing. Because it is liquid, this starter packs best in a rigid container. The recipe fits in a 2-cup freezer container.

MAKING THE TEA

- 6 cups water
- 6 black tea bags
- 1 recipe frozen Peach Iced Tea starter, thawed
- Ice

1. Bring the water to a boil in a medium saucepan over medium heat. Turn off the heat, add the tea bags, cover the pan, and let steep for 5 minutes. Remove and discard the tea bags. Allow the tea to completely cool.
2. Combine the tea with the starter in a pitcher. Stir well, then serve over ice in glasses (preferably with straws for stirring).

Cilantro Lime Sauce

Cilantro is one of those "feast or famine" herbs in my garden. We have baskets overflowing with it early in the season, but it dries up once summer's heat sets in. When cilantro is in abundance, I blend it into this vibrant sauce that I serve with breakfast burritos, or I stir it into cooked rice.

YIELD: 1 CUP

This recipe can be doubled or tripled.

- 2 cups firmly packed fresh cilantro leaves and stems
- ¼ cup freshly squeezed lime juice
- 1 tablespoon avocado oil or other neutral oil
- 1 tablespoon water
- 1 teaspoon honey or sugar
- ½ teaspoon finely grated lime zest
- ⅛ teaspoon sea salt

1. Combine the cilantro, lime juice, oil, water, honey, lime zest, and salt in a blender. Blend on high until smooth but with some dark green cilantro flecks still intact, about 30 seconds. Use the tamper or a spatula to help push down the cilantro if needed.
2. **TO FREEZE:** Freeze immediately. Because it blends down into a relatively small amount, this sauce packs best in rigid containers; I prefer to freeze it in small 4-ounce glass jars or in individual cubes.

Chimichurri-Style Sauce

I'm a lover of fresh parsley (I put the stuff on everything when it's growing fresh!), so this vibrant sauce is a staple in my freezer. Used traditionally for topping grilled meats, this herb-packed green sauce can be stirred in while cooking or served as a raw topping at the table. It adds a refreshing hit of acidity and a tangy burst of flavor to steak, fish, grilled veggies, or roasted potatoes.

YIELD: 1¾ CUPS

This recipe can be doubled or tripled.

- 2 cups finely chopped fresh flat-leaf parsley
- 1 tablespoon finely grated fresh garlic
- 2 teaspoons dried oregano
- 1 teaspoon finely grated red onion
- ½ teaspoon crushed red pepper
- ¼ teaspoon sea salt
- ¾ cup extra-virgin olive oil
- 3 tablespoons red wine vinegar
- 2 tablespoons freshly squeezed lemon juice

1. Stir together the parsley, garlic, oregano, onion, red pepper, and salt in a small mixing bowl or pint jar, then stir in the oil, vinegar, and lemon juice. Let the mixture sit for 15 minutes, and stir again.
2. **TO FREEZE:** Freeze immediately to retain a brighter green color. Because the recipe makes a relatively small amount, this sauce packs best in rigid containers; I prefer 4-ounce glass jars.
3. **TO SERVE:** Bring to room temperature for 10 minutes before serving so that the oil, if solidified, can melt back into a liquid. Chimichurri can turn brown the longer it sits. This is a reaction between the vinegar and herbs; it isn't harmful and doesn't affect the flavor.

TIP ❄ While you can use a food processor to chop the parsley, the quality will be best when hand chopped with a sharp knife. A food processor can bruise the herbs, which isn't a big deal if you're eating the sauce fresh but can affect its quality when preserving it for a longer time.

Rustic Kale Pesto

I call this "rustic" because the kale stems give it a slightly fibrous look, and it tastes like something you'd be served on a quaint farm in the countryside. Pairing it with crispy-fried potatoes and eggs is my favorite way to eat it, but it can also be swirled through pasta or heirloom beans, or served with chicken. Because the kale is blanched, this pesto retains a vibrant green color and flavor.

YIELD: 2 CUPS

Do not double. To increase yield, make consecutive batches.

- 12 large stalks "dinosaur" or lacinato-type kale
- 2 garlic cloves, peeled
- ⅓ cup grated Parmesan cheese
- ⅓ cup extra-virgin olive oil
- 2 teaspoons freshly squeezed lemon juice
- ¼ teaspoon sea salt

1. Bring a large pot of water to a rolling boil.
2. Cut the kale into thirds, including the stems. Place the kale and garlic in the boiling water and cook, stirring occasionally, until the kale is just tender, about 4 minutes. Drain the kale and garlic in a colander for 1 minute.
3. The kale will be warm and still a little wet, which will help it blend. Combine the kale and garlic in a food processor along with the Parmesan, oil, lemon juice, and salt. Process until it forms a loose paste, about 1 minute.
4. **TO FREEZE:** Cool completely before freezing. Because it is thick, this pesto packs best in rigid containers. Consider freezing smaller portions in an ice cube tray or silicone mold.

Sweet Pepper Relish

A condiment of epic importance in our household, we use this daily for topping our fried eggs. We also serve it on hamburgers, grilled cheese, and hot dogs or even mix it into tuna salad. The best part about this relish? It's customizable to whatever peppers you have, and the heat level can be dialed up or down depending on what you like.

YIELD: 4 CUPS

This recipe can be doubled or tripled.

- 7 cups finely chopped sweet bell peppers and jalapeños (see Note)
- 1 small yellow onion, finely chopped
- ½ cup sugar
- ¼ cup apple cider vinegar
- ¼ cup distilled white vinegar
- 1 teaspoon sea salt

1. Combine the peppers, onion, sugar, vinegars, and salt in a large pot over medium heat. Bring to a boil, then simmer, stirring occasionally, until the peppers are tender and most of the liquid has evaporated, about 30 minutes.
2. **TO FREEZE:** Cool completely before freezing. This relish benefits from being refrigerated overnight before freezing so that the flavors can meld. It packs best in rigid containers; I prefer 8-ounce straight-sided glass jars.

NOTE: *This is a very adaptable recipe, but my preferred ratio is 75 percent colorful bell peppers (green, red, yellow, and orange) and 25 percent jalapeños. I typically use about 5 large bell peppers and 10 jalapeños, which makes a moderately spicy relish. You can also incorporate poblanos and any specialty peppers. To prepare the peppers, remove the seeds and ribs and then cut them into large pieces. Pulse in a food processor until finely chopped but not puréed, then measure out 7 cups. Work in batches if needed.*

Tomatillo Avocado Salsa

The secret to a tomatillo salsa that holds up well in the freezer and doesn't tiptoe into enchilada sauce territory is to cook the tomatillos but leave the peppers, onions, and garlic raw. This one is blended with avocado to make a zippy and creamy dip for chips or for drizzling on fish tacos or fajitas. It comes out of the freezer with a smooth texture and a sprightly fresh flavor.

YIELD: 3 CUPS

This recipe can be doubled.

- 1 tablespoon avocado oil or other neutral oil
- 1 pound whole tomatillos, husks removed and rinsed (about 6 medium)
- 1 large ripe avocado, roughly chopped
- ½ small yellow onion, roughly chopped
- 1 jalapeño, deseeded and roughly chopped
- 1 garlic clove, minced
- 2 tablespoons chopped fresh cilantro
- 1 tablespoon freshly squeezed lime juice
- ¼ teaspoon sea salt

1. Heat the oil in a large skillet over medium-high heat and add the tomatillos in a single layer. Cook, stirring occasionally, until the tomatillos have turned from bright green to a lighter drab green and are browning on all sides, about 10 minutes. Turn off the heat and let the tomatillos cool in the pan for 10 minutes.
2. Combine the tomatillos, avocado, onion, jalapeño, garlic, cilantro, lime juice, and salt in a blender. Blend on high until mostly smooth with a few chunks left, about 30 seconds.
3. **TO FREEZE:** Refrigerate immediately and allow the salsa to cool for 1 hour before freezing. This salsa packs well in freezer bags or rigid containers.

Fire-Roasted Tomato, Corn & Black Bean Salsa

Broiling the tomatoes until the skins are charred black is quick, adds a fire-roasted flavor, and causes the skins to crumble instead of turn into big stringy pieces. Win-win-win! The addition of black beans and fresh sweet corn makes this the heartiest of salsas for serving with salty tortilla chips.

YIELD: ABOUT 10 CUPS

This recipe can be doubled or tripled.

- 5 pounds paste tomatoes or other meaty tomatoes (see Note)
- 1 large green bell pepper
- 1 large poblano pepper or additional green bell pepper
- 5 jalapeños, deseeded
- 1 large yellow onion
- 1 large red onion
- 1 tablespoon avocado oil or other neutral oil
- 4 garlic cloves, minced
- ⅓ cup freshly squeezed lime juice
- 3 tablespoons distilled white vinegar
- 2 teaspoons sea salt
- 2 cups fresh sweet corn kernels (about 2 large ears)
- 1 (15-ounce) can black beans, drained and rinsed

1. Position an oven rack in the middle of the oven and preheat the broiler.
2. Cut the tomatoes in half from top to bottom and place them skin-side up in a single layer on a large sheet pan (do not use parchment paper). Use multiple pans if needed. Broil for 10 to 15 minutes, until the tomatoes turn charred black on the top. Rotate the pans if needed for even charring, or remove any tomatoes that finish charring before the others.
3. Cool to a safe handling temperature, then transfer the tomatoes to the bowl of a food processor, including the charred skin and any liquid from the pan. Pulse until just puréed, about 30 seconds. Work in batches if needed. Pour the tomato purée into a bowl and set aside.
4. Cut the bell pepper, poblano, jalapeños, and onions into large pieces. Place them in the bowl of a food processor and pulse until finely chopped but not puréed, about 30 seconds. Work in batches if needed.
5. Heat the oil in a large pot over medium heat. Add the peppers and onions, and sauté, stirring occasionally, until tender, about 12 minutes.
6. Stir in the puréed tomatoes, along with the garlic, lime juice, vinegar, and salt. Bring to a boil, then simmer gently, stirring occasionally, until the salsa has thickened and is reduced by 25 percent, about 45 minutes. Make sure to scrape the bottom of the pan when stirring so that the salsa doesn't stick and burn.
7. Stir in the corn and simmer for 15 minutes. Turn off the heat and stir in the black beans.
8. **TO FREEZE:** Cool completely before freezing. This salsa benefits from being refrigerated overnight before freezing so that the flavors can meld. It packs well in freezer bags or rigid containers.

NOTE: *No need to remove the skins or seeds of the tomatoes. Paste tomatoes will yield a thicker sauce, but you can substitute meaty heirloom types in this recipe.*

Versatile Roasted Cherry Tomato Sauce

Every year I plant way too many cherry tomato plants, and every year I end up with more tomatoes than I can handle. I probably won't change my ways, either—I just adore those little tomatoes so much! Thankfully they sauce well if you roast them in the oven and have a powerful blender. This is a plain, slightly sweet sauce that bends however you need it to. Use it as a base for marinara sauce, tomato soup, Indian dishes, chili, and more.

YIELD: ABOUT 4 CUPS

This recipe can be doubled but requires an additional pan.

- 8 cups whole cherry tomatoes, or paste tomatoes cut into 2-inch pieces
- 1 tablespoon extra-virgin olive oil
- ½ teaspoon sea salt

1. Preheat the oven to 425°F (220°C).
2. Place the tomatoes in a glass or ceramic 13- by 9-inch baking pan, and toss with the oil and salt.
3. Bake for 50 to 60 minutes, until the tomatoes are bubbling and starting to brown on top.
4. Cool to a safe handling temperature, then transfer the tomatoes to a high-speed blender, including any liquid from the pan. Blend on high until smooth, about 30 seconds.
5. **TO FREEZE:** Cool completely before freezing. This sauce packs well in freezer bags or rigid containers.

Garden Veggie Marinara Sauce

This is a "use what you've got" sauce recipe that is exceptionally fast to whip up and loaded with fresh veggies. Roasting brings out the natural sweetness in vegetables, so if you're a fan of slightly sweet tomato sauce, you'll enjoy this one. Use it wherever you would use a traditional marinara; it's excellent with Italian meatballs.

YIELD: ABOUT 6 CUPS

This recipe can be doubled but requires an additional pan.

- 10 cups chopped tomatoes, in 2-inch pieces (about 3½ pounds whole; see Notes)
- 5 cups chopped assorted vegetables, in 2-inch pieces (see Notes)
- 2 garlic cloves, peeled
- 2 tablespoons extra-virgin olive oil
- 1 teaspoon sea salt
- 1 tablespoon chopped fresh basil
- 1 tablespoon finely chopped fresh parsley

1. Preheat the oven to 400°F (200°C).
2. Combine the tomatoes, assorted vegetables, and garlic on an 18- by 13-inch rimmed sheet pan. Toss with the oil and salt, then spread in an even layer.
3. Bake for 45 to 60 minutes, until the vegetables are tender and starting to brown.
4. Cool to a safe handling temperature, then transfer the vegetables to a blender, including any liquid from the pan. Add the basil and parsley, and blend on high until smooth, about 45 seconds.
5. **TO FREEZE:** Cool completely before freezing. This sauce benefits from being refrigerated overnight before freezing so that the flavors can meld. It packs well in freezer bags or rigid containers.

NOTES: *Any tomatoes work well in this recipe: paste, heirloom varieties, or large meaty cherry tomatoes. No need to remove the skins or seeds—just core the tomatoes and cut them into 2-inch pieces.*

Possible vegetables include onions, sweet bell peppers, eggplant, zucchini, yellow squash, green beans, fennel, winter squash, and carrots. The more variety of vegetables, the better! Just don't use too many peppers, as that pushes the flavor profile toward salsa instead of marinara. My preferred blend is 2 cups zucchini, 1 cup bell peppers, 1 cup eggplant, ½ cup green beans, and ½ cup carrots.

Roasted Butternut Squash Tomato Sauce

Squash gives this sauce a sweetness that reminds me of my childhood favorite, O-shaped spaghetti in a can. And it's perfect for re-creating a homemade version of that. (Don't forget to add the cut-up hot dogs!) For a more grown-up option, serve with penne and Italian sausage. I like to melt in an extra knob of butter when heating it up, then top it with a good dusting of fontina or Asiago cheese.

YIELD: ABOUT 5 CUPS

This recipe can be doubled but requires an additional pan.

- 10 cups chopped paste tomatoes or other meaty tomatoes, in 2-inch pieces (about 3½ pounds whole)
- 3 cups peeled, chopped butternut squash, in 1-inch pieces
- 1 small yellow onion, quartered
- 2 garlic cloves, peeled
- 1 tablespoon chopped fresh sage
- 2 teaspoons chopped fresh thyme
- 2 tablespoons melted butter or extra-virgin olive oil
- 1 teaspoon sea salt
- ¼ teaspoon freshly ground black pepper

1. Preheat the oven to 400°F (200°C).
2. Combine the tomatoes, squash, onion, garlic, sage, and thyme on an 18- by 13-inch rimmed sheet pan. Toss with the butter, salt, and pepper, then spread in an even layer.
3. Bake for 55 to 60 minutes, until the vegetables are tender and starting to brown.
4. Cool to a safe handling temperature, then transfer the vegetables to a blender, including any liquid from the pan. Blend on high until smooth, about 45 seconds.
5. **TO FREEZE:** Cool completely before freezing. This sauce benefits from being refrigerated overnight before freezing so that the flavors can meld. It packs well in freezer bags or rigid containers.

Winter Veggie Sauce

Inspired by a friend who can't eat tomatoes, this versatile sauce is based in carrots, squash, and beets. It's an earthy, hearty sauce that can be used as a marinara alternative for tomato-heavy recipes like lasagna and chili. It also pairs well with meats like baked chicken, beef roast, or meatballs. I'm always amazed at how tomato-esque this sauce tastes!

YIELD: 5 CUPS

This recipe can be doubled or tripled.

- 1 tablespoon extra-virgin olive oil
- 1 small yellow onion, diced
- 2 garlic cloves, minced
- 2 cups water
- 3 cups peeled, chopped butternut squash (or similar), in 1-inch pieces
- 1½ cups peeled, chopped beets, in 1-inch pieces
- 3 medium carrots, diced
- 1 teaspoon dried basil
- 1 teaspoon dried oregano
- 1 teaspoon sea salt
- ½ teaspoon dried rosemary
- ½ teaspoon dried thyme
- ¼ teaspoon freshly ground black pepper
- 2 teaspoons lemon juice, fresh or bottled
- 2 teaspoons red wine vinegar

1. Heat the oil in a large pot over medium heat. Add the onion and sauté until just tender, about 7 minutes. Add the garlic and cook for 3 minutes longer.
2. Stir in the water, squash, beets, carrots, basil, oregano, salt, rosemary, thyme, and pepper. Bring to a boil, then cover and simmer gently, stirring occasionally, until the veggies are tender, about 40 minutes. Turn off the heat and stir in the lemon juice and vinegar.
3. Cool to a safe handling temperature, then use an immersion blender or transfer to a countertop blender and blend on high until almost smooth with a little bit of texture remaining.
4. **TO FREEZE:** Cool completely before freezing. This sauce benefits from being refrigerated overnight before freezing so that the flavors can meld. It packs well in freezer bags or rigid containers.

Spicy Roasted Carrot Dip

This dip eats like creamy hummus but is made from roasted carrots. Serve it with veggies, pita chips, or warm pita bread, or use it on a Mediterranean salad or grain bowl. When I'm serving this to company and want it to look a little more fancy, I swirl it in a bowl and add a drizzle of olive oil and a sprinkle of cumin seeds on top.

YIELD: 2 CUPS

This recipe can be doubled.

- 5 cups sliced carrots, in ½-inch rounds (about 2 pounds)
- 1 garlic clove, peeled
- 2 tablespoons extra-virgin olive oil or avocado oil
- 1 tablespoon harissa powder
- ½ teaspoon sea salt
- 1 tablespoon almond butter
- 1 tablespoon freshly squeezed lemon juice

1. Preheat the oven to 400°F (200°C). Line a large sheet pan with parchment paper.
2. Combine the carrots, garlic, oil, harissa, and salt in a large bowl and toss until the carrots are well coated. Transfer the mixture to the prepared pan and arrange in an even layer.
3. Bake for 45 to 50 minutes, until the carrots are tender and starting to brown.
4. Allow the carrots and garlic to cool for 10 minutes, then transfer to a food processor. Add the almond butter and lemon juice, and process until all the carrots are finely chopped, stopping to scrape down the sides of the bowl as necessary. Continue processing until the mixture forms a creamy consistency and flows freely in the bowl, about 1 minute.
5. **TO FREEZE:** Cool completely before freezing. This dish benefits from being refrigerated overnight before freezing so that the flavors can meld. Because it is thick, this dip packs best in rigid containers.

Street Corn Dip

There's a little bit of everything in this Mexican elote-inspired dip: It's smoky, creamy, tangy, salty, sweet, and spicy. Freshly grilled sweet corn is such a delicacy during summer, and freezing it for this dip is a prime way to preserve it. Serve the dip with tortilla chips, or use it as a topping for taco salad, shrimp tacos, or fajitas.

YIELD: 6 SERVINGS

This recipe can be doubled or tripled to make additional batches.

MAKING & FREEZING THE STARTER

- 3 large ears of sweet corn
- 2 teaspoons extra-virgin olive oil or avocado oil
- 1 jalapeño, deseeded and very finely diced
- 1 tablespoon finely chopped fresh cilantro
- 1 tablespoon freshly squeezed lime juice
- 2 teaspoons chili powder
- 1 teaspoon sea salt
- ½ teaspoon granulated garlic
- ½ teaspoon granulated onion

1. Preheat the grill to high. Remove the husks and silks from the corn, then brush each ear evenly with the oil.
2. Think of the ear as a square, and grill each of its four sides until about 25 percent of the kernels turn golden brown and charred, about 3 minutes on each side for a total of 12 minutes. Let each side fully brown before turning to the next side, and keep the grill lid closed between turnings.
3. Cool to a safe handling temperature, then cut the kernels from the cob.
4. Stir together the corn, jalapeño, cilantro, lime juice, chili powder, salt, garlic, and onion in a large mixing bowl.
5. **TO FREEZE:** Cool completely before freezing. This starter packs well in a freezer bag or rigid container. The recipe fits in a 1-quart freezer bag.

MAKING THE DIP

- 2 tablespoons mayonnaise
- 2 tablespoons sour cream
- ½ cup grated cotija cheese
- 1 recipe frozen Street Corn Dip starter, thawed
- 2 tablespoons chopped fresh cilantro (optional)
- Tortilla chips

1. Stir together the mayonnaise and sour cream in a large mixing bowl. Fold in the cheese and starter.
2. Spoon into a serving bowl and garnish with fresh cilantro, if desired. Serve with tortilla chips.

Cranberry Salsa & Cream Cheese Dip

A beloved appetizer where I live here in cranberry country, this unexpected "salsa" is poured over cream cheese and served with crackers. I like mine with a hint of fresh ginger, which brings together this unique combination of ingredients. Because of its big flavors, this dip is best served with plain water crackers.

YIELD: 8–10 SERVINGS

Do not double. To increase yield, make consecutive batches.

MAKING & FREEZING THE STARTER

- 2½ cups fresh cranberries
- ¼ cup sugar
- 3 tablespoons freshly squeezed lime juice
- 2 tablespoons very finely diced red onion
- 1 jalapeño, deseeded and very finely diced
- ½ teaspoon sea salt
- ¼ teaspoon grated fresh ginger

1. Combine the cranberries, sugar, lime juice, onion, jalapeño, salt, and ginger in the bowl of a food processor. Pulse until the cranberries are in pieces between the size of peas and rice, about 10 pulses.
2. Cover and refrigerate for 1 hour, stirring occasionally to help the flavors meld.
3. **TO FREEZE:** This starter packs well in a freezer bag or rigid container. The recipe fits in a 2-cup freezer container.

MAKING THE DIP

- 8 ounces cream cheese, softened
- 1 recipe frozen Cranberry Salsa & Cream Cheese Dip starter, thawed
- Water crackers

1. Spread the cream cheese on a serving plate in a circle about 1 inch thick.
2. Give the starter a stir, then spoon it over the top of the cream cheese, including any liquid from the container. Serve with crackers.

Eggplant Yogurt Dip

This is one of those dishes that adapts to any season; it's refreshing in warmer months and comforting during cooler months. The eggplant is roasted, then chopped and mixed with garlic and spices before freezing. Just thaw and stir in yogurt to make a creamy dip! Serve with pita chips or seedy whole-grain crackers for an instant appetizer, party dip, or accompaniment to Indian or Mediterranean meals.

YIELD: 4 SERVINGS

This recipe can be doubled or tripled to make additional batches.

MAKING & FREEZING THE STARTER

- 1 medium dark purple eggplant
- 1 tablespoon finely chopped fresh parsley
- 1 teaspoon freshly squeezed lemon juice
- ½ teaspoon finely grated fresh garlic
- ½ teaspoon ground cumin
- 1 teaspoon sea salt

1. Preheat the oven to 400°F (200°C). Line a large sheet pan with parchment paper.
2. Poke the eggplant several times with a thin sharp knife and place it on the prepared pan.
3. Bake for 55 to 60 minutes, until the eggplant is soft all the way through. It's okay if it gets a little brown or charred on the outside.
4. Cool to a safe handling temperature, then cut the eggplant open from top to bottom and peel back the skin. Use a spoon to scrape out the flesh from inside and measure out 1 packed cup. (Reserve any excess for another use.) Transfer the eggplant flesh to a cutting board and finely chop it, working the knife in both directions.
5. Stir together the eggplant, parsley, lemon juice, garlic, cumin, and salt in a mixing bowl.
6. **TO FREEZE:** Cool completely before freezing. This starter packs best in a rigid container. The recipe fits in a 1-cup freezer container.

MAKING THE DIP

- 1 recipe frozen Eggplant Yogurt Dip starter, thawed
- ½ cup plain whole-milk Greek yogurt
- 1 teaspoon extra-virgin olive oil
- Pita chips, crackers, or fresh veggies

Stir together the starter, yogurt, and oil in a mixing bowl. This dip can be served immediately or refrigerated overnight. Serve with pita chips, crackers, or fresh vegetables.

Creamy Baked Swiss Chard Dip

This recipe uses loads of Swiss chard and bakes up considerably creamy and cheesy. You'd never know it was frozen! Swiss chard tastes a lot like spinach but is easier to grow, if you ask me. It always has a place in my garden . . . and in my freezer in various forms. Use regular full-fat dairy products in this recipe, because they freeze and bake up better than their low-fat counterparts.

YIELD: 8 SERVINGS

This recipe can be doubled or tripled to make additional batches.

MAKING & FREEZING THE STARTER

- 4 cups firmly packed chopped Swiss chard leaves (about 15 large leaves; see Note)
- 8 ounces cream cheese, softened
- ¾ cup grated Parmesan cheese
- ¼ cup mayonnaise
- ¼ cup sour cream
- 1 teaspoon sea salt
- ½ teaspoon granulated garlic
- ½ teaspoon granulated onion

1. Steam blanch (page 140) the Swiss chard leaves for 3 minutes, tossing the greens around at the 90-second mark. Alternatively, blanch in boiling water for 2 minutes. Transfer the Swiss chard to a large baking sheet to cool.
2. Use your hands to squeeze out as much water as possible from the greens. I like to divide it into three equal piles and squeeze each pile in my fist until no more water comes out. Finely chop the Swiss chard and set it aside.
3. Place the cream cheese in a large bowl. Using a hand mixer or stand mixer fitted with a paddle attachment, beat the cream cheese on high until fluffy, about 1 minute. Add the Parmesan, mayonnaise, sour cream, salt, garlic, and onion, and beat on low until just combined. Finally, add the Swiss chard and beat until it is evenly mixed through.
4. **TO FREEZE:** This starter packs well in a freezer bag or rigid container. The recipe fits in a 1-quart freezer bag.

NOTE: *To prepare and measure the Swiss chard, tear the leaves from the center rib, then chop the leaves into 2- to 3-inch pieces. Pack them firmly into the measuring cup until you have 4 cups.*

MAKING THE DIP

- 1 recipe frozen Creamy Baked Swiss Chard Dip starter, thawed
- 4 ounces mozzarella cheese, shredded
- Tortilla chips, toasted baguette slices, or celery

1. Preheat the oven to 400°F (200°C).
2. Spread the starter evenly into an 8- by 6-inch (or similar) baking dish and top with the mozzarella cheese.
3. Bake for 25 to 30 minutes, until the dip is bubbly and the cheese is browning around the edges. Serve immediately with tortilla chips, toasted baguette slices, or celery.

Creamy Baked Swiss Chard Dip ready for the freezer

Fried Onion & Herb Dip

With this starter in your freezer, you're only a few ingredients away from an herby fried onion dip! It's equally good with potato chips, sweet potato chips, or veggies like carrots and celery, so I often serve it with all of the above.

YIELD: 6 SERVINGS

This recipe can be doubled or tripled to make additional batches.

MAKING & FREEZING THE STARTER

- 2 tablespoons butter
- 2 cups diced yellow onion (about 1 large)
- ½ teaspoon sea salt
- 2 tablespoons finely chopped fresh chives
- 2 tablespoons finely chopped fresh parsley

1. Melt the butter in a medium skillet over medium heat. Add the onion and salt, and sauté, stirring frequently, until the onion is golden brown, about 15 minutes.
2. Turn off the heat and let the onion cool for 10 minutes, then stir in the chives and parsley.
3. **TO FREEZE:** Cool completely before freezing. Because it cooks down into a relatively small amount, this starter packs best in a rigid container. The recipe fits in a 1-cup freezer container.

MAKING THE DIP

- 4 ounces cream cheese, softened
- ½ cup sour cream
- 2 tablespoons mayonnaise
- 1 recipe frozen Fried Onion & Herb Dip starter, thawed
- Potato chips, sweet potato chips, or vegetables

1. Place the cream cheese in a bowl and stir vigorously with a fork until it is smooth. Stir in the sour cream and mayonnaise.
2. Warm the starter by running the container under hot tap water, or by heating it in the microwave for 10 seconds, just until the butter melts and the onions become glossy; don't overheat.
3. Fold the starter into the cream cheese mixture and refrigerate for at least 1 hour or overnight before serving. Serve with chips or vegetables.

CHAPTER 4

MEAL STARTERS

A "meal starter" is the fresh portion of a dish cooked and then frozen. Come mealtime, the thawed starter is combined with cooked protein, rice, pasta, eggs, or other pantry ingredients to finish it. This approach conserves freezer space, makes quick work of dinner, and allows you to preserve produce in a useful way. I always appreciate having these almost-ready-to-go meals on hand!

Broccoli Fried Rice (page 121) comes together quickly with a thawed bag of starter, leftover cooked rice, eggs, and tamari.

Meal Starter Examples

If you need help visualizing what a meal starter looks like in real life, take Broccoli Fried Rice (page 121) as an example. This recipe works as a starter because it's composed of vegetables that freeze well in their blanched or cooked form. To make the meal starter, just sauté broccoli, onion, and carrots with a few seasonings, then freeze this mixture. To make the dish, warm the thawed starter in a skillet with leftover rice, scramble in a couple of eggs, and finish it with some soy sauce. Dinner is ready in 10 minutes!

Or how about Sloppy Joes (page 129), everyone's favorite sweet-and-tangy loose meat sandwich? This is a classic meal starter that people have been using for decades—just pour a can of sloppy joe mix onto some browned hamburger, stir it, and slap it on a bun! Only now we're doing it homemade and using the freezer. It's got the same nostalgic flavor you expect, but it is made from scratch with fresh ingredients like tomatoes, onions, and peppers.

How to Craft Your Own Meal Starter

This is a broad category, which means there are many opportunities to turn veggie-filled dinners into meal starters. This also makes it more difficult to give a set of instructions that are generally applicable to everything. Many veggies adapt well to this method of preservation, and those that are good when cooked and tender will do best.

A meal starter doesn't have to be elaborate. Think of it as anything that gives you a helping hand with dinner. In Apple, Onion & Sage Pulled Pork (page 114), apples and onions are sautéed with herbs and then frozen. Dropping a pork roast into a slow cooker and pouring the bag of starter over the top gets dinner started in less than 5 minutes.

For dishes with multiple ingredients, build your starter in a way that makes sense for each veggie. Root vegetables like carrots, beets, or potatoes should be cooked all the way through. Vegetables that are best when tender crisp or that have a short cooking time—think green beans, peas, peppers, or kale—should be added toward the end. Consider layering on more flavor by grilling or roasting the vegetables.

Ingredients like meat, broth, noodles, rice, beans, and dairy should be added on the back end. These foods will complete the dish and are stirred in when the meal starter is thawed and warmed for serving.

For inspiration, look at what your family loves to eat and see what lines up with what's fresh and in season. What convenience items do you buy from the store that you wish you could make instead?

Freezing Meal Starters

With potatoes. If using diced or sliced potatoes in your starter, waxy varieties will hold their shape and have the best texture. Large chunks of potatoes can develop a grainy texture once thawed, so dice them small, slice thin, or grate for the best texture in your finished dish.

With dairy. If your dish calls for dairy as a sauce component, adapt the recipe so that the dairy is added when the dish is thawed and prepared for heating and serving. Cheese does freeze well in a meal starter when it's baked in as part of a filling or topping, such as in Cheesy Fire-Roasted Poblano Breakfast Tacos (page 124).

Thawing & Heating Meal Starters

A meal starter will be best when thawed overnight in the refrigerator or with the cold-water method (see page 21). If your starter is partially thawed but still a little icy come dinnertime, it will easily thaw the rest of the way when you start to heat it for serving. Meal starters are best when used immediately after thawing, so don't let them sit for too long in their thawed state.

Be thoughtful and pay attention when heating meal starters. There's a lot of variety in this category, and each one requires something a little different. Meal starters with tender vegetables like broccoli are heated only briefly to warm through. Dishes like Slow Cooker Chicken Chile Verde (page 130) will cook for hours in the slow cooker and do just fine with that amount of heat.

A block of Thai-Inspired Pumpkin Veggie Curry (page 136), ready to thaw and eat

Apple, Onion & Sage Pulled Pork

This pulled pork is lightly sweet and gets a lot of flavor from the apples and onions. I like it plain as is, but it also excels in a more characteristic role served on buns with barbecue sauce. I typically serve this fall-time favorite dinner with a crisp salad and a savory rice pilaf.

YIELD: 1 BATCH OF STARTER, MAKES 6–8 SERVINGS

Do not double. To increase yield, make consecutive batches.

MAKING & FREEZING THE STARTER

- 2 tablespoons butter, extra-virgin olive oil, or lard
- 2 large sweet apples, cut into ¼- to ½-inch slices
- 1 medium yellow onion, cut into thin slices
- ⅓ cup chopped fresh sage leaves
- 1 bay leaf

1. Melt the butter in a large skillet over medium-high heat. Add the apples and onion, and sauté until the apples are just tender and starting to caramelize, about 8 minutes.
2. Turn off the heat and stir in the sage and bay leaf.
3. **TO FREEZE:** Cool completely before freezing. This starter packs best in a freezer bag. The recipe fits in a 1-quart freezer bag.

MAKING THE DISH

- 1 cup water
- 1 (4-pound) pork shoulder roast
- 2 teaspoons sea salt
- ½ teaspoon freshly ground black pepper
- 1 recipe frozen Apple, Onion & Sage Pulled Pork starter, thawed

1. Pour the water into the bottom of a 6-quart slow cooker. If the roast has a lot of fat on the top, cut off and discard most of it. Season the roast with the salt and pepper, then place it in the slow cooker. Spread the starter on top of the pork (some will fall off the sides; that's okay).
2. Cook on high until the roast is falling apart and tender, about 8 hours. Remove and discard the bay leaf, then shred the pork with two forks, incorporating the onions and apple into it.

TIP Instead of freezing the starter in step 3, you can make the pork and freeze the finished dish; the prepared pork is convenient to have on hand, too!

Apple, Onion & Sage Pulled Pork starter

"Apple" Cinnamon Zucchini Oatmeal

It may be unconventional, but turning zucchini into something that tastes like apples is a creative use for this versatile veggie. With a little help from cinnamon, sugar, and lemon juice, zucchini can transform into an apple alternative that is surprisingly enjoyable atop baked oatmeal. You'd never know you were eating a green vegetable!

YIELD: 1 BATCH OF STARTER, MAKES 8 SERVINGS

This recipe can be doubled or tripled to make additional batches.

MAKING & FREEZING THE STARTER

- 2 tablespoons butter
- 3 cups peeled, diced zucchini, in ½-inch pieces
- ¼ cup firmly packed brown sugar
- 2 tablespoons lemon juice, fresh or bottled
- 2 teaspoons ground cinnamon
- 1 teaspoon apple pie spice
- ⅛ teaspoon sea salt

1. Melt the butter in a medium saucepan over medium heat. Add the zucchini and sauté until tender, about 10 minutes.
2. Stir in the sugar, lemon juice, cinnamon, apple pie spice, and salt. Continue cooking until most of the liquid in the bottom of the pan has evaporated and forms a syrup, about 5 minutes.
3. **TO FREEZE:** Cool completely before freezing. Because it cooks down into a relatively small amount, this starter packs best in a rigid container. The recipe fits in a 1½-cup container.

MAKING THE DISH

- Cooking spray, for greasing the pan
- 2 cups milk or nondairy alternative
- ⅓ cup granulated sugar or honey
- 1 egg
- 1 teaspoon vanilla extract
- ½ teaspoon sea salt
- 2 cups old-fashioned oats
- 1 recipe frozen "Apple" Cinnamon Zucchini Oatmeal starter, thawed

1. Preheat the oven to 350°F (180°C). Grease a 9-inch square (or similar) baking pan with cooking spray.
2. Whisk together the milk, sugar, egg, vanilla, and salt in a large bowl. Stir in the oats and let sit for 10 minutes to hydrate.
3. Pour the oat mixture into the prepared pan and use a spatula to push the oats down into the liquid, making sure they are all submerged. Spoon the starter evenly over the oats.
4. Bake for 45 to 50 minutes, until the edges are just starting to turn golden brown. Serve warm.

Chicken Pot Pie

I usually bake this starter in a classic piecrust, as done here, but it will also work for chicken and dumplings, in a casserole dish with a biscuit topping, or with any other buttery pastry you can think to top it with! Because this starter will be baked into a pie in the oven, I only lightly cook the vegetables before freezing them.

YIELD: 1 BATCH OF STARTER, MAKES 6 SERVINGS

This recipe can be doubled or tripled to make additional batches.

MAKING & FREEZING THE STARTER

- 1 tablespoon butter or extra-virgin olive oil
- 1 medium yellow onion, diced
- 3 celery stalks, diced
- 2 garlic cloves, minced
- 1 cup water
- 2 large carrots, thinly sliced
- 1½ cups cut green beans, in ½-inch pieces
- ¾ cup sweet corn kernels, fresh or frozen
- ½ teaspoon dried rosemary
- ½ teaspoon dried sage
- ½ teaspoon dried thyme
- ½ teaspoon sea salt
- ¼ teaspoon freshly ground black pepper
- 2 tablespoons finely chopped fresh parsley

1. Melt the butter in a large pot over medium heat. Add the onion and celery, and sauté until almost tender, about 5 minutes. Add the garlic and cook for 3 minutes longer.
2. Stir in the water, carrots, beans, corn, rosemary, sage, thyme, salt, and pepper. Bring to a boil, then cover and simmer gently until the vegetables are blanched but not quite tender, about 5 minutes. Turn off the heat and stir in the parsley.
3. **TO FREEZE:** Cool completely before freezing. This starter packs well in a freezer bag or rigid container. The recipe fits in a 1-quart freezer bag.

MAKING THE DISH

- 2 prepared Flaky All-Butter Piecrusts (page 246)
- 2 tablespoons butter
- 2 tablespoons all-purpose flour or gluten-free flour blend
- 1 cup chicken broth
- 4 cups cooked, chopped chicken
- 1 recipe frozen Chicken Pot Pie starter, thawed
- Sea salt
- 1 egg, beaten

1. Preheat the oven to 425°F (220°C). Unwrap the discs of dough and allow them to sit at room temperature for 10 minutes.
2. Melt the butter in a medium pot over medium heat. Add the flour and stir frequently until it is cooked but not browning, about 3 minutes.
3. Slowly stream in the broth while whisking so that the flour doesn't clump. Bring to a simmer, stirring frequently, and cook until the mixture thickens, about 2 minutes.
4. Combine the chicken and starter in a large mixing bowl and fold in the thickened broth mixture. Because some broths are saltier than others, taste the mixture and add more salt if necessary.

Chicken Pot Pie starter

5. Place one disc of the dough between two pieces of parchment paper and use a rolling pin to roll it into a large circle about 12 inches in diameter and, more importantly, ⅛ inch thick. Repeat with the second disc.
6. Transfer one of the piecrusts to a 9-inch pie pan and press it into the bottom and sides. Leave about 1 inch of dough sticking out past the pan's edge, and trim off any excess. Roll the extra dough under until it's flush with the edge of the pan.
7. Spoon the filling into the crust and spread it in an even layer.
8. Cover with the second crust and pinch the edges together with the bottom crust to form the outer lip of the crust. Cut five 2-inch slits in the top to allow steam to escape. Brush the entire top and outer lip of the crust with the egg.
9. Bake for 20 minutes. Reduce the oven temperature to 375°F (190°C) and bake for 40 to 45 minutes longer, until the filling looks bubbly and the crust is golden brown.

Broccoli Fried Rice

Fried rice is an infinitely customizable dish, so make this recipe as written or adapt it however you like. Stir in cooked shrimp, throw in some frozen peas, sprinkle scallions on top, or add a squirt of hot sauce. You'll usually find me using this starter for breakfast fried rice: I double the eggs and stir in leftover crumbled breakfast sausage before serving.

YIELD: 1 BATCH OF STARTER, MAKES 4 SERVINGS

Do not double. To increase yield, make consecutive batches.

MAKING & FREEZING THE STARTER

- 1 tablespoon avocado oil or other neutral oil
- 4 cups chopped broccoli, in ¼- to ½-inch pieces
- 1 medium yellow onion, diced
- 2 medium carrots, shredded
- 2 garlic cloves, minced
- 2 teaspoons sesame seeds
- ¼ teaspoon ground ginger
- ¼ teaspoon crushed red pepper (optional)

1. Heat the oil in a large skillet over medium-high heat. Add the broccoli and onion, and sauté until almost tender, about 7 minutes. Stir in the carrots, garlic, sesame seeds, ginger, and red pepper, if using, and cook until the carrots are just tender, about 3 minutes longer.
2. Turn off the heat but leave the pan on the stove for 10 minutes; the vegetables will continue to soften a little more as they cool.
3. **TO FREEZE:** Cool completely before freezing. This starter packs well in a freezer bag or rigid container. The recipe fits in a 1-quart freezer bag.

MAKING THE DISH

- 2 tablespoons avocado oil or other neutral oil
- 3 cups cooked and cooled white rice
- 1 recipe frozen Broccoli Fried Rice starter, thawed
- 2 eggs, lightly beaten
- 3 tablespoons tamari or low-sodium soy sauce

1. Heat the oil in a large skillet over medium heat. Add the rice and starter, and sauté until the mixture is warmed through, about 4 minutes.
2. Move the mixture to the edges of the pan, creating an empty space in the center. Pour the eggs into the center of the pan and cook, stirring and chopping them into small pieces. Keep the eggs in the center of the pan until they are cooked through, about 2 minutes.
3. Stir the cooked eggs into the rice and broccoli, then stir in the tamari.

Egg Roll in a Bowl

How many cabbages is too many cabbages? I ask myself this every summer as I'm pushing an overloaded wheelbarrow back to the house. Thankfully this popular dish, which turns the savory insides of an egg roll into a proper meal, is a good way to put them up! Cooked cabbage behaves very well in the freezer, so this dish makes a great meal starter.

YIELD: 1 BATCH OF STARTER, MAKES 4 SERVINGS
Do not double. To increase yield, make consecutive batches.

MAKING & FREEZING THE STARTER

- 1 tablespoon avocado oil or other neutral oil
- 1 medium yellow onion, diced
- 6 cups thinly sliced green cabbage (about ½ medium head)
- 2 medium carrots, shredded
- 2 garlic cloves, minced
- ¼ cup tamari or low-sodium soy sauce
- 2 teaspoons sesame seeds
- ½ teaspoon ground ginger
- ¼ teaspoon crushed red pepper

1. Heat the oil in a large skillet over medium heat. Add the onion and sauté until tender, about 7 minutes. Stir in the cabbage and cook, stirring frequently, until it has wilted down a little, about 5 minutes. Stir in the carrots and garlic, and continue cooking until the cabbage is tender, about 5 minutes longer.
2. Whisk together the tamari, sesame seeds, ginger, and red pepper in a small bowl, then stir it into the cabbage mixture. Continue cooking, stirring frequently, until the cabbage wilts down a little more and the flavors have melded, about 2 minutes.
3. **TO FREEZE:** Cool completely before freezing. This starter packs well in a freezer bag or rigid container. Make sure to include any liquid from the pan. The recipe fits in a 1-quart freezer bag.

MAKING THE DISH

- 1 pound ground pork or lean ground beef, cooked, crumbled, and drained
- 1 recipe frozen Egg Roll in a Bowl starter, thawed
- Cooked white rice
- Sliced scallions (optional)
- Crispy fried onions (like French's; optional)

1. Combine the pork and starter (including all liquid from the bag) in a large skillet over medium heat. Cook, stirring occasionally, until the mixture is warmed through, about 5 minutes.
2. Serve over rice and garnish with scallions and crispy fried onions, if desired.

Sheet Pan Orange Chicken

If you've got a bumper crop of oranges, you'll want to fill your freezer with this sweet, umami-filled sauce. I've made this recipe with juicing oranges, navel oranges, and even tangerines, so go ahead and use whatever sweet orange citrus you've got.

YIELD: 1 BATCH OF STARTER, MAKES 4–6 SERVINGS

This recipe can be doubled or tripled to make additional batches.

MAKING & FREEZING THE STARTER

- ⅔ cup freshly squeezed orange juice
- ¼ cup tamari or low-sodium soy sauce
- ¼ cup sugar or honey
- ½ teaspoon orange zest
- ¼ teaspoon crushed red pepper
- ¼ teaspoon ground ginger
- 1 tablespoon toasted sesame oil
- 1 garlic clove, minced
- 1 tablespoon all-purpose flour or gluten-free flour blend

1. Stir together the orange juice, tamari, sugar, orange zest, red pepper, and ginger in a bowl, and set aside.
2. Heat the oil in a medium saucepan over medium heat. Add the garlic and sauté until fragrant but not browning, about 3 minutes. Stir in the flour and cook for 3 minutes longer.
3. Slowly stream in the orange juice mixture while whisking so that the flour doesn't clump. Bring to a boil, then simmer gently, stirring frequently, until the sauce thickens, about 2 minutes.
4. **TO FREEZE:** Cool completely before freezing. This starter packs best in a rigid container. The recipe just fits in a 1-cup container.

MAKING THE DISH

- 2½ pounds boneless, skinless chicken thighs, cut into 2-inch pieces
- 2 tablespoons avocado oil or other neutral oil
- ½ teaspoon sea salt
- 6 cups fresh or frozen broccoli florets
- 1 recipe frozen Sheet Pan Orange Chicken starter, thawed
- 2 teaspoons sesame seeds
- Cooked white rice

1. Preheat the oven to 425°F (220°C).
2. Place the chicken on a large sheet pan. Toss with the oil and salt, and spread in a single layer.
3. Bake for 25 to 30 minutes, until the chicken is cooked through and some of the juices have evaporated from the pan. Place the broccoli on top of the chicken in a single layer and return the pan to the oven. Bake for about 10 minutes, until the broccoli is just tender and the chicken is starting to get brown and crispy.
4. Immediately drizzle the starter over the chicken and broccoli, and toss with a spatula until they are well coated.
5. Sprinkle the sesame seeds evenly over the top and serve with rice.

Cheesy Fire-Roasted Poblano Breakfast Tacos

If you've never had a poblano, they're similar to a green bell pepper but with an earthier, more sophisticated, and slightly spicy taste. For this starter the charred peppers are topped with cheese, broiled until golden brown, then cut into pieces and frozen. Thaw and stuff them into corn tortillas with scrambled eggs for a memorable breakfast taco!

YIELD: 6 SERVINGS

This recipe can be doubled or tripled to make additional batches.

MAKING & FREEZING THE STARTER

- 8 large poblano peppers
- ½ teaspoon sea salt
- 8 ounces Monterey Jack cheese, shredded

1. Position an oven rack in the middle of the oven and preheat the broiler.
2. Place the peppers on a large sheet pan and broil them until most of the skin has charred black on top, about 5 minutes. Rotate the pan as needed for even charring. Flip the peppers and char on the second side.
3. Cool to a safe handling temperature, but work while they are still warm. Peel off the charred and uncharred skin; it's okay if you can't remove every little piece. Next, cut each pepper open from top to bottom and gently pull the stem out, removing most of the seeds with it. Remove any other seeds left inside.
4. Line a large sheet pan with parchment paper. Preheat the broiler again.
5. Open the pepper halves so that they lie flat, and place them skin-side down on the prepared pan. Make a "sheet" of peppers, placing them in a single layer so that the pieces are just touching.
6. Sprinkle the peppers evenly with the salt, then spread the cheese on top so it covers the entire pepper sheet. Broil until the cheese is golden brown, about 5 minutes.
7. **TO FREEZE:** Cool completely before freezing. Transfer the peppers and parchment paper to a cutting board and use a sharp knife or kitchen shears to cut into rectangles that are about 4 by 2 inches, cutting through both the peppers and the paper. This starter packs best in a freezer bag. Leaving the paper attached will keep the frozen rectangles separated.

MAKING THE DISH

- 1 teaspoon avocado oil or other neutral cooking oil
- 2 corn tortillas
- 2 rectangles frozen Cheesy Fire-Roasted Poblano Breakfast Tacos starter, thawed
- 1–2 eggs, scrambled

1. To make one serving of two tacos, heat the oil in a skillet over medium heat. Place the tortillas in the skillet and top each with a rectangle of the starter. Heat until the tortillas are starting to crisp and the filling is warmed through, about 4 minutes.
2. Remove from the skillet, top with the scrambled eggs, and immediately fold in half while still hot.

Cheesy Fire-Roasted Poblano Breakfast Tacos starter

Penne alla Vodka

This velvety tomato cream sauce spiked with vodka works exceptionally well as a meal starter. The fresh tomatoes and aromatics are cooked down and frozen, then the vodka, cream, and cheese are added when the starter is thawed and heated for serving. If you're not a pasta eater, serve this luxurious sauce with meatballs or baked chicken. I recommend doubling or tripling this recipe if you've got a lot of tomatoes to use up!

YIELD: 1 BATCH OF STARTER, MAKES 6 SERVINGS

This recipe can be doubled or tripled to make additional batches.

MAKING & FREEZING THE STARTER

- 1 tablespoon butter or extra-virgin olive oil
- ½ small yellow onion, finely diced
- 1 garlic clove, thinly sliced
- 8 cups chopped paste tomatoes or other meaty tomatoes, in 1-inch pieces (about 3 pounds whole)
- ½ teaspoon sea salt
- ⅛ teaspoon crushed red pepper
- 1 tablespoon chopped fresh basil

1. Melt the butter in a large pot over medium heat. Add the onion and garlic, and sauté until tender but not browning, about 5 minutes.
2. Stir in the tomatoes, salt, and red pepper. Bring to a boil, then simmer until the tomatoes are tender and juicy, about 5 minutes.
3. Make a mental note of how high the tomatoes are in the pot. Continue cooking, stirring occasionally, until the tomatoes have thickened and reduced by more than half and there's little to no liquid left in the bottom of the pot, about 1 hour. Make sure to scrape the bottom of the pot when stirring so the tomatoes don't stick and burn.
4. Turn off the heat and stir in the basil. Cool to a safe handling temperature, then transfer to a countertop blender and blend on high until smooth.
5. **TO FREEZE:** Cool completely before freezing. This starter packs well in a freezer bag or rigid container. The recipe fits in a 1-quart freezer bag.

MAKING THE DISH

- 1 recipe frozen Penne alla Vodka starter, thawed
- ¼ cup vodka
- ½ cup heavy whipping cream
- ⅓ cup grated Parmesan cheese, plus more for serving
- 1 pound penne pasta, cooked and drained

1. Combine the starter and vodka in a large pot over medium heat. Bring to a boil, then simmer until the sauce has thickened slightly and some of the alcohol has cooked off, about 7 minutes. Turn off the heat and stir in the cream and Parmesan.
2. Stir the pasta into the sauce and serve. Top each serving with an additional sprinkle of Parmesan.

Penne alla Vodka starter (top) and Shakshuka starter (bottom; page 128) ready for the freezer

Shakshuka

With this richly spiced tomato sauce already made and stashed in the freezer, Shakshuka is approachable any day of the week. I typically serve this with toasted buttered bread, but it leans well into Mexican flavors and pairs with tortilla chips and avocado, too.

YIELD: 1 BATCH OF STARTER, MAKES 4 SERVINGS

This recipe can be doubled or tripled to make additional batches.

MAKING & FREEZING THE STARTER

- 1 tablespoon extra-virgin olive oil
- 1 small yellow onion, diced
- 1 small red bell pepper, diced
- 2 garlic cloves, minced
- 4 cups diced paste tomatoes or other meaty tomatoes, in ½-inch pieces
- 1 tablespoon tomato paste
- 1 teaspoon sweet paprika
- ½ teaspoon ground cumin
- ½ teaspoon sea salt

1. Heat the oil in a large pot over medium heat. Add the onion and bell pepper, and sauté until tender, about 7 minutes. Add the garlic and cook for 3 minutes longer.
2. Stir in the tomatoes, tomato paste, paprika, cumin, and salt. Bring to a boil, then simmer, stirring occasionally, until the mixture has reduced by almost half and has thickened to the consistency of a typical marinara sauce, about 25 minutes.
3. **TO FREEZE:** Cool completely before freezing. This starter packs well in a freezer bag or rigid container. The recipe fits in a 1-quart freezer bag.

MAKING THE DISH

- 1 recipe frozen Shakshuka starter, thawed
- 8 eggs
- Sea salt
- Freshly ground black pepper
- 1 tablespoon finely chopped fresh parsley
- Toasted and buttered bread

1. Heat a large (10-inch or similar) skillet over medium heat. Add the starter and bring to a gentle simmer.
2. Use the back of a large spoon to make eight wells in the tomato mixture to cradle the eggs. Gently crack one egg into each of the wells.
3. Cover the pan and continue cooking until the eggs reach your desired doneness, about 4 minutes for runny yolks and 8 minutes for hard yolks.
4. Season the eggs with salt and pepper, then sprinkle the parsley evenly over the top. Serve with toasted and buttered bread.

Sloppy Joes

These were a staple on our family's dinner table and at every childhood birthday party I attended in the sloppy joes era of the 1980s and '90s. And for good reason—they're absolutely delicious! My homemade version is reminiscent of the popular canned mix but with a homegrown touch that's just as easy to use. Ground beef is standard, but try it with ground turkey or lentils for a Sloppy Jane or a Sloppy Lenny.

YIELD: 1 BATCH OF STARTER, MAKES 4–6 SERVINGS

This recipe can be doubled or tripled to make additional batches.

MAKING & FREEZING THE STARTER

- 1 tablespoon butter or extra-virgin olive oil
- 1 small yellow onion, finely diced
- 1 small green bell pepper, finely diced
- 1 garlic clove, minced
- 4 cups diced paste tomatoes or other meaty tomatoes, in ½-inch pieces
- 2 tablespoons tomato paste
- ¼ cup firmly packed brown sugar
- 2 teaspoons apple cider vinegar
- 1 teaspoon chili powder
- 1 teaspoon prepared yellow mustard
- 1 teaspoon Worcestershire sauce
- 1 teaspoon sea salt
- ¼ teaspoon freshly ground black pepper

1. Melt the butter in a large pot over medium heat. Add the onion and bell pepper, and sauté until tender, about 7 minutes. Add the garlic and cook for 3 minutes longer.
2. Stir in the tomatoes, tomato paste, sugar, vinegar, chili powder, mustard, Worcestershire, salt, and black pepper. Bring to a boil, then simmer, stirring occasionally, until the mixture has reduced by a little more than half and has formed a thick sauce, about 30 minutes.
3. **TO FREEZE:** Cool completely before freezing. This sauce benefits from being refrigerated overnight before freezing so that the flavors can meld. This starter packs well in a freezer bag or rigid container. The recipe fits in a 1-quart freezer bag.

MAKING THE DISH

- 2 pounds lean ground beef, cooked, crumbled, and drained
- 1 recipe frozen Sloppy Joes starter, thawed
- Hamburger buns

Combine the ground beef and starter in a large skillet over medium heat. Simmer gently, stirring occasionally, until heated through, about 10 minutes. Serve on buns.

Slow Cooker Chicken Chile Verde

With this sauce on hand, starting this meal takes three minutes of hands-on time, maybe five if you're being leisurely. The chicken simmers in the slow cooker with a flavorful green sauce until it's falling-apart tender. Shred the meat and serve it over rice or salad greens, in a taco shell, wrapped up in a burrito, or on tortilla chips. Finish it with all your favorite toppings like lettuce, tomatoes, and cheese. It's as versatile as it is delicious!

YIELD: 1 BATCH OF STARTER, MAKES 6–8 SERVINGS

This recipe can be doubled or tripled to make additional batches.

MAKING & FREEZING THE STARTER

- 1 tablespoon avocado oil or other neutral oil
- 1 small yellow onion, diced
- 1 large poblano pepper, diced
- 2 jalapeños, deseeded and diced
- 2 garlic cloves, minced
- 4 cups roughly chopped tomatillos, in 1- to 2-inch pieces (about 1 pound whole)
- ½ cup water
- 1 teaspoon sea salt
- 2 tablespoons chopped fresh cilantro

1. Heat the oil in a large pot over medium heat. Add the onion, poblano, and jalapeños, and sauté until just tender, about 7 minutes. Add the garlic and cook for 3 minutes longer.
2. Stir in the tomatillos, water, and salt. Bring to a boil, then cover and simmer gently, stirring occasionally, until thickened and saucy, about 20 minutes. Turn off the heat and stir in the cilantro.
3. Cool to a safe handling temperature, then use an immersion blender or transfer to a countertop blender and blend on high until lightly puréed but still maintaining a slightly chunky texture.
4. **TO FREEZE:** Cool completely before freezing. This starter packs well in a freezer bag or rigid container. The recipe fits in a 1-quart freezer bag.

MAKING THE DISH

- 3 pounds boneless, skinless chicken breasts
- 1 recipe frozen Slow Cooker Chicken Chile Verde starter, thawed
- Cooked white rice or tortilla chips
- Toppings: lettuce, tomato, shredded cheese, sour cream, avocado, diced red onion (optional)

1. Combine the chicken and starter in a 6-quart slow cooker. Cook on high until the chicken is tender and falling apart, about 4 hours.
2. Use two forks to shred the chicken, then mix the shredded chicken into the sauce.
3. Serve over white rice or tortilla chips and top with your choice of toppings, if desired.

Ratatouille & Sausage Pasta

Since my kitchen is bustling in summer with preserving the harvest on top of cooking meals from scratch, I like to streamline a recipe whenever I can. Roasting the vegetables not only adds a caramelized flavor, but it's quick and easy. This starter can be used in other ways, like spooned over baked chicken or white fish, or as a lasagna filling.

YIELD: 1 BATCH OF STARTER, MAKES 4 SERVINGS

Do not double. To increase yield, make consecutive batches.

MAKING & FREEZING THE STARTER

- 3 cups chopped paste tomatoes or other meaty tomatoes, in 1-inch pieces
- 2 cups diced eggplant, in ½-inch pieces
- 2 cups diced zucchini, in ½-inch pieces
- 1 medium yellow onion, diced
- 2 garlic cloves, thinly sliced
- 2 tablespoons extra-virgin olive oil
- 1 teaspoon sea salt

1. Preheat the oven to 425°F (220°C). Line an 18- by 13-inch rimmed sheet pan with parchment paper.
2. Combine the tomatoes, eggplant, zucchini, onion, and garlic on the prepared pan. Toss with the oil and salt, then spread in a single layer.
3. Bake for 40 to 45 minutes, until the vegetables are tender and turning golden brown.
4. **TO FREEZE:** Cool completely before freezing. This starter packs well in a freezer bag or rigid container. The recipe fits in a 1-quart freezer bag.

MAKING THE DISH

- 8 ounces dry fusilli pasta
- Sea salt
- 1 recipe frozen Ratatouille & Sausage Pasta starter, thawed
- 1 pound mild Italian sausage, cooked, crumbled, and drained
- Ricotta cheese

1. Cook the pasta until al dente in salted water according to the directions on the package. Reserve ½ cup of the starchy cooking water before draining.
2. While the pasta is draining, return the pot to the stove and add in the starter, sausage, and reserved pasta water. Cook over medium heat, stirring occasionally, until the mixture is warmed through, about 5 minutes. Stir in the pasta and cook for 1 minute longer.
3. Serve and top each helping with a spoonful of cheese.

Supreme Pizza Casserole

With sweet peppers, onions, and tomatoes, this casserole tastes just like a supreme pizza. It seems like you can never go wrong covering ingredients with cheese and baking them in the oven! I like a protein-filled meal, so I use more meat and less pasta in the finished dish, but you can flip that and use half the sausage and double the pasta instead.

YIELD: 1 BATCH OF STARTER, MAKES 6–8 SERVINGS

This recipe can be doubled or tripled to make additional batches.

MAKING & FREEZING THE STARTER

- 1 tablespoon extra-virgin olive oil
- 3 garlic cloves, minced
- 6 cups diced paste tomatoes or other meaty tomatoes, in ½-inch pieces (about 2½ pounds whole)
- 1 teaspoon dried basil
- 1 teaspoon dried oregano
- 1 teaspoon sea salt
- ⅛ teaspoon crushed red pepper
- 1 large red onion, cut in half and then into ¼-inch slices
- 1 large green bell pepper, cut into ¼-inch strips
- 1 large red bell pepper, cut into ¼-inch strips

1. Heat the oil in a large pot over medium heat. Add the garlic and sauté until fragrant but not browning, about 3 minutes.
2. Stir in the tomatoes, basil, oregano, salt, and red pepper. Bring to a boil, then simmer, stirring occasionally, until the tomatoes have thickened to the consistency of a typical marinara sauce, about 35 minutes.
3. Stir in the onion and bell peppers, and cook until they are just tender and wilted into the sauce, about 5 minutes.
4. **TO FREEZE:** Cool completely before freezing. This starter packs well in a freezer bag or rigid container. The recipe fits in a 1-quart freezer bag.

MAKING THE DISH

- Cooking spray, for greasing the pan
- 8 ounces penne pasta, cooked and drained
- 2 pounds mild Italian sausage, cooked, crumbled, and drained
- 1 recipe frozen Supreme Pizza Casserole starter, thawed
- 8 ounces mozzarella cheese, shredded
- 4 ounces sliced pepperoni
- 1 (6-ounce) can sliced black olives (optional)

1. Preheat the oven to 375°F (190°C). Grease a 13- by 9-inch baking pan with cooking spray.
2. Fold together the pasta, sausage, and starter in a large mixing bowl. Pour the mixture into the prepared pan and spread in an even layer. Top with the cheese, then arrange the pepperoni and black olives, if using, on top.
3. Bake for 30 to 35 minutes, until the cheese is melted and starting to brown.

Zucchini Pasta

When I saw Deb Perelman of *Smitten Kitchen* tossing cooked zucchini with pasta (she credits Julia Child for the inspiration), I knew I could turn the idea into a freezer-friendly way to preserve this abundant summer veggie. My version of this dish eats like a cacio e pepe, which is a rustic dish of pasta tossed with Parmesan cheese and black pepper—only I've added a whole lot of zucchini (and it's excellent!).

YIELD: 1 BATCH OF STARTER, MAKES 4 SERVINGS

This recipe can be doubled or tripled to make additional batches.

MAKING & FREEZING THE STARTER

- 1 tablespoon extra-virgin olive oil
- 1 garlic clove, minced
- 5 cups shredded zucchini (2–3 medium)
- ½ teaspoon sea salt
- 2 tablespoons finely chopped fresh basil

1. Heat the oil in a large pot over medium heat. Add the garlic and sauté until it is fragrant but not browning, about 3 minutes.
2. Stir in the zucchini and salt. Cook, stirring occasionally, until the zucchini becomes soft and translucent and the liquid in the bottom of the pot has mostly evaporated, about 15 minutes. Turn off the heat and stir in the basil.
3. **TO FREEZE:** Cool completely before freezing. This starter packs well in a freezer bag or rigid container. The recipe fits in a 1-quart freezer bag.

MAKING THE DISH

- 8 ounces dry spaghetti
- Sea salt
- 1 recipe frozen Zucchini Pasta starter, thawed
- ½ cup grated Parmesan cheese, plus more for serving
- 2 tablespoons butter, cut into 8 pieces
- ½ teaspoon freshly ground black pepper

1. Cook the pasta until al dente in salted water according to the package directions. Reserve ¼ cup of the starchy cooking water before draining.
2. Combine the starter and reserved pasta water in a large pot over medium heat. Bring to a simmer, then add the spaghetti. Use tongs to fold the pasta around in the sauce, and use a silicone spatula to help scrape the bottom and sides of the pot as needed.
3. Fold in half of the Parmesan. Once it's incorporated, fold in the remaining half. Turn off the heat and stir in the butter and pepper. Serve and top with an extra sprinkle of Parmesan.

Thai-Inspired Pumpkin Veggie Curry

I could eat veggies tossed in a rich curry sauce just about every day. My favorite combination is pumpkin, red bell pepper, and spinach, but you can adapt this starter recipe to other veggies as well. I use Thai Kitchen brand red curry paste because it's easy to find and fairly mild. Proceed with caution if the one you're using is more potent.

YIELD: 1 BATCH OF STARTER, MAKES 4 SERVINGS

This recipe can be doubled or tripled to make additional batches.

MAKING & FREEZING THE STARTER

- 1 tablespoon avocado oil or other neutral oil
- 2 garlic cloves, minced
- 2 tablespoons red curry paste
- ½ cup water, plus more if needed
- 3 cups peeled, diced kabocha or butternut squash, in ½-inch pieces (about 1 medium)
- 1 medium yellow onion, cut in half and then into ¼-inch slices
- 1 large red bell pepper, cut into ¼-inch strips
- 2 cups firmly packed chopped spinach, Swiss chard, or kale leaves (see Note)
- 2 tablespoons chopped fresh basil
- ½ teaspoon salt

1. Heat the oil in a large pot over medium heat. Add the garlic and curry paste, and sauté until fragrant but not browning, about 3 minutes.
2. Stir in the water and squash. Bring to a boil, then cover and simmer, stirring occasionally, until the squash is almost tender, about 10 minutes. There should still be a small amount of water in the bottom of the pot; if it is dry, add ¼ cup more. Stir in the onion and bell pepper, cover, and continue cooking until they are just wilted and the squash is tender, about 5 minutes.
3. Fold in the spinach, then turn off the heat and stir in the basil and salt.
4. **TO FREEZE:** Cool completely before freezing. This starter packs well in a freezer bag or rigid container. The recipe fits in a 1-quart freezer bag.

NOTE: *To prepare and measure the spinach, Swiss chard, or kale, tear the leaves from the center rib, then chop the leaves into 2- to 3-inch pieces. No need to remove the ribs if using baby greens. Pack them firmly into the measuring cup until you have 2 cups.*

MAKING THE DISH

- 1 recipe frozen Thai-Inspired Pumpkin Veggie Curry starter, thawed
- ½ cup heavy whipping cream or canned coconut milk
- 1 can chickpeas, drained and rinsed
- White rice

Combine the starter (including all liquid from the bag), cream, and chickpeas in a large skillet over low heat. Cook, stirring occasionally, until the mixture is warmed through, about 10 minutes. Serve over rice.

CHAPTER 5

VEGETABLE SIDE DISHES

Deciding what to have for dinner every single night of the week can sometimes feel like a monotonous chore, so having a freezer stocked with veggies that are already seasoned, full of flavor, and just waiting to be served is such a relief! A quick shopping trip through the freezer is all it takes to put dinner together.

Cooking Vegetable Side Dishes for the Freezer

Vegetables are usually best when blanched or cooked in some way before freezing, though there is a bit of nuance here, depending on what you want for the finished dish. Each vegetable is different, but there are recurring themes among similar types of produce. Veggies that can easily become mushy—like broccoli, zucchini, and green beans—are best when parcooked or blanched before freezing. Side dishes that are based in root vegetables, like Balsamic Roasted Beets (page 145), should be cooked all the way through.

BLANCHING

All vegetables contain enzymes that cause them to deteriorate over time. Freezing slows this process but does not stop it completely, and most vegetables need to be heated or blanched to deactivate these enzymes. Blanching is done by briefly steaming vegetables or submerging them in boiling water, then cooling them rapidly to stop the cooking. Not only do blanched vegetables have better color and flavor, but they retain more nutrients over time than raw. Roasting, grilling, and parcooking also accomplish this same goal.

To steam blanch, place a steamer insert in a pot, then fill with enough water to cover the bottom of the pot but not so much that it touches the steamer insert. Cover and bring to a boil, then place the prepared vegetables in the steamer insert; don't overcrowd the pot. Replace the lid, then start the timer and cook for the time indicated in the recipe. Use tongs to toss the vegetables at the halfway point so that they cook evenly. Transfer to a bowl with ice water to cool for several minutes, then transfer to a towel-lined pan to dry.

To blanch with boiling water, bring a large pot of water to a rolling boil. Place the prepared vegetables in the boiling water, being careful not to overcrowd the pot. When the water returns to a boil, start the timer and cook for the time indicated in the recipe. (If it takes more than 1 minute for the water to return to a boil, you've added too many veggies; add fewer next time.) Transfer the veggies to a bowl with ice water to cool for several minutes, then transfer to a towel-lined pan to dry.

Crafting Your Own Veggie Side Dishes

Vegetables that are meant to be eaten soft and tender will make the best frozen side dishes. A fresh lettuce salad is obviously not going to freeze well, but Zucchini Peanut Noodles (page 169), which are crisp-tender spiralized zucchini with a sweet peanutty sauce, will be fantastic.

If a vegetable freezes well in its plain form, like sweet corn or broccoli, it will also freeze well with bells and whistles on. In Parmesan Ranch Green Beans & Broccoli (page 148), the blanched vegetables are coated with olive oil and a ranch herb blend

BE CAUTIOUS WITH LEMON JUICE

Flavoring with lemon juice can discolor some types of green vegetables like broccoli and green beans. Lemon zest is fine to use before freezing, but in general it's best to use fresh lemon juice when the vegetables are heated and served.

Tossing blanched cauliflower with olive oil and curry powder before freezing makes for a quick and easy side dish later!

before going into the freezer. They roast from frozen, so it takes just a minute to pour them onto a pan and slide them into the oven. In addition to being quick on the dinner side of things, the seasoning sticks better to the veggies before they're frozen. Pre-seasoning these classic freezer vegetables adds a lot of interest and convenience to your dinners.

Take the veggies you already like to eat and get creative with flavoring them before they go into the freezer. While I appreciate having plain diced potatoes, they're even better with peppers and onions added for Oven-Roasted Potatoes O'Brien (page 166). Here's how I think about crafting this dish for the freezer: I want the potatoes to be fully cooked but the peppers and onions only briefly heated. This means I roast the potatoes until tender and add the other vegetables during the last few minutes of cooking. Instead of blanching the peppers and onions in boiling water, we let the heat of the oven parcook them. Each vegetable is cooked according to how it will freeze best, and when reheated the potatoes will turn golden brown and the onions and peppers will be tender. If you need even more guidance for crafting your own veggie sides for the freezer, my first book, *Freeze Fresh*, has in-depth information on the best way to prep every individual vegetable for freezing.

Try combining multiple in-season veggies or herbs for extra flavor and convenience. For example, zucchini is ripe at the same time as tomatoes, and together they make Tomato Butter Sauce Zucchini Noodles (page 167). Green beans and sweet corn can be frozen together as Garlic Butter Green Beans & Corn (page 159). Cooked rice freezes wonderfully and can be combined with many different types of vegetables for a two-in-one side dish, like in Buttered Zucchini Rice (page 170).

Have you seen it in the frozen foods aisle at your local grocery store? Chances are you can freeze it yourself!

Freezing Vegetable Side Dishes

With root vegetables. Root vegetables freeze very well if you treat them right. Potatoes will change their texture slightly when thawed, but this can be masked by shredding, mashing, or cutting them into small pieces. There is no noticeable texture change in dishes like Hash Brown Waffles (page 163).

Colorful beets, sweet potatoes, and carrots can be frozen in many ways. Turning them into a mash is always a good option. Dishes like Sweet Potato Casserole Cups (page 173) will come out of the freezer exactly as they went in. Beets are a hero in the

Root vegetables like sweet potatoes freeze well after being cooked and mashed.

Oven-Roasted Potatoes O'Brien (page 166) is precooked before freezing. When reheated in the oven the potatoes will be crispy on the outside and soft on the inside.

freezer, maintaining their firm texture in most preparations; they're especially good in the Shredded Beet Salad (page 146).

With dairy. Like we've talked about in previous chapters, dairy *can* be frozen in dishes under the right circumstances. The best-use case is when cheese is stirred into a dish that is baked either before or after being frozen. In Cheesy Mashed Cauliflower & Potatoes (page 157), the cheese is stirred into the mashed veggies and frozen, then baked in a casserole dish after being thawed. In Onion Cheddar Hash Brown Casserole Squares (page 164), shredded cheese is folded into shredded potatoes and baked into squares that freeze and reheat impeccably.

Thawing & Heating Vegetable Side Dishes

Frozen veggies prefer to be thawed overnight in the refrigerator or with the cold-water method (see page 21). Vegetables are best when used immediately after thawing, so don't let them sit for too long in their thawed state. My ideal timing is to have the veggies almost thawed with a few ice crystals left when it's time to cook dinner. In some instances I aim to cook the vegetables right from frozen, like in BBQ-Seasoned Cauliflower (page 152).

The most important thing to remember when heating vegetable side dishes is simply to pay attention. Turn your back for a few minutes too long, and tender vegetables can turn to mush. Dishes with potatoes and other root vegetables will be fully cooked and simply need warming. Side dishes with veggies like cabbage, broccoli, cauliflower, and green beans will be heated until just tender, which usually takes only a short time. That's part of their usefulness—they're quick to reheat, but it also means that they can become overdone if you're not watchful.

Smashed Lemon Butter Asparagus

I'm always looking for ways to preserve asparagus, especially when I can condense a lot of it into a little space—like this! Smashed asparagus is soft but not mushy and has hints of that snappy asparagus texture. We usually eat this as a side dish, but I've also stirred it into pasta and risotto.

YIELD: 3–4 SERVINGS

Do not double. To increase yield, make consecutive batches.

- 1 tablespoon butter
- 3 cups diced asparagus, in ½-inch pieces (about 1 pound)
- ¼ cup water
- ¼ teaspoon sea salt
- 2 teaspoons freshly squeezed lemon juice
- ½ teaspoon finely grated lemon zest

1. Melt the butter in a medium saucepan over medium heat. Add the asparagus, water, and salt. Cook uncovered, stirring occasionally, until the asparagus is just tender and most of the liquid has evaporated from the bottom of the pan, about 10 minutes for medium-size spears. Don't overcook; the asparagus should still be bright green when done. Turn off the heat and stir in the lemon juice and zest.
2. Use a handheld masher to lightly crush the asparagus into a chunky mash. It won't turn creamy like mashed potatoes, but it will break apart into smaller pieces. Transfer the asparagus to a plate or pan to cool.
3. **TO FREEZE:** Cool completely before freezing. Because it cooks down into a relatively small amount, this dish packs best in a rigid container. The recipe fits in a 1½-cup container.
4. **TO SERVE:** Place the thawed Smashed Lemon Butter Asparagus in a small saucepan, along with any liquid from the container. Cook over low heat, stirring almost continuously, until just heated through, about 3 minutes; don't overheat. Alternatively, this dish can be heated gently in a microwave.

Balsamic Roasted Beets

Of all the root vegetables to freeze, beets are one of the most stellar. These are lightly sweet and tangy from the balsamic vinegar, and they have a firm yet tender texture after being thawed. Serve them warm with roasted meats and breakfast dishes like eggs and sausage, or cold on top of a green salad.

YIELD: 4 SERVINGS

This recipe can be doubled or tripled.

- 8 cups peeled, chopped beets, in 1-inch pieces (about 5 medium-large)
- 2 tablespoons extra-virgin olive oil
- ½ teaspoon sea salt
- 1 tablespoon balsamic vinegar

1. Preheat the oven to 400°F (200°C). Line a large sheet pan with parchment paper.
2. Place the beets on the prepared pan. Toss with the oil and salt, then spread in a single layer.
3. Bake for 45 to 50 minutes, until just tender and starting to brown on the bottom. Drizzle the vinegar over the beets and toss until they are coated. Return to the oven and bake for 10 minutes longer.
4. **TO FREEZE:** Cool completely before freezing. These beets pack best in a freezer bag. The recipe fits in a 1-quart freezer bag.
5. **TO SERVE:** Heat the thawed beets in a microwave, or in a 400°F (200°C) oven until warmed through, about 10 minutes. Alternatively, this dish can be served cold.

Shredded Beet Salad

Is it a condiment? Is it a side dish? Yes! This salad is reminiscent of pickled beets but with a little less pickled-ness. It's incredibly fresh tasting, even out of the freezer. Use it to add a pop of brightness to salads or grain bowls, or simply serve a spoonful on your plate for an instant veggie side dish.

YIELD: 6 SERVINGS

This recipe can be doubled or tripled.

- 2 tablespoons freshly squeezed orange juice
- 2 tablespoons red wine vinegar
- 1 tablespoon sugar or honey
- ¼ teaspoon sea salt
- 3 cups cooked, shredded beets (about 3 medium-large; see Note)

1. Combine the orange juice, vinegar, sugar, and salt in a large bowl. Add the beets and use a silicone spatula to fold them around gently until they are evenly coated.
2. **TO FREEZE:** This salad packs well in a freezer bag or rigid container. The recipe fits in a 1-quart freezer bag or a 3-cup container.
3. **TO SERVE:** Thaw overnight in the refrigerator or with the cold-water method (see page 21), and serve cold.

NOTE: *Steam or boil beets until cooked through and just tender, about 30 minutes; cut very large beets in half before cooking. Chill for 4 hours or overnight in the refrigerator before shredding. No need to peel the beets; it's easier to hold them for shredding with the peels on.*

Savory Seasoned Broccoli

Frozen broccoli is a dinnertime staple for us, but it can sometimes feel a bit boring. That's when I whip out a bag of this! It's still quick to prepare, going straight from frozen to roasting in the oven, but the savory spice blend adds more pep and zing to the meal.

YIELD: 4 SERVINGS

This recipe can be doubled or tripled.

MAKING & FREEZING

- 6 cups broccoli florets
- 1 tablespoon extra-virgin olive oil
- ½ teaspoon sea salt
- ¼ teaspoon chili powder
- ¼ teaspoon granulated garlic
- ¼ teaspoon granulated onion
- ⅛ teaspoon ground coriander
- ⅛ teaspoon ground cumin

1. Steam blanch (see page 140) the broccoli for 4 minutes, tossing it around at the 2-minute mark. (Alternatively, blanch the broccoli in boiling water for 3 minutes.) Move immediately to an ice bath and chill for 2 minutes. Drain as much water from the broccoli as possible, then transfer to a towel-lined pan to cool and dry. Work in batches if needed.
2. Stir together the oil, salt, chili powder, garlic, onion, coriander, and cumin in a large mixing bowl. Add the broccoli and fold with a silicone spatula until it is evenly coated.
3. **TO FREEZE:** Freeze immediately. This broccoli packs best in a freezer bag. The recipe fits in a 1-quart freezer bag.

SERVING

1. Preheat the oven to 425°F (220°C). Line a large sheet pan with parchment paper.
2. Allow the broccoli to thaw just slightly at room temperature, so that it can be separated into pieces, about 10 minutes. Place the broccoli on the prepared pan and spread in an even layer.
3. Bake for 20 to 25 minutes, until the broccoli turns golden brown.

TIP ❄ Use the stem as well as the florets! The stem of a broccoli head gets woody at the bottom, but it is tender and sweet toward the top and great for freezing and eating.

Parmesan Ranch Green Beans & Broccoli

I often have beans and broccoli ripening at the same time, and they partner together well with ranch-y herbs and spices. My favorite part about this dish is how the Parmesan cheese turns all golden and toasted in the oven. This is a "busy evening special," as I call it, because it is just one bag from the freezer, requires very little work, and delivers two different veggies.

YIELD: 4 SERVINGS

This recipe can be doubled or tripled.

MAKING & FREEZING

- 4 cups broccoli florets
- 2 cups cut green beans, in 3-inch pieces
- 2 tablespoons extra-virgin olive oil
- 1 teaspoon dried parsley
- ½ teaspoon granulated garlic
- ½ teaspoon granulated onion
- ½ teaspoon sea salt
- 2 tablespoons grated Parmesan cheese

1. Steam blanch (see page 140) the broccoli for 4 minutes, tossing it around at the 2-minute mark. (Alternatively, blanch the broccoli in boiling water for 3 minutes.) Move immediately to an ice bath and chill for 2 minutes. Drain as much water from the broccoli as possible, then transfer to a towel-lined pan to cool and dry. Work in batches if needed.
2. Steam blanch the green beans for 3 minutes, tossing them around at the 90-second mark. (Alternatively, blanch the beans in boiling water for 2 minutes.) Move immediately to an ice bath and chill for 2 minutes. Drain as much water from the beans as possible, then transfer to a towel-lined pan to cool and dry.
3. Stir together the oil, parsley, garlic, onion, and salt in a large mixing bowl. Add the broccoli and green beans, and fold with a silicone spatula until they are evenly coated. Sprinkle on the Parmesan and fold again to incorporate it.
4. **TO FREEZE:** Freeze immediately. These vegetables pack best in a freezer bag. The recipe fits in a 1-quart freezer bag.

SERVING

1. Preheat the oven to 425°F (220°C). Line a large sheet pan with parchment paper.
2. Allow the vegetables to thaw just slightly at room temperature, so that they can be separated into pieces, about 10 minutes. Place them on the prepared pan and spread in an even layer.
3. Bake for 20 to 25 minutes, until the vegetables turn golden brown.

Southern Fried Cabbage

This is a popular cabbage dish made with bacon, onions, vinegar, and spices. It's got a *lot* of flavor and goes well with a variety of main dishes like roasted chicken, white fish, and smoked sausage. Cooked cabbage is always great fare for the freezer: It wilts down significantly so it's very space saving, and it comes out tasting good, too.

YIELD: 4 SERVINGS

Do not double. To increase yield, make consecutive batches.

- 1 tablespoon butter or extra-virgin olive oil
- 3 slices thick-cut bacon, diced
- 8 cups thinly sliced green cabbage (about 1 medium head; see Note)
- ½ medium yellow onion, diced
- 2 teaspoons apple cider vinegar
- 1 teaspoon firmly packed brown sugar
- ½ teaspoon granulated garlic
- ½ teaspoon sea salt
- ¼ teaspoon dried thyme
- ¼ teaspoon freshly ground black pepper
- ¼ teaspoon sweet paprika

1. Melt the butter in a large skillet over medium heat. Add the bacon and sauté until crisp, about 10 minutes.
2. Stir in the cabbage and onion, and continue cooking, stirring occasionally, until the cabbage is tender and starting to brown, about 12 minutes.
3. Stir in the vinegar, sugar, garlic, salt, thyme, pepper, and paprika, and cook for 3 minutes longer.
4. **TO FREEZE:** Cool completely before freezing. This cabbage packs well in a freezer bag or rigid container. The recipe fits in a 1-quart freezer bag or a 3-cup container.
5. **TO SERVE:** Place the thawed cabbage and a splash of water (about 1 tablespoon) in a medium saucepan over medium heat. Cover and cook, stirring occasionally, until warmed through, about 5 minutes. Alternatively, this dish can be heated in a microwave.

NOTE: *I like the cabbage to be thinly sliced but not in long strands. To prepare it, I cut the head in half and remove the core. I place each half cut-side down and slice from top to bottom into 3 or 4 strips, then slice into thin, short strips.*

Maple Roasted Carrots

Roasting carrots brings out their natural sweetness and makes them all golden, brown, and delicious. This cooking technique also draws out some of their moisture, which gives them a better texture out of the freezer. A touch of butter and maple syrup makes this side dish ready to thaw, heat, and serve!

YIELD: 6–8 SERVINGS

This recipe can be doubled.

- 8 cups peeled, cut carrots, in 1- to 2-inch pieces (about 2 pounds; see Note)
- 2 tablespoons butter, melted
- ½ teaspoon sea salt
- 2 tablespoons maple syrup

1. Preheat the oven to 400°F (200°C). Line a large sheet pan with parchment paper.
2. Place the carrots on the prepared pan. Toss with the butter and salt, then spread in a single layer.
3. Bake for 35 to 40 minutes, until just tender and starting to brown on the bottom. Drizzle the maple syrup over the carrots and toss until they are coated. Return to the oven and bake for 5 minutes longer.
4. **TO FREEZE:** Cool completely before freezing. These carrots pack best in a freezer bag. Make sure to include any sauce from the pan. The recipe fits in a 1-quart freezer bag.
5. **TO SERVE:** Place the thawed carrots and a splash of water (about 1 tablespoon) in a medium saucepan over medium heat. Cover and cook, stirring occasionally, until warmed through, about 5 minutes. Alternatively, this dish can be heated in a microwave.

NOTE: *I like to cut the carrots into big blocky pieces with multiple sides so that they hold on to the most flavor. I call this "jeweling" them, because they look like jewels with multiple facets. Make one diagonal cut, then turn the carrot a quarter turn and cut the next piece, turn again and cut, and so on.*

TIP When thawing, peel the bag away from the carrots while they're still frozen and put them right into a pot. That way you don't lose any of that precious maple butter to the inside of the bag.

BBQ-Seasoned Cauliflower

Cauliflower is an incomparable blank canvas, always willing to take on whatever bold seasonings you give it. And when frozen with a light coating of oil and spices, it is ready to roast straight from the freezer. I let the cauliflower thaw just enough to break into individual pieces while the oven preheats, then dump it on a pan without a second thought.

YIELD: 4 SERVINGS

This recipe can be doubled or tripled.

MAKING & FREEZING

- 6 cups cauliflower florets (about 1 medium head)
- 1 tablespoon avocado oil or extra-virgin olive oil
- ½ teaspoon chili powder
- ½ teaspoon granulated garlic
- ½ teaspoon granulated onion
- ½ teaspoon sea salt
- ¼ teaspoon freshly ground black pepper
- ¼ teaspoon sweet paprika

1. Steam blanch (see page 140) the cauliflower for 4 minutes, tossing it around at the 2-minute mark. (Alternatively, blanch for 3 minutes in boiling water.) Move immediately to an ice bath and chill for 2 minutes. Drain as much water from the cauliflower as possible, then transfer to a towel-lined pan to cool and dry. Work in batches if needed.
2. Stir together the oil, chili powder, garlic, onion, salt, pepper, and paprika in a large mixing bowl. Add the cauliflower and fold with a silicone spatula until it is evenly coated.
3. **TO FREEZE:** Freeze immediately. This cauliflower packs best in a freezer bag. The recipe fits in a 1-quart freezer bag.

SERVING

1. Preheat the oven to 425°F (220°C). Line a large sheet pan with parchment paper.
2. Allow the cauliflower to thaw just slightly at room temperature so that it can be separated into pieces, about 10 minutes. Place them on the prepared pan and spread in an even layer.
3. Bake for 25 to 28 minutes, until the cauliflower is turning brown on the bottom.

BBQ-Seasoned Cauliflower (bottom) and Curry-Seasoned Cauliflower (top; page 154) ready for the freezer

Curry-Seasoned Cauliflower

Roasted cauliflower has a sweet and slightly nutty aroma that goes really well with a vibrant curry powder. It's a fast and flavorful side dish that I like to serve with baked chicken, pork tenderloin, or Indian cuisine.

YIELD: 4 SERVINGS

This recipe can be doubled or tripled.

MAKING & FREEZING

- 6 cups cauliflower florets (about 1 medium head)
- 1 tablespoon avocado oil or extra-virgin olive oil
- 1 teaspoon curry powder
- ½ teaspoon granulated garlic
- ½ teaspoon sea salt
- ¼ teaspoon freshly ground black pepper

1. Steam blanch (see page 140) the cauliflower for 4 minutes, tossing it around at the 2-minute mark. (Alternatively, blanch for 3 minutes in boiling water.) Move immediately to an ice bath and chill for 2 minutes. Drain as much water from the cauliflower as possible, then transfer to a towel-lined pan to cool and dry. Work in batches if needed.
2. Stir together the oil, curry powder, garlic, salt, and pepper in a large mixing bowl. Add the cauliflower and fold with a silicone spatula until it is evenly coated.
3. **TO FREEZE:** Freeze immediately. This cauliflower packs best in a freezer bag. The recipe fits in a 1-quart freezer bag.

SERVING

1. Preheat the oven to 425°F (220°C). Line a large sheet pan with parchment paper.
2. Allow the cauliflower to thaw just slightly at room temperature so that it can be separated into pieces, about 10 minutes. Place the cauliflower on the prepared pan and spread in an even layer.
3. Bake for 25 to 28 minutes, until the cauliflower is turning brown on the bottom.

Coconut Cauliflower Rice

Every time I make this creamy cauliflower rice, I remember just how good it is and pledge to make it more often. The light coconut flavor is my favorite for pairing with Indian, Asian, or Hawaiian dishes.

YIELD: 4 SERVINGS

This recipe can be doubled or tripled.

- ¾ cup canned full-fat coconut milk
- ½ teaspoon sea salt
- 4 cups riced cauliflower (see Note)

1. If your coconut milk separates into a thick cream on top with a liquid layer below, use about an equal portion of each. Combine the coconut milk and salt in a medium saucepan over medium heat. Bring to a simmer, and then stir in the cauliflower. Cover and cook, stirring frequently, until the cauliflower is just tender, about 4 minutes; replace the cover between stirrings.
2. Transfer the cauliflower to a plate, including any liquid from the pan. Spread it in an even layer to cool.
3. **TO FREEZE:** Cool completely before freezing. This cauliflower rice packs well in a freezer bag or rigid container. The recipe fits in a 1-quart freezer bag or a 3-cup container.
4. **TO SERVE:** Place the thawed cauliflower rice in a medium saucepan, along with any liquid from the container. Cook over low heat, stirring almost continuously, until just heated through, about 3 minutes; don't overheat. Alternatively, this dish can be heated gently in a microwave.

NOTE: *To rice the cauliflower, cut the cauliflower into florets and place them in a food processor. Pulse until most of the cauliflower is the size of peas; err on the side of the pieces being too large rather than too small.*

STAUB
STAUB

Cheesy Mashed Cauliflower & Potatoes

These potatoes are creamy and cheesy with just a hint of buttery cauliflower in the background. Because the cauliflower adds extra moisture, these potatoes reheat best when baked in the dry heat of an oven. This also makes them an ideal topping for shepherd's pie.

YIELD: 8 SERVINGS

This recipe can be doubled or tripled.

MAKING & FREEZING

- 6 cups peeled, chopped starchy or all-purpose potatoes, in 2-inch pieces (about 2½ pounds whole)
- 4 cups cauliflower florets (about ½ large head)
- 4 ounces cream cheese, cut into 8 pieces
- 3 tablespoons butter
- 1 teaspoon sea salt
- 4 ounces medium-sharp cheddar cheese, shredded
- 2 tablespoons chopped fresh chives

1. Place the potatoes in a large pot and fill it with cold water to about 3 inches above the potatoes. Bring to a boil over medium heat, then simmer until the potatoes are half cooked, about 8 minutes. Add the cauliflower and continue cooking until both the potatoes and cauliflower are tender, about 10 minutes longer.
2. Drain the vegetables, then return them to the pot while they're still warm. Add the cream cheese, butter, and salt, and use a handheld masher to mash and stir the potato mixture until it is almost smooth with a few lumps left. Fold in the cheddar cheese and chives.
3. **TO FREEZE:** Cool completely before freezing. This mixture packs well in freezer bags or rigid containers. The recipe fits in a 1-gallon freezer bag or can be split into two 1-quart freezer bags for smaller portions.

SERVING

1. Preheat the oven to 400°F (200°C).
2. Spoon the thawed cauliflower and potatoes into a casserole dish; use a small size for half of this recipe, or an 8-inch square dish (or similar) for the whole recipe.
3. Bake for 35 to 40 minutes, until heated through and turning golden around the edges.

Tomato & Feta Green Beans

Serve this if you have company you want to impress! It eats like a fancy side dish but is surprisingly easy to throw together. The green beans are tender and make the perfect vehicle for saucy tomatoes, salty feta, and crunchy walnuts.

YIELD: 4 SERVINGS

This recipe can be doubled or tripled to make additional batches.

MAKING & FREEZING THE STARTER

- 1 tablespoon extra-virgin olive oil
- ½ medium yellow onion, diced
- 2 garlic cloves, minced
- 1 cup diced paste tomatoes or other meaty tomatoes, in ½-inch pieces
- ¾ teaspoon sea salt
- 5 cups cut green beans, in 2-inch pieces

1. Heat the oil in a large skillet over medium heat. Add the onion and sauté until tender, about 7 minutes. Add the garlic and cook for 3 minutes longer.
2. Stir in the tomatoes and salt. Simmer, stirring occasionally, until the tomatoes have reduced and there's just a little moisture in the bottom of the pan, about 5 minutes.
3. Stir in the green beans and continue cooking until they are heated through but still crisp, about 10 minutes.
4. **TO FREEZE:** Cool completely before freezing. This dish packs best in a freezer bag. The recipe fits in a 1-quart freezer bag.

MAKING THE DISH

- 1 recipe frozen Tomato & Feta Green Beans starter, thawed
- ¼ cup crumbled feta cheese
- ¼ cup chopped walnuts

1. Place the starter in a large skillet, including any liquid from the bag. Cook over medium heat, stirring occasionally, until heated through, about 5 minutes.
2. Sprinkle the cheese and walnuts over the top and serve.

Garlic Butter Green Beans & Corn

Here are two quintessential summer veggies in one dish! Both love being slathered in butter, garlic, and herbs, and together they make a terrific duo. This recipe works well naturally since sweet corn and green beans tend to be in season at the same time.

YIELD: 4 SERVINGS

This recipe can be doubled or tripled.

- 2 tablespoons butter
- 2 garlic cloves, minced
- 2 tablespoons water
- 3 cups cut green beans, in 1-inch pieces
- 2 cups fresh sweet corn kernels (about 2 large ears)
- 1 tablespoon finely chopped fresh basil
- 1 tablespoon finely chopped fresh parsley
- 1 teaspoon sea salt

1. Melt the butter in a large pot over medium heat. Add the garlic and sauté until fragrant but not browning, about 3 minutes.
2. Stir in the water, green beans, and corn. Cover and cook, stirring occasionally, until the corn is just tender and the beans turn bright green, about 10 minutes; replace the cover between stirrings.
3. Remove the pot from the heat and stir in the basil, parsley, and salt.
4. **TO FREEZE:** Cool completely before freezing. These vegetables pack best in a freezer bag. The recipe fits in a 1-quart freezer bag.
5. **TO SERVE:** Place the thawed beans and corn, along with any liquid from the bag, in a medium saucepan. Cover and cook over medium heat, stirring occasionally, until the vegetables are warmed through, about 5 minutes. Alternatively, this dish can be heated in a microwave.

Smothered Green Beans

I typically prefer my frozen green beans to have a little snap left in them, but this recipe is an exception to that. Once thawed, these lightly seasoned beans bake in the oven until very tender. Their soft texture helps soak up that sweet and smoky sauce.

YIELD: 4–6 SERVINGS

This recipe can be doubled or tripled.

MAKING & FREEZING

- 6 cups cut green beans, in 2-inch pieces
- 1 teaspoon extra-virgin olive oil or avocado oil
- 3 slices thick-cut bacon, diced
- 3 tablespoons firmly packed brown sugar
- 3 tablespoons tamari or low-sodium soy sauce
- 1 teaspoon granulated garlic

1. Steam blanch (see page 140) the green beans for 3 minutes, tossing them around at the 90-second mark. (Alternatively, blanch for 2 minutes in boiling water.) Move immediately to an ice bath and chill for 2 minutes. Drain as much water from the beans as possible, then transfer to a towel-lined pan to cool and dry.
2. Heat the oil in a large skillet over medium heat. Add the bacon and sauté until crisp, about 10 minutes. Turn off the heat and stir in the sugar, tamari, and garlic until a glaze forms. Let cool for 10 minutes.
3. Use a silicone spatula to fold the beans into the bacon glaze until they are evenly coated.
4. **TO FREEZE:** Cool completely before freezing. This dish packs best in a freezer bag. Make sure to include all the glaze from the pan. The recipe fits in a 1-quart freezer bag.

SERVING

1. Preheat the oven to 375°F (190°C).
2. Place the thawed green beans, including any liquid from the bag, in an 8-inch square (or similar) glass or ceramic baking dish. Cover tightly with foil.
3. Bake for 30 to 35 minutes, until the beans are starting to bubble.

Hash Brown Waffles

Crunchy on the outside and creamy in the middle, these hash browns reheat in the toaster just like a frozen waffle. This recipe is largely hands-off, but each one requires a couple of cycles in the waffle maker. Having a batch of these going while I'm doing the dishes or making dinner is the perfect time to exercise my multitasking abilities.

YIELD: FIVE 5-INCH WAFFLES

Do not double. To increase yield, make consecutive batches.

- 4 cups peeled, shredded potatoes (any variety; about 1¼ pounds whole)
- 1 egg
- 2 tablespoons butter, melted
- 1 teaspoon sea salt
- ½ teaspoon granulated garlic
- ½ teaspoon granulated onion
- ¼ teaspoon freshly ground black pepper
- Cooking spray, for greasing the waffle iron

1. Preheat a standard waffle iron.
2. Spread the potatoes in an even layer about ½ inch thick on a clean kitchen tea towel. Roll up the towel, squeezing out as much water from the potatoes as possible.
3. Whisk together the egg, butter, salt, garlic, onion, and pepper in a large mixing bowl, then fold in the potatoes.
4. Grease the waffle iron with cooking spray. Spread the batter ½ inch thick on the waffle iron; it won't spread like waffle batter, so spread the batter in the size you want the finished hash brown to be. Close the lid firmly and cook until browned, about two cycles in most waffle irons.
5. **TO FREEZE:** Cool completely before freezing. These waffles pack best in a freezer bag. There is no need to flash freeze, as these don't stick together in the bag.
6. **TO SERVE:** Heat the waffles from frozen in a toaster until warmed through, one or two toaster cycles.

TIP Hash Brown Waffles and Onion Cheddar Hash Brown Casserole Squares (page 164) are good opportunities to use and preserve russet potatoes. These starchy potatoes don't freeze well in most other preparations, but they do wonderfully in these two recipes!

Onion Cheddar Hash Brown Casserole Squares

These are my emergency "I need a dinner side dish now" potatoes—a lifesaver on busy nights! They can be heated from frozen in just a few minutes, and they go with everything. It doesn't get much better than the combo of potatoes and cheese, but this recipe works without the cheese as well.

YIELD: 12 SERVINGS

Do not double. To increase yield, make consecutive batches.

- 8 cups peeled, shredded potatoes (any variety; about 2½ pounds)
- 3 tablespoons butter
- 1 medium yellow onion, diced
- 2 tablespoons all-purpose flour or gluten-free flour blend
- 1 cup whole or 2% milk
- 2 teaspoons sea salt
- ¼ teaspoon freshly ground black pepper
- 8 ounces mild cheddar cheese, shredded

1. Immediately place the shredded potatoes in a large bowl filled with cold water; allow the potatoes to soak for 10 minutes.
2. Preheat the oven to 425°F (220°C). Line a 13- by 9-inch baking pan with parchment paper: Cut a piece of parchment paper a bit bigger than the pan. Crumple it up in your hands, then uncrumple it and press it into the bottom and up the sides of the pan.
3. Melt the butter in a large pot over medium heat. Add the onion and sauté until tender, about 7 minutes. Stir in the flour and cook for 3 minutes longer.
4. Slowly stream in the milk while whisking so that the flour doesn't clump. Continue whisking while the mixture comes to a simmer and thickens, about 2 minutes. Turn off the heat and stir in the salt and pepper.
5. Pour the potatoes into a colander and let them drain for 3 minutes, then fold them into the warm sauce. Reserve about 1 cup of the cheese for topping, and fold the rest into the potato mixture.
6. Pour the potato mixture into the prepared pan. Sprinkle the reserved cheese evenly over the top. Cover tightly with foil.
7. Bake for 40 minutes. Remove the foil and bake uncovered for 40 to 45 minutes longer, until the potatoes are tender and golden brown along the edges.
8. **TO FREEZE:** Cool completely before freezing. Cut into 12 squares and flash freeze by placing them in a single layer on a parchment paper–lined pan. Transfer the squares to a freezer bag for storage.
9. **TO SERVE:** Heat thawed or partially thawed squares in a toaster oven or microwave.

Oven-Roasted Potatoes O'Brien

A common offering in the frozen foods section of any grocery store, these are golden crispy nuggets of potato with peppers and onions. They're traditionally served for breakfast, but I use them for any meal of the day. Because they are cut in larger pieces, it's extra important to use a waxy variety of potato so they aren't mealy once thawed.

YIELD: 8 SERVINGS

This recipe can be doubled or tripled.

MAKING & FREEZING

- 10 cups peeled, diced waxy potatoes, in ½-inch pieces (about 3½ pounds whole)
- 2 tablespoons extra-virgin olive oil
- 1½ teaspoons sea salt
- 1 teaspoon dried oregano
- ½ teaspoon granulated garlic
- ¼ teaspoon freshly ground black pepper
- ¼ teaspoon sweet paprika
- 1 medium yellow onion, diced
- 1 medium green bell pepper, diced
- 1 medium red bell pepper, diced

1. Preheat the oven to 425°F (220°C).
2. Place the potatoes on a large sheet pan. Toss with the oil, salt, oregano, garlic, black pepper, and paprika, then spread in a single layer.
3. Bake for 30 to 35 minutes, until tender. Sprinkle the onion and bell peppers evenly on top of the potatoes and bake for an additional 10 minutes, until the onion and peppers are warmed through. Stir the peppers and onion into the potatoes.
4. **TO FREEZE:** Cool completely before freezing. These potatoes pack best in freezer bags. The recipe fits in a 1-gallon freezer bag or can be split into two 1-quart freezer bags for smaller portions.

SERVING

1. Preheat the oven to 425°F (220°C). Line a large sheet pan with parchment paper.
2. Place the thawed or partially thawed potato mixture on the prepared pan in a single layer. Use the entire recipe or a smaller portion.
3. Bake for 25 to 30 minutes, until the potatoes start to turn golden brown but before the onions and bell peppers begin to burn.

Tomato Butter Sauce Zucchini Noodles

Zucchini has the amazing ability to cook down and pack into very little space, which I always appreciate. This recipe starts with 6 cups of zucchini and ends up as 2 cups for the freezer! With lots of butter, garlic, and fresh tomatoes, these "zoodles" make for an incredibly flavorful side dish.

YIELD: 2–4 SERVINGS

This recipe can be doubled or tripled.

- 6 cups lightly packed spiral-cut zucchini noodles (about 3 medium)
- 1 teaspoon sea salt
- 2 tablespoons butter
- 2 garlic cloves, thinly sliced
- 1½ cups diced paste tomatoes or other meaty tomatoes, in ½-inch pieces
- ¼ cup grated Parmesan cheese
- 1 tablespoon finely chopped fresh parsley
- 1 teaspoon freshly squeezed lemon juice

1. Line a large bowl with a clean tea towel and place the zucchini spirals in it. Sprinkle with the salt and gently toss them around. Let the zucchini sit for 15 minutes, tossing it occasionally.
2. Gather up the towel around the zucchini, forming it into a ball. Twist and tighten the top of the towel with one hand while using your other hand to squeeze the liquid out of the zucchini ball. Tighten and squeeze, tighten and squeeze, until you've released about 1 cup of liquid and only a few drops still come out. Discard the liquid.
3. Melt the butter in a large nonstick skillet over medium heat. Add the garlic and sauté until fragrant but not browning, about 3 minutes. Stir in the tomatoes and cook, stirring occasionally, until they have softened, about 5 minutes.
4. Add the zucchini noodles and cook, stirring frequently, until they are warmed through, about 3 minutes. Turn off the heat and stir in the Parmesan, parsley, and lemon juice. Immediately transfer the zucchini noodles to a plate to cool.
5. **TO FREEZE:** Cool completely before freezing. Because they cook down into a relatively small amount, these noodles pack best in a rigid container. The recipe fits in a 2-cup container.
6. **TO SERVE:** Heat a small nonstick skillet over medium heat. Add the thawed noodles and cook, stirring frequently, until just warmed through, about 3 minutes. Alternatively, this dish can be heated in a microwave.

Tomato Butter Sauce Zucchini Noodles (page 167) and Zucchini Peanut Noodles ready for the freezer

Zucchini Peanut Noodles

These peanutty "zoodles" are a fun and unexpected use for zucchini, and you'd never know they were frozen! Sweating the long strands of zucchini and lightly cooking them locks in a firm but tender texture, even when thawed. Flavored zucchini noodles are one of my favorite dishes to pack into 1-cup serving containers for lunches.

YIELD: 2–4 SERVINGS

This recipe can be doubled or tripled.

- 6 cups lightly packed spiral-cut zucchini noodles (about 3 medium)
- ¾ teaspoon sea salt
- 2 tablespoons smooth unsweetened peanut butter
- 1 tablespoon tamari or low-sodium soy sauce
- 1 tablespoon freshly squeezed lime juice
- 1 tablespoon sugar or honey
- ⅛ teaspoon ground ginger
- Pinch of crushed red pepper
- 2 teaspoons toasted sesame oil
- 1 garlic clove, minced
- 2 tablespoons chopped roasted and salted peanuts
- 1 teaspoon sesame seeds

1. Line a large bowl with a clean tea towel and place the zucchini spirals in it. Sprinkle with the salt and gently toss them around. Let the zucchini sit for 15 minutes, tossing it occasionally.
2. Gather up the towel around the zucchini, forming it into a ball. Twist and tighten the top of the towel with one hand while using your other hand to squeeze the liquid out of the zucchini ball. Tighten and squeeze, tighten and squeeze, until you've released about 1 cup of liquid and only a few drops still come out. Discard the liquid.
3. Stir together the peanut butter, tamari, lime juice, sugar, ginger, and red pepper in a small bowl, and set aside.
4. Heat the oil in a large nonstick skillet over medium heat. Add the garlic and sauté until fragrant but not browning, about 3 minutes. Add the peanut butter mixture and bring the sauce just to a simmer.
5. Stir in the zucchini noodles and cook, stirring frequently, until they are warmed through, about 4 minutes; there isn't a lot of sauce, so use a spatula to wiggle them into it. The zucchini noodles will wilt into the sauce once they warm up.
6. Turn off the heat and stir in the peanuts and sesame seeds. Immediately transfer the zucchini noodles to a plate to cool.
7. **TO FREEZE:** Cool completely before freezing. Because they cook down into a relatively small amount, these noodles pack best in a rigid container. The recipe fits in a 2-cup container.
8. **TO SERVE:** I prefer to serve these thawed zucchini noodles cold. Alternatively, this dish can be heated in a microwave or nonstick skillet.

Buttered Zucchini Rice

Thanks to recipes like this one, I never feel overwhelmed with a big harvest of zucchini. There's a whopping 6 cups of it in this veggie-loaded side dish! Toasting the rice in butter and then cooking it in chicken broth adds a savory flavor that goes really well with the zucchini.

YIELD: 8–10 SERVINGS

This recipe can be doubled or tripled.

- 4 tablespoons butter
- 2 cups long-grain rice (like basmati)
- 6 cups shredded zucchini
- 1 small yellow onion, diced
- 1½ teaspoons sea salt
- 3½ cups chicken broth

1. Melt 1 tablespoon of the butter in a large pot over medium heat. Add the uncooked rice and sauté, stirring occasionally, until it starts to turn golden brown and smells nutty, about 10 minutes. Pour all of the rice onto a plate and set aside.
2. Return the pot to the stove over medium heat and add the remaining 3 tablespoons of butter. Once it melts, stir in the zucchini, onion, and ½ teaspoon of the salt. Cook, stirring occasionally, until the zucchini is soft and wilted and there is little to no liquid left on the bottom of the pot, about 20 minutes.
3. Stir in the broth, toasted rice, and the remaining 1 teaspoon salt. Bring to a boil, then cover the pot and reduce the heat to low. Cook for 10 minutes, then with the lid still on, turn off the heat and let sit until the rice is just tender, about 5 minutes longer; don't overcook.
4. Pour the rice mixture onto a baking pan to cool quickly. Use a fork to fluff the rice and distribute the zucchini.
5. **TO FREEZE:** Cool completely before freezing. This dish packs well in freezer bags or rigid containers. The recipe fits in a 1-gallon freezer bag or can be split into two 1-quart freezer bags for smaller portions.
6. **TO SERVE:** Heat the thawed rice in the microwave, or in a covered pot on the stove with a splash of water, until just warmed through.

TIP Turn this recipe into a starter instead! While I find having the prepared rice most useful, this can also be frozen as a starter. Cook the zucchini and onion in step 2, then freeze. To make the rice, start at step 1, then skip to step 3 and add the thawed zucchini mixture at that point.

Sweet Potato, Apple & Bacon Hash

Sweet potato and apple both lean into the sweet and savory world, which is probably why they work together so well in this dish. If you're someone who enjoys the great outdoors, this is a good one to prep for camping or reheating over an open fire.

YIELD: 4 SERVINGS

Do not double. To increase yield, make consecutive batches.

- 1 tablespoon butter or extra-virgin olive oil
- 8 ounces bacon, diced
- 5 cups peeled, diced sweet potatoes, in ½-inch pieces (about 2 medium)
- 1 large apple, diced
- 1 medium yellow onion, diced
- 1 teaspoon sea salt
- ½ teaspoon ground oregano
- ½ teaspoon ground sage
- ¼ teaspoon granulated garlic
- ¼ teaspoon granulated onion
- ¼ teaspoon freshly ground black pepper
- ⅛ teaspoon ground cinnamon
- ⅛ teaspoon ground turmeric

1. Melt the butter in a large skillet over medium heat. Add the bacon and sauté until crispy, about 12 minutes. Remove the bacon from the pan and set aside.
2. Add the sweet potatoes to the pan with the bacon grease. Sauté for 5 minutes to give them a head start, then add the apple and yellow onion. Sauté, stirring occasionally, until the sweet potatoes are tender, about 15 minutes longer.
3. In a small bowl, stir together the salt, oregano, sage, garlic, granulated onion, pepper, cinnamon, and turmeric. Stir it into the sweet potato mixture along with the reserved bacon, and cook for 1 minute.
4. **TO FREEZE:** Cool completely before freezing. This hash packs best in a freezer bag. The recipe fits in a 1-quart freezer bag.
5. **TO SERVE:** This dish can be heated in the microwave, in the oven at 400°F (200°C) for 15 minutes, or in a large nonstick skillet or well-seasoned cast-iron pan over medium heat.

Sweet Potato Casserole Cups

These creamy sweet potatoes are topped with pecan streusel and baked in individual portions. Using a silicone muffin pan means they can go right into the freezer, and once frozen they will pop right out. The topping here is flexible, so if you hold strong feelings about sweet potato casserole, don't worry—they can be dressed up however you prefer!

YIELD: 10 SERVINGS

This recipe can be doubled but requires an additional muffin pan.

FOR THE SWEET POTATOES

- 6 cups peeled, chopped sweet potatoes, in 1-inch pieces (about 2 medium)
- ⅓ cup whole milk or half-and-half
- 4 tablespoons butter, melted
- 2 large eggs, beaten
- 2 tablespoons firmly packed brown sugar
- 1 teaspoon vanilla extract
- 1 teaspoon sea salt

FOR THE STREUSEL

- ¼ cup all-purpose flour or gluten-free flour blend
- 2 tablespoons granulated sugar
- ¼ cup chopped pecans
- 2 tablespoons butter, melted

1. To make the sweet potatoes, bring a large pot of water with a steamer insert to a boil. Place the sweet potatoes in the basket and steam for 10 minutes. Toss them around and cook for 10 minutes longer, until they are tender and can be easily pierced with a fork.
2. Transfer the sweet potatoes to a large mixing bowl and use a handheld masher to mash them until smooth. Let the sweet potatoes cool for 10 minutes. Stir in the milk, butter, eggs, brown sugar, vanilla, and salt, and use a whisk to whip until incorporated and smooth.
3. Preheat the oven to 400°F (200°C).
4. To make the streusel topping, stir together the flour, granulated sugar, and pecans in a bowl, then stir in the butter to form a crumbly dough.
5. Divide the sweet potato mixture evenly among 10 muffin cups, filling each one to the top. (A silicone muffin pan works best, but you can use a metal muffin pan with parchment paper liners.) Smooth out the tops, then sprinkle the streusel mixture evenly over each cup. Push the streusel lightly into the sweet potato so that it sticks.
6. Bake for 30 to 35 minutes, until the streusel is turning golden brown.
7. **TO FREEZE:** Cool completely before freezing. Freeze the casserole cups directly in the silicone muffin pan for 4 hours or overnight, until completely frozen. Pop out and transfer to a freezer bag for storage. For a metal pan with paper liners, allow the cups to cool, then transfer to a baking pan and flash freeze.
8. **TO SERVE:** Heat the thawed or partially thawed cups in a toaster oven or microwave. If using paper liners, remove before reheating.

CHAPTER 6

FRUIT BAKES & FRUIT SAUCES

I've never met a cooked fruit dish that didn't shine in the freezer! They take up less space than their raw fruit counterparts, they go with just about any meal, and when served warm they feel like an instant comfort food.

Making Baked Fruits for the Freezer

I always appreciate how uncomplicated it is to bake up a pan of fruit. It can be roasted to caramelize and intensify the flavors or baked in a dish to soften and thicken like pie filling. Unlike raw fruit, which tends to give off a lot of liquid when thawed, heating the fruit sets the pectin and concentrates the juices, so it stays firmer and less watery. Cooked fruit comes out of the freezer very close to how it went in.

For roasted fruit I use parchment paper to help collect the juices and ensure the fruit doesn't stick to the pan, like in Roasted Plums (page 193). Fruit can be cut into smaller pieces, slices, or even halves, like Almond Cookie Crumble Baked Peaches (page 190).

Baked fruit, which is reminiscent of pie filling, can be thickened with a small amount of all-purpose flour, gluten-free flour blend, tapioca flour, or modified cornstarch. Toss the fresh fruit with the starch before pouring it into a deep baking dish, like in Cranberry Raspberry Baked Apples (page 180). To help tighten up the juices, I use about 1 tablespoon (give or take) of thickener for every 4 cups of prepared fruit. You can forgo any flour or thickener, and the fruit will bake up juicier, which is also a fine way to enjoy it.

If adding sweetener, do so before the dish goes into the oven so the sugar and fruit juices can mingle and form a sauce. Toss the fruit with granulated sugar, brown sugar, honey, maple syrup, or whatever sweetener you prefer. Fruit can be roasted or baked without sweetener as well.

Making Fruit Sauces for the Freezer

A simple fruit sauce is one of the easiest things to prepare and is nearly impossible to mess up! Cook the fruit down in a pot until it's tender, then decide if you want it very chunky, lightly smashed, or puréed smooth. (I almost always prefer a chunky fruit sauce.)

Just about any fruit or combination of fruits can be sauced. Put together different in-season fruits for unique sauces, and add spices and flavorings like cinnamon and vanilla. In Strawberry Rhubarb Sauce (page 195), I add orange juice and zest, which makes this sauce taste almost tropical. In Cranberry Pear Sauce (page 192), I combine two of my favorite fall fruits with a hint of cinnamon for one very cozy sauce. With the help of the freezer, you can even combine fruits from different seasons.

Because acidity levels are not a concern with freezing like they are with canning, you can safely combine fruits with vegetables, like apples and beets in Sweet Beet Applesauce (page 182). Feel free to experiment, because it's hard to go wrong!

I've also found a handful of specialty fruit sauces that freeze well, like Chocolate Cherry Ice Cream Sauce (page 184) and Spiced Pumpkin Butter (page 196). They are a little bit more complex to make than a simple fruit sauce, but having these fancy sauces in the freezer is well worth the effort!

Freezing Cooked Fruits

Preserving cooked fruit couldn't be simpler. After it has cooled, spoon into containers and freeze. As part of a two-person household, I often freeze fruit sauces and baked fruit in 2-cup containers. For specialty fruit sauces like No-Fuss Lemon Curd (page 185), I like to use 4-ounce glass jars so I can take just a little bit out of the freezer at a time. For larger families, freeze in the container size that meets your needs.

Because they are soft, cooked fruits generally pack well in both rigid containers and freezer bags. I freeze in both, but I do find it easier to scrape a thicker sauce out of a rigid container.

Thawing Cooked Fruits

While most frozen foods thaw best overnight in the refrigerator or with the cold-water method (see page 21), baked fruits and fruit sauces are one of the few things that thaw well in the microwave. This is because these types of dishes are already cooked soft and are often served warm. However, if the sauce will be eaten cold, it should not be thawed with heat. Specialty fruit sauces and raw fruit sauces, like Honey Vanilla Orange Slices (page 188), should not be thawed with heat, either. Cooked fruits will keep in the refrigerator for up to a week after being thawed.

Using Cooked Fruits

Cooked fruits can be eaten cold or warm. Baked fruit that is thickened with starch will have the best texture when gently heated in the microwave or on the stovetop before serving.

Besides the classic "eat it with a spoon" way to enjoy cooked fruit, there are an impressive number of uses for it.

- Spoon over ice cream.
- Serve on top of angel food or pound cake, nestled into pillows of whipped cream.
- Pair with rich breakfast foods like bacon, sausage, and eggs.
- Use as a sweet topping for pancakes and waffles.
- Stir into oatmeal or yogurt.
- Serve alongside a savory meal like beef or pork roast.
- Use as a meal filler—particularly welcome in households with children or ravenous teenagers.
- Add to baked goods for a boost of flavor and nutrients; try the Choose-Your-Own-Sauce Muffins on page 199.

Adding the zest and juice of an orange to Strawberry Rhubarb Sauce (page 195) gives it a bright, tropical flavor.

Cinnamon Breakfast Apples

This recipe was born out of my desire to eat apple pie filling straight from the container instead of cooking it into a pie. Think of this as a less-sweet pie filling, meant to be eaten alongside eggs and sausage for brunch or with pork chops for dinner. These apples are soft and spiked with cinnamon and lightly sweet, so feel free to increase the sugar a little if you like them on the sweeter side or if your apples are especially tart.

YIELD: 6 CUPS

This recipe can be doubled or tripled.

- 2 tablespoons butter
- 10 cups peeled, chopped apples, in 1-inch pieces (about 8 large; see Note)
- 2 tablespoons water
- 3 tablespoons firmly packed brown sugar
- 1 tablespoon all-purpose flour or gluten-free flour blend
- 2 teaspoons ground cinnamon
- ⅛ teaspoon sea salt

1. Melt the butter in a large pot over medium heat, then add the apples and water. Cover and cook, gently folding and stirring the apples with a silicone spatula every few minutes, until the apples are just tender, about 12 minutes; replace the cover between stirrings.
2. Mix together the sugar, flour, cinnamon, and salt in a small bowl, then fold it into the apples. Cook, stirring frequently, until the flour thickens into a light glaze, about 3 minutes. Turn off the heat, cover the pot, and let the apples sit for 15 minutes to soften a little bit more.
3. **TO FREEZE:** Cool completely before freezing. These apples pack well in freezer bags or rigid containers.
4. **TO SERVE:** This dish is best when served warm; heat briefly in the microwave or in a pot on the stove before serving.

NOTE: *Make sure to use apples that hold their shape when cooked so that you don't end up with applesauce. Apples that are crisp or dense, or that are commonly used for pie, work well here.*

Cranberry Raspberry Baked Apples

Once baked, this combination of fall fruits feels a lot like an apple pie filling. It's a little sweet and a little tart, with a charming red color and fruity flavor from the berries. There's just enough sauciness to make it feel dessertlike, so I generally eat it plain as is.

YIELD: 6 CUPS

This recipe can be doubled but requires an additional pan.

- Cooking spray, for greasing the pan
- 10 cups peeled, chopped apples, in 1-inch pieces (about 8 large; see Note)
- 2 cups raspberries, fresh or frozen
- 1 cup halved cranberries, fresh or frozen
- 3 tablespoons all-purpose flour or gluten-free flour blend
- ¼ teaspoon sea salt
- ½ cup maple syrup or granulated sugar
- 3 tablespoons butter, cut into 6 pieces

1. Preheat the oven to 375°F (190°C). Grease a 13- by 9-inch glass or ceramic baking pan with cooking spray.
2. Combine the apples, raspberries, cranberries, flour, and salt in a large mixing bowl. Use a silicone spatula to fold the fruit until it's evenly coated with the flour. Drizzle the maple syrup over the fruit and toss again until it is coated.
3. Pour the fruit mixture into the prepared pan and distribute the pieces of butter evenly across the top.
4. Bake for 30 minutes, then remove the pan from the oven. Stir the fruit, taking care to bring the fruit and juices that are on the bottom of the pan to the top and allowing the drier fruit on top to move to the bottom. Press the fruit down gently so that it sinks back into the juices. Bake for 20 to 25 minutes longer, until just starting to bubble around the edges.
5. **TO FREEZE:** Cool completely before freezing. These apples pack well in freezer bags or rigid containers.
6. **TO SERVE:** This dish is best when served warm; heat briefly in the microwave or in a pot on the stove before serving.

NOTE: *Make sure to use apples that hold their shape when baked so that you don't end up with applesauce. Apples that are crisp or dense, or that are commonly used for pie, work well here.*

Sweet Beet Applesauce

Beets are such a stunning vegetable, turning whatever they touch to a vibrant hue of red (including your hands!). This is a sauce for beet lovers, as the vegetable's flavor really holds strong paired with apples and cinnamon. I prefer this sauce more on the chunky side, so I lightly crush it with a handheld masher after it's cooked.

YIELD: 4 CUPS

This recipe can be doubled or tripled.

- 12 cups peeled, chopped apples, in 1-inch pieces (about 10 large)
- 2 cups peeled, chopped beets, in 1-inch pieces
- ¼ cup water
- 1 teaspoon ground cinnamon
- 1 teaspoon vanilla extract
- ⅛ teaspoon sea salt

1. Combine the apples, beets, and water in a large pot over medium heat. Cover and cook, stirring occasionally, until the apples and beets start to release their juices and soften, about 20 minutes; replace the cover between stirrings.
2. Stir in the cinnamon, vanilla, and salt. Continue cooking, uncovered, until the apples and beets are fully soft and easily mashed, about 15 minutes.
3. Use a handheld masher to gently crush the mixture to a mashed but chunky consistency.
4. **TO FREEZE:** Cool completely before freezing. This applesauce packs well in freezer bags or rigid containers.

Sweet Beet Applesauce and Fall Harvest Applesauce ready for the freezer

Fall Harvest Applesauce

This is a great example of why I cherish the freedom that comes with freezing. A recipe like this could not be safely canned in a home kitchen (it's too thick to be heated properly), but it is spectacular for the freezer! Thanks to the warm spices, this tastes like applesauce with a hint of pumpkin pie. I usually cook this up on the stove, but it also works in a slow cooker.

YIELD: 4 CUPS

This recipe can be doubled or tripled.

- 12 cups chopped apples, peeled or unpeeled, in 1-inch pieces (about 10 large)
- 2 cups peeled, chopped winter squash, in 1-inch pieces
- 1 large carrot, diced
- ¼ cup water
- 1 teaspoon apple pie spice
- 1 teaspoon ground cinnamon
- ⅛ teaspoon sea salt

1. Combine the apples, squash, carrot, and water in a large pot over medium heat. Cover and cook, stirring occasionally, until the apples and veggies start to release their juices and soften, about 20 minutes; replace the cover between stirrings.
2. Stir in the apple pie spice, cinnamon, and salt. Continue cooking, uncovered, until the apples and veggies are fully soft and easily mashed, about 15 minutes.
3. Cool to a safe handling temperature, then use an immersion blender or transfer to a countertop blender and blend on high until smooth. Work in batches if needed.
4. **TO FREEZE:** Cool completely before freezing. This applesauce packs well in freezer bags or rigid containers.

Chocolate Cherry Ice Cream Sauce

Preserve those beautiful dark sweet cherries in a rich chocolate fudge sauce! Spoon over vanilla ice cream, or turn it into a proper sundae by adding a crunchy topping like crushed amaretti cookies or toasted almonds.

YIELD: 3 CUPS

This recipe can be doubled or tripled.

- 4 cups pitted whole sweet cherries
- 1 tablespoon water
- ½ cup sugar
- ½ cup unsweetened cocoa powder
- ⅛ teaspoon sea salt
- 1 teaspoon vanilla extract

1. Combine the cherries and water in a medium saucepan over low heat. Cook, stirring frequently, until the cherries have released some of their juices, about 5 minutes. Use a handheld masher to crush the cherries into small pieces.
2. Stir together the sugar, cocoa powder, and salt in a small bowl, then stir the mixture into the cherries along with the vanilla. Bring to a boil, then simmer gently until the sauce thickens slightly, about 2 minutes.
3. **TO FREEZE:** Cool completely before freezing. This sauce packs best in rigid containers.

No-Fuss Lemon Curd

I call this "no-fuss" because it's a simple recipe for a down-to-earth kitchen. It uses whole eggs instead of just the yolks, and I don't bother straining it because I don't mind a few lumps. If you're looking for a very bold and punchy lemon curd that freezes like a dream and comes together easily, this is it!

YIELD: 3 CUPS

Do not double. To increase yield, make consecutive batches.

- 5 eggs
- ¾ cup sugar
- ¾ cup freshly squeezed lemon juice
- 1 tablespoon finely grated lemon zest
- ⅛ teaspoon sea salt
- 6 tablespoons butter, cut into 12 pieces

1. In a large glass bowl, whisk together the eggs and sugar until they are frothy and well blended, about 2 minutes. Then whisk in the lemon juice, lemon zest, and salt.
2. Fill a medium saucepan with several inches of water and bring to a boil over medium heat.
3. Reduce the heat so that the water is just simmering gently. Place the bowl with the lemon mixture on top of the pan, making sure the bottom of the bowl doesn't touch the water. Stir continuously until the mixture thickens to the consistency of a pudding, about 15 minutes. Periodically use a silicone spatula to scrape the bottom and sides of the bowl; this will prevent lumps in the finished curd.
4. Remove from the heat and stir in the butter, continuously whisking until it has melted and becomes incorporated.
5. Pour the warm lemon curd into a heatproof bowl or directly into the containers it will be frozen in (I like 8-ounce glass jars). Immediately place a piece of plastic wrap on the entire surface of the curd to prevent a skin from forming.
6. **TO FREEZE:** Refrigerate overnight before freezing to allow the curd to firmly set. This curd packs best in rigid containers.
7. **TO SERVE:** Thaw overnight in the refrigerator; do not thaw in the microwave or with heat.

Cranberry Orange Relish

This chopped cranberry sauce has a hint of apple and orange, which makes it pleasantly sweet and refreshing. It's served raw, and I love the pop of color and freshness it adds to a weeknight meal. For a real treat, use it in the Cranberry Orange Fluff Salad on page 187.

YIELD: 3 CUPS

Do not double. To increase yield, make consecutive batches.

- 1 large orange
- 3 cups fresh cranberries
- 1 small red apple, diced
- ½ cup sugar
- ⅛ teaspoon sea salt

1. Zest the orange with a rasp grater and measure out ½ teaspoon of the zest. Peel the orange, remove as much white pith as you reasonably can, then break the fruit into segments.
2. Combine the orange zest and segments, cranberries, apple, sugar, and salt in the bowl of a food processor. Pulse until the cranberries are in pieces between the size of peas and rice, about 10 pulses.
3. **TO FREEZE:** Refrigerate for 1 hour before freezing, stirring occasionally to help the fruit macerate. This relish packs well in freezer bags or rigid containers. The recipe fits in a 1-quart freezer bag.

BONUS USE FOR RELISH

Cranberry Orange Fluff Salad

We call this a "salad" here in the Midwest, though there's not a green vegetable anywhere in sight. Finely chopped cranberries, oranges, and apples (made easy by using the Cranberry Orange Relish on page 186) are folded into whipped cream with marshmallows and walnuts. This pretty pink salad is a staple at our holiday table.

YIELD: 8–10 SERVINGS

- 1 cup heavy whipping cream
- 1 tablespoon sugar
- ½ teaspoon vanilla extract
- 1 recipe frozen Cranberry Orange Relish (page 186), thawed
- 1 cup mini marshmallows
- ⅓ cup roughly chopped toasted walnuts

1. Combine the cream, sugar, and vanilla in a large bowl. Using a hand mixer or stand mixer fitted with a whisk attachment, whisk on high speed until the whipped cream forms stiff peaks, about 5 minutes.
2. Stir together the relish (including any liquid from the container), marshmallows, and walnuts in a large mixing bowl, and then fold in the whipped cream. Refrigerate for 10 minutes or up to 1 hour before serving.

Honey Vanilla Orange Slices

These sweet and floral orange slices come out of the freezer having a similar texture to store-bought canned mandarin oranges (only better because you made them yourself!). A little vanilla and honey bring out their best character, but feel free to leave them plain instead. Once the oranges are eaten, use any leftover syrup for flavoring cocktails or sparkling water.

YIELD: 2 CUPS

This recipe can be doubled or tripled.

- 1 (2-inch) strip orange zest
- 1 tablespoon water
- 1 tablespoon honey
- ¼ teaspoon vanilla extract
- 2 cups supremed orange segments and their juices (about 2 pounds whole; see Note)

1. Combine the zest, water, honey, and vanilla in a large mixing bowl, stirring until the honey dissolves, about 1 minute.
2. Fold in the oranges and let them sit at room temperature to macerate for 30 minutes.
3. **TO FREEZE:** Remove the zest strip before freezing. These oranges pack best in a rigid container.

NOTE: *Navel oranges can become bitter when juiced or frozen, so use a juicing variety like Valencia. The membrane around the orange segments will be tough if frozen, so it needs to be removed.*

To supreme, use a sharp knife to cut a small slice from the top and bottom of the orange so it sits flat on the cutting board. Cut the rind and all the white pith away from the orange flesh. Remove each segment by carefully cutting right next to the membrane on each side of it. Work over a large bowl to collect the juices, and once all the segments have been removed, squeeze out any remaining juice from the innards of the orange. Measure out 2 cups of segments and juice.

Maple Cinnamon Roasted Peaches

I can't think of a better trio than peaches + maple syrup + cinnamon. If you're lucky enough to live in a climate where peaches grow, this is an exceptional way to process your harvest. You can eat these peaches straight out of the container, serve over biscuits with sweetened whipped cream for peach shortcake, or enjoy them with yogurt or oatmeal.

YIELD: 5 CUPS

This recipe can be doubled or tripled.

- 8 cups chopped peaches, in 1- to 2-inch pieces (about 6 large)
- 3 tablespoons maple syrup
- 2 tablespoons butter, melted
- ½ teaspoon ground cinnamon
- ⅛ teaspoon sea salt

1. Preheat the oven to 400°F (200°C). Line a large sheet pan with parchment paper.
2. Place the peaches on the prepared pan. Toss with the maple syrup, butter, cinnamon, and salt, then spread in a single layer.
3. Bake for 20 minutes, then give the peaches a stir to recoat them in the sauce, and spread in a single layer again. Bake for 10 to 15 minutes longer, until the peaches are tender and starting to caramelize.
4. **TO FREEZE:** Cool completely before freezing. These peaches pack well in freezer bags or rigid containers. Make sure to include any sauce from the pan.
5. **TO SERVE:** This dish is best when served warm; heat briefly in the microwave or in a pot on the stove before serving.

Almond Cookie Crumble Baked Peaches

These peaches feel elegant, but they're easy to make and are suitable for everyday life. Just make sure to use freestone peaches so that they split nicely into halves. They're stuffed with an almond filling that bakes up golden brown and has the texture of a soft baked cookie. Serve them cold for breakfast with yogurt or warm for dessert with vanilla ice cream.

YIELD: 10 SERVINGS

This recipe can be doubled or tripled.

- ½ cup raw almonds
- ⅓ cup sugar
- 2 tablespoons old-fashioned oats
- ⅛ teaspoon sea salt
- 4 tablespoons cold butter, cut into 8 pieces
- 1 teaspoon almond extract
- ½ teaspoon vanilla extract
- 5 large freestone peaches

1. Preheat the oven to 400°F (200°C). Line a large sheet pan with parchment paper.
2. Combine the almonds, sugar, oats, and salt together in the bowl of a food processor. Pulse until the mixture is finely ground, about 1 minute. Add the butter, almond extract, and vanilla, and pulse again until the mixture forms a crumbly dough.
3. Cut the peaches in half from top to bottom along their natural ridge, then remove the pit.
4. Place the peaches cut-side up on the prepared pan. Divide the almond mixture evenly among the peaches, gently pressing it into the pit cavities and spreading it over the cut surface of the fruit.
5. Bake for 40 to 45 minutes, until the topping is golden brown.
6. **TO FREEZE:** Cool completely before freezing. Flash freeze by placing the peaches in a single layer on a parchment paper-lined pan. Freeze for 4 hours or overnight, until completely frozen. Transfer to a freezer bag for storage.

Raspberry Peach Sauce

Making sauce is one of my favorite ways to work through a big bushel of peaches, and adding a handful of raspberries makes them even better! I like to leave the skins on for this chunky sauce because there is a lot of flavor there, but you can peel them if you'd like.

YIELD: 6 CUPS

This recipe can be doubled or tripled.

- 8 cups chopped peaches, in ½- to 1-inch pieces (about 6 large)
- 2 cups raspberries, fresh or frozen
- 2 tablespoons sugar or honey, plus more as needed

1. Place the peaches in a large pot and use a handheld masher to crush them into smaller pieces, about the size of peas. Place the pot over medium heat and bring the peaches to a simmer.
2. Stir in the raspberries and sugar. Continue cooking uncovered, stirring occasionally, until the peaches are tender, about 12 minutes. Because some fruits are tarter than others, taste the sauce and add more sugar if needed.
3. **TO FREEZE:** Cool completely before freezing. This sauce packs well in freezer bags or rigid containers.

Cranberry Pear Sauce

Pears and cranberries have an inherent rustic quality that I just love; they both feel like workhorse fruits with no frills. Together they cook into a sauce that's sweet and tart with big, chunky pieces of soft pear. The cranberries melt into the background in the loveliest way and give the sauce a rosy pink hue.

YIELD: 5 CUPS

This recipe can be doubled or tripled.

- 8 cups peeled, chopped pears, in 1- to 2-inch pieces (about 8 large)
- 2 cups cranberries, fresh or frozen
- ¼ cup water
- ¼ cup sugar
- ¼ teaspoon ground cinnamon
- ⅛ teaspoon sea salt

1. Combine the pears, cranberries, and water in a large pot over medium heat. Cover and cook, stirring occasionally, until the pears have started to soften, about 15 minutes; replace the cover between stirrings.
2. Stir in the sugar, cinnamon, and salt. Continue cooking, uncovered, until the pears are soft, about 10 minutes. I like to leave this sauce chunky, but you can mash it with a handheld masher or blend it for a smoother sauce.
3. **TO FREEZE:** Cool completely before freezing. This sauce packs well in freezer bags or rigid containers.

Roasted Plums

I love a fresh plum, but I think I love a cooked plum even more. Roasting mellows their sweet-tart taste, intensifies their floral quality, and turns them into a considerably useful frozen fruit. They can be chopped and baked into muffins, used to top a bowl of oatmeal, layered into a yogurt parfait with crunchy granola, or served as a side dish next to a beef roast.

YIELD: 2½ CUPS

This recipe can be doubled or tripled.

- 6 cups chopped plums, in 2-inch pieces (about 2 pounds whole)
- 2 tablespoons honey
- 2 tablespoons butter, melted
- ½ teaspoon ground cinnamon
- ⅛ teaspoon sea salt

1. Preheat the oven to 425°F (220°C). Line a large sheet pan with parchment paper.
2. Place the plums on the prepared pan. Toss with the honey, butter, cinnamon, and salt, then spread in a single layer.
3. Bake for 30 to 35 minutes, until the plums are tender and starting to caramelize.
4. **TO FREEZE:** Cool completely before freezing. These plums are delicate but pack well in freezer bags or rigid containers. Make sure to include any sauce from the pan.
5. **TO SERVE:** This dish is best when served warm; heat briefly in the microwave or in a pot on the stove before serving.

Raspberry Honey Butter Pancake Sauce

Everything you could want on your breakfast cakes, all rolled into one sauce! I call this a "pancake" sauce, but it's also worthy of your waffles, French toast, Dutch babies, and even ice cream. Serve slightly warmed, and try it with a dollop of whipped cream on top.

YIELD: 2 CUPS

This recipe can be doubled or tripled.

- 4 cups raspberries
- 1 tablespoon water
- 3 tablespoons butter, cut into 6 pieces
- ⅓ cup honey, plus more as needed
- ½ teaspoon vanilla extract

1. Combine the raspberries and water in a medium saucepan over medium heat. Cover and cook, stirring occasionally, until the raspberries have softened and started to release their juices, about 5 minutes. Continue cooking, uncovered, until the raspberries have reduced and thickened slightly, about 5 minutes longer.
2. Turn off the heat and whisk in the butter until it is fully melted and incorporated, about 1 minute. Stir in the honey and vanilla. Because some raspberries are sweeter than others, taste the sauce and add 1 to 2 more tablespoons of honey if needed.
3. **TO FREEZE:** Cool completely before freezing. This sauce packs best in rigid containers.
4. **TO SERVE:** This dish is best served warm; heat briefly in the microwave or in a pot on the stove before serving.

Strawberry Rhubarb Sauce

Fruit sauces often focus on late-season fall fruits, but this sunny combination of early season strawberries and rhubarb is deserving of a little freezer space. A hint of orange enhances the flavor of both fruits and gives them a tropical note. I like my sauce tart, so go ahead and add a little more sugar if you like it sweeter. It's superb eaten plain as is, but try it in the Choose-Your-Own-Sauce Muffins on page 199.

YIELD: 8 CUPS

This recipe can be doubled or tripled.

- 8 cups cut strawberries, halved if medium and quartered if large
- 4 cups chopped rhubarb, in ½-inch pieces
- ½ cup sugar or honey
- ¼ cup freshly squeezed orange juice
- 1 teaspoon finely grated orange zest
- ⅛ teaspoon sea salt

1. Combine the strawberries, rhubarb, sugar, juice, zest, and salt in a large pot over medium heat. Bring to a gentle simmer and cook, stirring occasionally, until the rhubarb is soft, about 10 minutes. Stir gently to keep the rhubarb intact.
2. **TO FREEZE:** Cool before freezing. This sauce packs well in freezer bags or rigid containers.

Spiced Pumpkin Butter

This pumpkin spread is perfection on a toasted, buttered English muffin where it can settle into the nooks and crannies. While this does take a while to cook down, it's mostly hands-off. I save pumpkin butter for a rainy day when I'll be putzing around the house and can stop by every hour to give it a good stir. Try it in the Pumpkin Chocolate Granola on page 198, or add a spoonful to your coffee with cream and sugar for a pumpkin spice latte.

YIELD: 4 CUPS

Do not double. To increase yield, make consecutive batches.

- 8 cups roasted pumpkin or winter squash purée (see Note)
- 1 cup apple juice or cider
- ½ cup firmly packed brown sugar
- 2 teaspoons pumpkin pie spice
- 1 teaspoon ground cinnamon
- 1 teaspoon vanilla extract
- ⅛ teaspoon salt

1. Combine the pumpkin purée, apple juice, sugar, pumpkin pie spice, cinnamon, vanilla, and salt in a 6-quart slow cooker. Cover and cook on high for 2 hours.

2. Uncover and continue cooking, stirring every hour or so, until the mixture is so thick that it sticks to a spoon when held upside down, 8 to 10 hours longer. Stir gently so you don't get pumpkin up the sides of the slow cooker where it will stick and burn, or scrape it down before it does. It's okay if the pumpkin butter forms a skin on top between stirrings; just mix it in. Some slow cookers run much hotter than others, so cooking times may vary.

3. **TO FREEZE:** Cool completely before freezing. Because it is thick, this butter packs best in rigid containers. A little goes a long way with pumpkin butter, so I prefer to freeze it in 1-cup containers.

NOTE: *To make roasted pumpkin or winter squash purée, preheat the oven to 400°F (200°C). Cut the squash in half and place the halves cut-side down on a large baking sheet. Bake for 45 to 75 minutes (depending on size), until the squash is soft, which you can feel by poking the rind. Allow the squash to cool to a safe handling temperature, then use a spoon to scoop out and discard the seeds and guts. Scoop out the flesh and process in a food processor or blender until smooth, about 30 seconds.*

TIP ❄ All pumpkins are squash, but not all winter squashes are pumpkins. Pumpkins are simply members of the squash family that are round, orange, and ribbed. While each different type of winter squash has its own characteristics, most orange-fleshed sweet types (think butternut, buttercup, kabocha, Hubbard) are interchangeable and can be used when a recipe calls for pumpkin. Just don't use pumpkins meant for carving, because they don't have as much flavor.

BONUS USE FOR SAUCE

Pumpkin Chocolate Granola

Smooth dark chocolate is great friends with pumpkin and warm spices like cinnamon and cloves. Using fruit butter to craft a granola not only adds flavor but also produces those highly desirable large chunky clusters. I refer to this as a "snacking granola" because I like to eat it dry as a sweet treat.

YIELD: 8–10 SERVINGS

- ½ cup frozen Spiced Pumpkin Butter (page 196), thawed
- ½ cup unsweetened and unsalted almond butter
- ½ cup maple syrup
- 2 tablespoons butter
- 1 teaspoon ground cinnamon
- 1 teaspoon pumpkin pie spice
- 1 teaspoon vanilla extract
- ¼ teaspoon sea salt
- 3 cups old-fashioned oats
- ½ cup pepitas (pumpkin seeds)
- ½ cup chopped walnuts or pecans
- ⅓ cup semisweet or dark chocolate chips

1. Preheat the oven to 250°F (120°C). Line an 18- by 13-inch rimmed sheet pan with parchment paper.
2. Combine the pumpkin butter, almond butter, maple syrup, butter, cinnamon, pumpkin pie spice, vanilla, and salt in a medium saucepan over medium heat. Cook, stirring frequently, until it is just starting to simmer, about 4 minutes. If there are almond butter chunks, break them up.
3. Combine the oats, pepitas, and walnuts in a large mixing bowl. Pour the warm pumpkin butter mixture over the top, and mix until all the oats are coated. Pour the mixture onto the prepared pan, and spread into a thin, even layer that covers the entire pan.
4. Bake for 30 to 35 minutes, until the mixture starts to look dry on top. Use a spatula to flip the granola in several sections, then break it into 1- to 2-inch chunks. Continue baking for about 2 hours longer, stirring and flipping every 30 minutes, until the granola is just starting to darken. It may seem soft but will become dry and crunchy once cooled. Cool to room temperature on the pan.
5. Place the chocolate chips in a small glass bowl and microwave on high for 90 seconds, or until just melted, stopping every 15 seconds to stir. Drizzle the melted chocolate in a thin stream evenly over the granola. Once the chocolate has hardened, about 2 hours, transfer the granola to an airtight container for storage.

BONUS USE FOR SAUCE

Choose-Your-Own-Sauce Muffins

This adaptable muffin takes its flavor and moisture from whatever cooked fruit sauce you happen to have on hand. These are a "weekday" muffin for me, which means they're straightforward and quick to make. They always turn out a little different, but they're always good. If your sauce is on the tart side, top the muffins with a sprinkle of coarse sugar before baking.

YIELD: 12 MUFFINS

- ½ cup granulated sugar
- ¼ cup avocado oil or other neutral oil
- 4 tablespoons butter, melted
- 2 eggs
- 1 teaspoon vanilla extract
- 1½ cups frozen fruit sauce, thawed (see Note)
- 1½ cups all-purpose flour or gluten-free flour blend
- 1 teaspoon baking powder
- ½ teaspoon baking soda
- ½ teaspoon sea salt
- 1 tablespoon coarse sugar, for topping (optional)

1. Preheat the oven to 375°F (190°C). Line a standard 12-cup muffin pan with paper liners.
2. Combine the granulated sugar, oil, butter, eggs, and vanilla in a large bowl. Using a hand mixer or stand mixer fitted with a paddle attachment, beat together on low speed until combined, about 1 minute. Add the fruit sauce and beat on low until just incorporated, about 15 seconds. Scrape down the sides and bottom of the bowl with a spatula as needed.
3. Stir together the flour, baking powder, baking soda, and salt in a bowl, then add it to the fruit sauce mixture and beat on low speed until just combined.
4. Divide the batter evenly among the muffin cups, filling each one almost full. Top each with a sprinkle of coarse sugar, if desired.
5. Bake for 20 to 22 minutes, until a toothpick inserted in the center of a muffin comes out clean. Cool for 10 minutes in the pan, then remove them to finish cooling.

NOTE: *Use a chunky fruit sauce or a smooth puréed one. Try these muffins with Sweet Beet Applesauce (page 182), Fall Harvest Applesauce (page 183), Raspberry Peach Sauce (page 191), Cranberry Pear Sauce (page 192), or Strawberry Rhubarb Sauce (page 195). I like to add ½ teaspoon of ground cinnamon with the dry ingredients to muffins made with an apple- or pear-based sauce.*

CHAPTER 7

LONG-COOKED JAMS & PRESERVES

In long-cooked jam, fruit is cooked down with sugar and a hint of lemon juice until it naturally becomes thick and jammy—no additional pectin needed. This style of jam has a distinct handmade artisan quality and is notably flavorful, with the deeper flavor notes of the concentrated fruit developing. And, of course, it freezes beautifully!

Making Long-Cooked Jams

These jams are not hard to make (trust me, anyone can do this!), but they do take a watchful eye. To make this style of jam, the general formula I follow for one batch of jam is: 8 cups of prepared fruit + 2 cups of sugar + 1 tablespoon of lemon juice.

There's a bit of wiggle room here depending on the fruit, but this formula is a good starting place. The fruit and sugar mixture simmers until it reaches a temperature of about 220°F (104.4°C), which can take anywhere from 30 minutes to 1 hour. Generally I've found the faster and hotter you can cook a jam without it boiling over or scorching on the bottom, the better the finished jam will be. Use a large pot, which will allow the jam to boil rapidly without boiling over; an 8-quart stockpot works well. Depending on the fruit type, the jam might set a little softer or a little firmer.

To determine if your jam is done, drop a dollop of hot jam on a chilled plate. If it holds its shape after you run your finger through it, it's done.

The art of making this style of jam lies in watching and testing to gauge doneness. It's fascinating to watch the way a jam bubbles and observe how it changes as it gets close to setting. Being able to read the jam and know when it's ready is a skill I've enjoyed developing.

Since jam can become jammy in the range of 217°F (102.7°C) to 221°F (105°C), depending on the fruit, it's helpful to use a "chilled plate test" when the jam is getting close. I keep a glass or ceramic plate in the freezer, then take it out and drop a small dollop of the hot jam onto it. After letting it cool for 30 seconds, I swirl the dollop around with my finger and watch as it starts to gel (or not, if it's not done). The cold plate cools the jam quickly and allows me to see what the texture will be like once it's in the jar.

Checking doneness this way helps ensure your jam will gel before you jar it up. One convenient detail about freezing jam instead of canning it is that you're not looking for the lid to seal. If you misjudge doneness and the jam is not thick enough, just dump it back in the pot and cook it a little longer.

One wild card recipe in this chapter is the Roasted Peach & Amaretto Jam on page 215. It's the only recipe where the fruit is roasted in the oven instead of simmered on the stovetop. Roasting is another method of long-cooking jam that intensifies the peach flavor and caramelizes some of the sugar.

FREEZING JAM VS. FREEZER JAM

Note that when I talk about freezing jam, I don't mean traditional "freezer jams," where crushed fruit is mixed with warmed pectin and a wild amount of sugar. That type of jam isn't my personal preference, though as the name implies, it does freeze well. The truth is that just about any jam, jelly, or preserves can be frozen with great success. Pectin holds its gel in the freezer, whether it comes naturally from a fruit or is added from a box.

ADDING SUGAR

Sugar is the difference between making a jam and making a fruit sauce. While it is tempting to try to reduce the amount of sugar significantly, that won't yield good results. Sugar is what gives the finished jam the lustrous, glassy appearance we're looking for.

Regular organic granulated sugar is my preferred choice for artisan jam because it doesn't overpower the flavor of the fruit. I sometimes substitute honey for a portion of the sugar to help bring out the floral notes in the fruit, like in Strawberry Vanilla Jam (page 218).

ADDING UNIQUE FLAVORS

Freezing jam comes with a vast amount of freedom to experiment without worrying about the acidity level needed to safely can it. Small-batch preserves are a great place to let your creativity run! Combine different types of fruit, or add flavors like lavender, hot peppers, ginger, herbs, alcohol, or even nuts to your jam. Consider if you should add these ingredients toward the beginning of cooking so their flavors can bloom (as with peppers or cinnamon) or if they should be stirred in at the end of cooking to preserve their delicate flavor (like fresh herbs, florals, or alcohol).

MAKING JAM WITH FROZEN FRUIT

Can you use previously frozen fruit to make jam? Yes! This works very well for long-cooked jams. Make sure to include both the fruit and any juice it gives off

Let your creativity run! Making small-batch jams for the freezer allows you to experiment with unique flavor additions.

during thawing. Using frozen fruit also enables you to combine fruits and flavors that might not be in season at the same time of year.

DOUBLING JAM RECIPES

Can you double long-cooked jam and preserve recipes? Generally, no. With this style of jam, small batches are the key to success. A larger amount of fruit takes longer to concentrate and develop the pectin, which results in overcooked and duller-tasting jam. If you want to increase your yield, it's better to have two separate small batches going at the same time. One exception is the Old-Fashioned Grape Jam recipe on page 212. Grapes have a lot of juice and are high in pectin, so this type of jam cooks quickly and doesn't suffer from a slightly longer cooking time when doubled.

Peanut Butter & Jam Cookies (page 223) with Strawberry Vanilla Jam (page 218) are a delightful way to use homemade jam!

Freezing & Thawing Jams

Long-cooked jams, jellies, and preserves are one of the few things I prefer to freeze in a glass jar; I think they deserve an elegant container! I've never had a small, straight-sided glass jar of jam break, which is probably because most of the moisture is cooked out and the preserves don't expand and put pressure on the glass very much once frozen. Jam can also be frozen in rigid plastic containers, like a "freezer jam" container. Because jam is so sticky, do not freeze it in freezer bags.

To freeze, allow the jam to cool slightly, but not so much that it starts setting in the pot. Ladle into jars and chill overnight in the refrigerator before freezing so that it properly sets.

To thaw a jar of jam, place it in the refrigerator overnight; never thaw a frozen glass container with heat. A jar of long-cooked jam will typically keep in the refrigerator for a month.

Using Freezer Jams & Preserves

One of the most enjoyable aspects about making artisan jams is discovering fun ways to utilize them. Naturally you can spread them on toast and peanut butter sandwiches, but there are oodles of other tasty options. Use a spoonful to sweeten and flavor a bowl of yogurt, or try Overnight Oats with Jam (page 221). Serve fig or tart cherry jam on a cheese board with Brie and chèvre, or make a jammy treat like Peanut Butter & Jam Cookies (page 223) or Oatmeal Shortbread Jam Bars (page 222).

Blueberry Lemon Jam

This jam is thick with chunks of fruit and has a deep-cooked blueberry taste with just a hint of lemon. It's good on morning toast, but it's superb when baked into desserts like hand pies or used for Overnight Oats with Jam (page 221). I prefer it bright and cheery, but adding a hint of cinnamon (about ⅛ teaspoon) gives it a cozier, Christmassy, cold-weather vibe.

YIELD: 4 CUPS

Do not double. To increase yield, make consecutive batches.

- 8 cups blueberries
- 2 cups sugar
- 3 tablespoons freshly squeezed lemon juice
- ⅛ teaspoon sea salt
- ½ teaspoon finely grated lemon zest
- ½ teaspoon vanilla extract

1. Chill a small ceramic or glass plate in the freezer.
2. Combine the blueberries, sugar, lemon juice, and salt in large pot (8-quart or slightly larger) over medium-low heat. Cook, stirring frequently, until the blueberries have released some of their juices, about 8 minutes.
3. Increase the heat to medium-high and continue cooking, keeping the blueberry mixture at a rolling boil and stirring occasionally, until it has a thick, jammy appearance and reaches a temperature of 218°F (103.3°C) to 220°F (104.4°C), about 30 minutes. Use a silicone spatula to scrape down the sides of the pot occasionally, and be watchful, as the mixture can foam up and boil over.
4. Remove the plate from the freezer and place a small spoonful of the hot jam on it. Let it sit for about 30 seconds, then drag your finger through it, noting the consistency. If the jam is not forming a gel, cook for a few minutes longer and test again with the chilled plate.
5. Remove the pan from the heat once the jam is setting—that is, when it reaches the consistency of jam on the chilled plate. Stir in the lemon zest and vanilla.
6. **TO FREEZE:** Allow the jam to cool slightly, but not so much that it starts setting in the pan. Ladle into jars and chill overnight in the refrigerator before freezing. Because it is thick, this jam packs best in rigid containers.

Tart Cherry Preserves

Tart cherries make a wonderful fruit spread that tastes just like a cherry pie—and it's a great way to cook down cherries into something useful that doesn't take up a ton of freezer space. Serve these unique preserves as a topping on cheesecake or as part of a cheese board, or use them in Oatmeal Shortbread Jam Bars (page 222).

YIELD: 4 CUPS

Do not double. To increase yield, make consecutive batches.

- 8 cups pitted whole tart cherries
- 2¼ cups sugar
- 1 tablespoon lemon juice, fresh or bottled
- ⅛ teaspoon sea salt

1. Chill a small ceramic or glass plate in the freezer.
2. Combine the cherries, sugar, lemon juice, and salt in a large pot (8-quart or slightly larger) over medium-low heat. Cook, stirring frequently, until the cherries have released some of their juices, about 10 minutes.
3. Increase the heat to medium-high and continue cooking, keeping the cherry mixture at a rolling boil and stirring occasionally, until it has a thick, jammy appearance and reaches a temperature of 219°F (103.8°C) to 220°F (104.4°C), about 30 minutes. Use a silicone spatula to scrape down the sides of the pot occasionally, and be watchful, as the mixture can foam up and boil over.
4. Remove the plate from the freezer and place a small spoonful of the hot preserves on it. Let it sit for about 30 seconds, then drag your finger through it, noting the consistency. If the preserves are not forming a gel, cook for a few minutes longer and test again with the chilled plate.
5. Remove the pan from the heat once the preserves are setting—that is, when they reach the consistency of jam on the chilled plate.
6. **TO FREEZE:** Allow the preserves to cool slightly, but not so much that they start setting in the pan. Ladle into jars and chill overnight in the refrigerator before freezing. Because it is thick, this recipe packs best in rigid containers.

Orange Jam

This citrus "jam" is more texturally interesting than jelly and less work than marmalade, which can also turn out overly sweet. It's a chunky jam that has a beautiful, glassy appearance and a sweet, punchy orange flavor. I typically use navel oranges, but this recipe can be made with other orange-colored citrus like mandarins or tangerines.

YIELD: 3 CUPS

Do not double. To increase yield, make consecutive batches.

- 6 cups chopped oranges, in ¼- to ½-inch pieces (about 6 large; see Note)
- 2 cups sugar
- 1 tablespoon water
- ⅛ teaspoon sea salt
- 1 teaspoon finely grated orange zest

1. Chill a small ceramic or glass plate in the freezer.
2. Combine the oranges, sugar, water, and salt in a large pot (6- to 8-quart) over medium-low heat. Cook, stirring frequently, until the oranges have released some of their juices, about 5 minutes.
3. Increase the heat to medium-high and continue cooking, keeping the citrus mixture at a rolling boil and stirring occasionally, until it has a thick, jammy appearance and reaches a temperature of 217°F (102.7°C) to 218°F (103.3°C), about 50 minutes. There will be just a small amount of liquid left in the bottom of the pot. Use a silicone spatula to scrape down the sides of the pot occasionally, and be watchful, as the mixture can foam up and boil over.
4. Remove the plate from the freezer and place a small spoonful of the hot jam on it. Let it sit for about 30 seconds, then drag your finger through it, noting the consistency. Orange jam turns into more of a thick fruit spread than a classic gel and is best when it sets a little on the softer side. If it is still runny, cook for a few minutes longer and test again on the chilled plate.
5. Remove the pan from the heat once the jam is setting—that is, when it reaches the consistency of jam on the chilled plate. Stir in the orange zest.
6. **TO FREEZE:** Allow the jam to cool slightly, but not so much that it starts setting in the pan. Ladle into jars and chill overnight in the refrigerator before freezing. Because it is thick, this jam packs best in rigid containers.

NOTE: *To prepare the oranges, peel them and break them into segments, removing as much of the white pith as possible without being too meticulous. Remove any seeds, chop into pieces, and measure out 6 cups.*

Fig & Honey Preserves

Forget the toast—these fancy preserves are begging to be served with cheese! My favorite way to eat these preserves is spread on a seedy cracker with some aged white cheddar. I always keep mini jars of this in the freezer for adding to a cheese or charcuterie board.

YIELD: 5–6 CUPS

Do not double. To increase yield, make consecutive batches.

- 12 cups chopped figs, in ½-inch pieces (about 4 pounds whole)
- 2 cups sugar
- 1 cup honey
- ¼ cup lemon juice, fresh or bottled
- ¼ teaspoon sea salt

1. Chill a small ceramic or glass plate in the freezer.
2. Combine the figs, sugar, honey, lemon juice, and salt in a large pot (8-quart or slightly larger) over medium-low heat. Cook, stirring frequently, until the figs have released some of their juices, about 15 minutes.
3. Increase the heat to medium-high and continue cooking, keeping the fig mixture at a rolling boil and stirring occasionally, until it has a thick, jammy appearance and reaches a temperature of 218°F (103.3°C) to 220°F (104.4°C), about 45 minutes. Use a silicone spatula to scrape down the sides of the pot occasionally, and be watchful, as the mixture can foam up and boil over.
4. Remove the plate from the freezer and place a small spoonful of the hot preserves on it. Let it sit for about 30 seconds, then drag your finger through it, noting the consistency. If the preserves are not forming a gel, cook for a few minutes longer and test again with the chilled plate.
5. Remove the pan from the heat once the preserves are setting—that is, when they reach the consistency of jam on the chilled plate.
6. **TO FREEZE:** Allow the preserves to cool slightly, but not so much that they start setting in the pan. Ladle into jars and chill overnight in the refrigerator before freezing. Because it is thick, this recipe packs best in rigid containers.

Old-Fashioned Grape Jam

This recipe is a teeny bit fussy but not difficult. And I think good jam is worth fussing over! While it's tempting to take the easier road and turn grapes into jelly, grape jam feels a little more special. Popping the grapes out of their skins is the kind of old-fashioned task that people used to do while sitting out on the porch in a rocking chair. It's harder to find the time for that sort of thing in this modern world, but well worth it when you can.

YIELD: 2–3 CUPS

This recipe can be doubled.

- 5 pounds dark purple grape clusters (like Concord; about 1 heaping gallon bucket of clusters)
- 1¾ cups sugar
- 1 tablespoon lemon juice, fresh or bottled
- ⅛ teaspoon sea salt

Use a small bowl set in a larger bowl to make removing grape skins quick and easy.

1. Wash the grapes and remove them from the stems. Discard any grapes that are shriveled or rotten.
2. Remove the skins from about half of the grapes by squeezing each one. I find it works best to fill a large bowl with grapes and nestle a small bowl into the center of them. Squeeze the skins off and place the skins in the small bowl, letting the innards fall into the big bowl with the rest of the grapes. Work with both hands to speed things up. Work until you have 2 cups of grape skins. Once you have enough, you can stop; the rest of the grapes will be cooked with the skins still on. Set the grape skins aside until step 6.
3. Place the grape innards along with the remaining intact grapes in a large pot (6- to 8-quart) over medium heat. Bring to a boil, then simmer, stirring frequently, until the grape flesh dissolves and the seeds are released, about 20 minutes. Use a handheld masher to crush the grapes and help release the seeds.
4. Set a fine-mesh sieve over a large bowl. Ladle the grape mixture into the sieve and let it strain for 30 minutes, stirring the skins and seeds around occasionally to help them drain. Make sure to collect any juice and pulp from the bottom side of the sieve.

5. Chill a small ceramic or glass plate in the freezer.
6. Give the pot a quick rinse and return it to the stove. Measure 3 cups of grape juice (you should have slightly more than that) and combine it with the sugar, lemon juice, salt, and reserved grape skins in the pot. Bring to a boil over medium-high heat. Keep the grape mixture at a rolling boil and stir occasionally, until it has a thick, jammy appearance and reaches a temperature of 218°F (103.3°C) to 220°F (104.4°C), about 30 minutes.
7. Remove the plate from the freezer and place a small spoonful of the hot jam on it. Let it sit for about 30 seconds, then drag your finger through it, noting the consistency. If the jam is not forming a gel, cook for a few minutes longer and test again with the chilled plate.
8. Remove the pan from the heat once the jam is setting—that is, when it reaches the consistency of jam on the chilled plate.
9. **TO FREEZE:** Allow the jam to cool slightly, but not so much that it starts setting in the pan. Ladle into jars and chill overnight in the refrigerator before freezing. Because it is thick, this jam packs best in rigid containers.

Grape Jam Potluck Meatballs

A common party and potluck offering here in the Midwest is a slow cooker full of meatballs swimming in a grape chili sauce. It sounds peculiar, but they're guaranteed to be a hit! The sweet-and-tangy sauce is reminiscent of barbecue sauce with a more complex flavor, always prompting people to ask, "Yum, what is that?" The secret, of course, is the grape jam.

YIELD: 8–12 SERVINGS

FOR THE MEATBALLS

- 1 slice white sandwich bread, finely chopped
- ¼ cup whole or 2% milk
- 1 egg
- ½ small yellow onion, finely chopped
- 2 garlic cloves, minced
- 1 teaspoon sea salt
- ¼ teaspoon freshly ground black pepper
- 2 pounds lean ground beef

FOR THE GRAPE SAUCE

- ½ cup frozen Old-Fashioned Grape Jam (page 212), thawed
- ½ cup water
- ¼ cup tomato paste
- 1 tablespoon grated yellow onion
- 1 tablespoon apple cider vinegar
- 1 teaspoon prepared yellow mustard
- ½ teaspoon granulated garlic
- ¼ teaspoon crushed red pepper
- ¼ teaspoon sea salt

1. To make the meatballs, preheat the oven to 400°F (200°C). Line a large sheet pan with parchment paper.
2. Combine the bread and milk in a large mixing bowl and allow it to sit and hydrate for 5 minutes.
3. Add the egg, chopped onion, garlic, salt, and black pepper to the bread mixture and stir until it forms a slurry. Stir in the ground beef, using a fork to mix until it is well combined.
4. Form the mixture into balls of about 1½ tablespoons each, rolling them between your palms. Work with light hands and take care not to overwork or compact the meatballs to ensure they stay tender. Evenly space the meatballs on the prepared pan.
5. Bake for 25 to 30 minutes, until the meatballs are cooked through and starting to brown.
6. To make the grape sauce, combine the jam, water, tomato paste, grated onion, vinegar, mustard, garlic, red pepper, and salt in a large pot over medium heat. Bring to a gentle simmer, stirring frequently as the sauce heats. Continue simmering until the sauce thickens, about 5 minutes.
7. Add the meatballs and toss to coat. Serve immediately or keep warm in a slow cooker on low.

TIP Use this sauce with store-bought frozen meatballs instead! Just brown them up in the oven before combining them with the sauce.

Roasted Peach & Amaretto Jam

This recipe is a riff on the peach jam recipe from my first book, *Freeze Fresh*. Baking this jam in the oven caramelizes and concentrates the peaches, and the amaretto liqueur highlights their flavor. This is one of the best jams for baked goods, and it's my favorite to use in jam-centric holiday cookies like thumbprints and Linzer tarts.

YIELD: 4 CUPS

Do not double. To increase yield, make consecutive batches.

- 10 cups peeled and chopped peaches, in about 1-inch pieces (about 5 pounds whole; see Note)
- 3 cups sugar
- 2 tablespoons lemon juice, fresh or bottled
- ¼ teaspoon sea salt
- ¼ cup amaretto liqueur, like Disaronno

1. Preheat the oven to 350°F (180°C).
2. Combine the peaches, sugar, lemon juice, and salt in a large pot over medium heat. Use a handheld masher to break the peaches into smaller pieces, about the size of peas, while they come to a boil. Simmer gently just until the sugar is dissolved, about 5 minutes.
3. Transfer the mixture to an 18- by 13-inch rimmed sheet pan and spread the peaches in an even layer. The pan will be very full, so be careful when moving it.
4. Bake for 90 minutes, stirring every 30 minutes with a silicone spatula. Make sure the peaches around the edges and in the corners get mixed to the center, as they will start to caramelize first. After each stirring, spread the peaches back into an even layer that fills the entire pan.
5. Bake for 10 to 30 minutes longer, stirring every 10 minutes during this final leg of cooking. The jam is done when it is thick (like the consistency of jam) and has a glassy appearance; it will thicken more once it cools.
6. Stir the amaretto into the jam on the pan.
7. **TO FREEZE:** Allow the jam to cool slightly, but not so much that it starts setting in the pan. Ladle into jars and chill overnight in the refrigerator before freezing. Because it is thick, this jam packs best in rigid containers.

NOTE: *To peel the peaches, cut a small "X" on the bottom and place them two or three at a time in boiling water for 30 to 60 seconds. Cool to a safe handling temperature and peel, working while the peaches are still warm. The peels should come off easily; if they don't, try boiling the peaches for up to 1 minute longer. Underripe peaches don't peel well, so make sure you're working with ripe, juicy ones!*

Almost-Seedless Raspberry Jam

This is everything you want a jam to be: light and fruity, yet somehow rich with berry notes . . . and it has just enough seeds to let you know it's raspberry. That's the secret to a good raspberry jam! Remove the seeds so that they aren't overpowering, but add just a few back in so it feels authentically raspberry.

YIELD: 3 CUPS

Do not double. To increase yield, make consecutive batches.

- 10 cups raspberries
- 2 tablespoons water
- 2 cups sugar
- 2 tablespoons lemon juice, fresh or bottled
- ⅛ teaspoon sea salt

1. Chill a small ceramic or glass plate in the freezer.
2. Combine the raspberries and water in a large pot (8-quart or slightly larger) over medium heat. Bring to a boil, then simmer, stirring occasionally, until the raspberries become juicy and have broken down, about 12 minutes.
3. Set a fine-mesh sieve over a large bowl and pour the hot berry mixture into the sieve. Use the back of a metal spoon to stir the berries, scraping them across the bottom of the sieve and working them through the mesh. Keep working the berries until most of the pulp and juice are in the bowl below and just seeds are left in the sieve. There should be only about ½ cup of seedy pulp left when you're done. Stop periodically and use a spatula to scrape off and collect any pulp stuck on the bottom of the sieve. Work in batches, if needed. Reserve 1½ teaspoons of the seeds and discard the rest.
4. Pour the raspberry purée back into the pot, and stir in the sugar, lemon juice, salt, and reserved seeds. Bring to a boil over medium-high heat. Keep the raspberry mixture at a rolling boil, stirring occasionally, until it has a thick, jammy appearance and reaches a temperature of 218°F (103.3°C) to 220°F (104.4°C), about 45 minutes. Use a silicone spatula to scrape down the sides of the pot occasionally, and be watchful, as the mixture can foam up and boil over.
5. Remove the plate from the freezer and place a small spoonful of the hot jam on it. Let it sit for about 30 seconds, then drag your finger through it, noting the consistency. If the jam is not forming a gel, cook for a few minutes longer and test again with the chilled plate.
6. Remove the pan from the heat once the jam is setting—that is, when it reaches the consistency of jam on the chilled plate.
7. **TO FREEZE:** Allow the jam to cool slightly, but not so much that it starts setting in the pan. Ladle into jars and chill overnight in the refrigerator before freezing. Because it is thick, this jam packs best in rigid containers.

Strawberry Vanilla Jam

As a strawberry jam enthusiast, I've spent a lot of time making (and eating!) the stuff. This recipe has a few specific details that make it one of the best stovetop jams I've had. Simmering the berries for too long can dampen their flavor, so I cook this jam hot and fast to retain a fresher strawberry taste. Gently baking the berries beforehand draws out their juices, which reduces the boiling time needed for the jam to set. Using honey and vanilla adds back in some of the bright floral notes of a fresh-picked berry, which gives this jam a full-bodied flavor. It's a truly spectacular strawberry jam!

YIELD: 5 CUPS

Do not double. To increase yield, make consecutive batches.

- 10 cups cut strawberries, small berries cut in half and medium and large berries cut in quarters (about 3½ pounds whole)
- 2 cups sugar
- 1 cup honey
- 2 tablespoons lemon juice, fresh or bottled
- ¼ teaspoon sea salt
- ½ vanilla bean or 1 teaspoon vanilla bean paste

1. Preheat the oven to 250°F (120°C). Mix together the strawberries and sugar in a 13- by 9-inch glass or ceramic baking pan.
2. Bake for 1 hour, until the strawberries have released a lot of their liquid. Use a handheld masher to crush about half of the berries into smaller pieces.
3. Chill a small ceramic or glass plate in the freezer.
4. Pour the juicy strawberry mixture into a large pot (8-quart or slightly larger). Stir in the honey, lemon juice, and salt. Bring to a boil over medium-high heat. Keep the strawberry mixture at a rolling boil and stir frequently, until it has a thick, jammy appearance and reaches a temperature of 218°F (103.3°C) to 220°F (104.4°C), about 30 minutes. (If it takes much longer than this, you likely aren't cooking it hot and fast enough, and the jam will lose some of its bright flavor.) The jam will be very frothy and threaten to boil over during the first half of cooking, so watch it closely. Make sure to scrape the bottom of the pot when stirring, and be careful, as the jam can spit and spatter.
5. Remove the plate from the freezer and place a small spoonful of the hot jam on it. Let it sit for about 30 seconds, then drag your finger through it, noting the consistency. If the jam is not forming a gel, cook for a few minutes longer and test again with the chilled plate.
6. Remove the pan from the heat once the jam is setting—that is, when it reaches the consistency of jam on the chilled plate. Cut the vanilla bean in half lengthwise and scrape the seeds from inside with the tip of a small knife. Stir the vanilla seeds into the hot jam.
7. **TO FREEZE:** Allow the jam to cool slightly, but not so much that it starts setting in the pan. Ladle into jars and chill overnight in the refrigerator before freezing. Because it is thick, this jam packs best in rigid containers.

Heirloom Tomato Jam

Able to succeed in whatever savory role you give it, this sweet and complex tomato jam is delicious when spread on a grilled cheese sandwich, served next to roast beef, or offered on a charcuterie board. And it never misses when poured over a block of cream cheese and served with crackers! This is the appetizer I'm always asked to bring to holiday parties . . . and once you make it, you will always be asked to bring it, too.

YIELD: 4 CUPS

Do not double. To increase yield, make consecutive batches.

- 12 cups diced heirloom slicing tomatoes, in ½-inch pieces (about 5 pounds whole; see Note)
- 2½ cups granulated sugar
- ½ cup firmly packed brown sugar
- 5 tablespoons lime juice, fresh or bottled
- 1 teaspoon sea salt
- ¾ teaspoon ground ginger
- ½ teaspoon ground cinnamon
- ½ teaspoon crushed red pepper
- ⅛ teaspoon ground cloves

1. Combine the tomatoes, sugars, lime juice, salt, ginger, cinnamon, red pepper, and cloves in a large pot (8-quart or slightly larger) over medium heat. Bring to a boil, then simmer, stirring occasionally, until the jam has thickened and reduced by 75 percent, about 2 hours. Make sure to scrape the bottom of the pot when stirring, especially toward the end of cooking, so the tomatoes don't stick and burn.
2. **TO FREEZE:** Allow the jam to cool slightly, but not so much that it starts setting in the pan. Ladle into jars and chill overnight in the refrigerator before freezing. Because it is thick, this jam packs best in rigid containers.

NOTE: *Don't peel or deseed the tomatoes for this recipe, as they both give flavor and texture to the jam. If you don't have enough heirloom slicing tomatoes (big, round, flavorful types), you can substitute half paste tomatoes.*

TIP Consider dicing and freezing the tomatoes during summer so that you can make this jam later in the season or during winter. To make the jam from frozen tomatoes, thaw and include all the liquid they release.

BONUS USE FOR JAM

Overnight Oats with Jam

I'm continually looking for new and exciting ways to use the jams I've so lovingly crafted. Overnight oats are an excellent vehicle for them! They're especially good with conventional flavors like blueberry, strawberry, peach, and cherry. Just a spoonful is all you need to infuse sweetness and flavor throughout the oatmeal.

YIELD: 1 SERVING

- ⅓ cup old-fashioned oats
- 1 teaspoon chia seeds
- Pinch of sea salt
- ⅔ cup milk or nondairy alternative
- 1 tablespoon frozen long-cooked jam, thawed

1. Stir together the oats, chia seeds, and salt in an 8-ounce jar (or similar container). Stir in the milk, then top with the jam.
2. Cover and refrigerate for 8 hours or overnight before serving.

BONUS USE FOR JAM

Oatmeal Shortbread Jam Bars

Having a freezer full of splendid jams is the ultimate homemade convenience for throwing together a dessert like this one. Most of the work is already done, and the bars will be fantastically delicious, thanks to your prepping ahead. Use whatever fruit jam you like; I haven't met one that didn't work well in this buttery oatmeal shortbread cookie base.

YIELD: 16 SERVINGS

- ¾ cup all-purpose flour or gluten-free flour blend
- ⅔ cup old-fashioned oats
- ½ cup firmly packed brown sugar
- ½ teaspoon baking powder
- ½ teaspoon sea salt
- ½ cup (1 stick) cold butter, cut into small pieces
- 1 teaspoon vanilla extract
- 1 cup frozen long-cooked jam, thawed

1. Preheat the oven to 350°F (180°C). Line an 8-inch square metal baking pan with parchment paper: Cut two strips that fit snuggly inside the bottom of the pan and up the sides, and overlap them going in opposite directions.
2. Combine the flour, oats, sugar, baking powder, and salt in a large bowl. Add the butter. Using your hands, rub the butter into the dry ingredients until the mixture is the size of peas and it sticks together in a clump when you squeeze it. Alternatively, use a pastry cutter. Stir in the vanilla.
3. Reserve ¾ cup of the dough, and press the remainder into the prepared pan, packing it down firmly and evenly to form the base crust.
4. Spread the jam evenly over the top of the crust, then crumble the reserved dough evenly on top.
5. Bake for 45 to 50 minutes, until the crust is browning around the edges. Cool completely, then use the parchment paper to lift the bars out of the pan for cutting.

BONUS USE FOR JAM

Peanut Butter & Jam Cookies

This is a soft peanut butter thumbprint cookie with a spot of jam in the center. Strawberry, raspberry, and grape are the best choices, but whatever flavor you enjoy in your PB&J will taste good in these cookies. Some jams stay right where you put them as a dollop in the middle of the cookie, and some will spread a little. I adore the way that the Strawberry Vanilla Jam (page 218) bubbles up across the surface of the cookie, looking all glassy and fancylike.

YIELD: ABOUT 30 COOKIES

- ½ cup (1 stick) butter, at room temperature
- ½ cup granulated sugar, plus more for coating
- ¼ cup firmly packed brown sugar
- ¾ cup smooth unsweetened peanut butter
- 1 egg
- 1 teaspoon vanilla extract
- 1¼ cups all-purpose flour or gluten-free flour blend
- 1 teaspoon baking soda
- ½ teaspoon sea salt
- ⅔ cup frozen long-cooked jam, thawed

1. Preheat the oven to 350°F (180°C). Line a large sheet pan with parchment paper.
2. Combine the butter and sugars in a large bowl. Using a hand mixer or stand mixer fitted with a paddle attachment, beat together on high speed until combined, about 1 minute.
3. Add the peanut butter, egg, and vanilla, and continue beating until fluffy, about 2 minutes. Scrape down the sides and bottom of the bowl with a spatula as needed.
4. Stir together the flour, baking soda, and salt in a bowl, then add it to the peanut butter mixture and beat on low speed until just combined.
5. Fill a small bowl with a few spoonfuls of granulated sugar, and use more as needed.
6. Roll the cookie dough into balls, using about 1 tablespoon of dough each, then toss them in the sugar to coat. Arrange the balls 2 inches apart on the prepared pan.
7. Use the very tip of your thumb to make a deep indent in the center of each dough ball. Spoon ½ teaspoon of jam into each indent. The jam should sit just below the surface of the cookie; if it doesn't, make the holes a little deeper or bigger.
8. Bake for 14 to 16 minutes, until the cookies are just turning golden brown around the edges. Cool for 5 minutes on the pan, and then remove them to finish cooling.

CHAPTER 8

PIE, CRISP, CRUMBLE & COBBLER FILLINGS

Having ready-made filling on hand means that a homemade pie is just a rolling pin away! And while I absolutely adore pie, I often find myself making a crisp or crumble instead. It's a bit easier and usually satisfies the same taste buds. Most of the "pie" fillings in this chapter are versatile and will flex into crisp, crumble, or cobbler as well.

Making Cooked Pie Fillings for the Freezer

Making a freezer pie filling involves getting the fruit to release some of its juices, and then gently cooking it with sugar and starch to form a thickened filling. Voilà, filling ready for a pie anytime! Depending on the fruit, you'll use either heat or maceration to extract the juices.

PRECOOKING TECHNIQUE

This heating or precooking technique works best for fruits that are firm and that brown easily when cut, like apples and pears. It also works for blueberries, too, because the heat will burst their thick outer skin and allow the juices to come out.

Step 1: Make the dry mix. Start by stirring together the sugar, thickener, and any dry spices like cinnamon in a bowl. I make the dry mix first so that I'm not tearing through cupboards looking for an ingredient while my fruit overcooks on the stove. (This recommendation does indeed come from experience!)

It's very important that you mix the starch and sugar together. If you stir starch by itself into hot fruit, it will form little flour balls that are nearly impossible to dissolve. When starch and sugar are combined, the sugar breaks up the starch and prevents it from clumping, allowing it to dissolve effortlessly.

Step 2: Prepare the fruit. Peel, core, remove pits, and cut the fruit into pieces if needed. It's important to follow the cutting size recommendation on each recipe. For example, in Apple Pie Filling (page 232), if the apple slices are too thin, they can fall apart after being heated, frozen, and baked. In general, bigger pieces tend to work better than small ones for this type of filling.

Step 3: Put the fruit in a pot and start cooking. Use a large, covered pot so the heat gets trapped and the top layer of fruit cooks at a similar rate to the fruit on the bottom. A little bit of water or lemon juice helps create steam and gets things going before the fruit starts to release its own juice.

Step 4: Watch for the fruit to release its juices. As the fruit cooks, stir and fold it around occasionally. A silicone spatula works best for this, since it's gentle on the fruit. Watch the pot carefully; it's crucial that you notice when the fruit starts to release some of its juices. Most fruits will soften and let go of some juices after 5 to 10 minutes of cooking. Err on the

Apple Pie Filling (page 232) has tender, lightly cooked apples and a thickened texture before going into the freezer.

side of less done than more; it's better to *undercook* a pie filling than it is to *overcook* it. Once the fruit has softened slightly and there's a layer of juice in the bottom of the pot, it's time to add the sweetener and thickener.

Step 5: Add the dry mix to thicken. Add in the prepared dry mix and fold the fruit around almost continuously with a silicone spatula, making sure to scrape the bottom and sides of the pot. It usually takes just 1 to 2 minutes for the filling to thicken. It will lightly thicken at first and become more gooey as all the starch molecules bind up with the juices. It should look like a typical baked pie filling when it's done.

Step 6: Cool. Remove the pot from the heat immediately and pour the filling onto a baking pan to cool.

MACERATING TECHNIQUE

Delicate fruits like peaches, strawberries, raspberries, and plums can be turned into pie fillings with a very similar method. Instead of using heat, which can cause these fruits to turn into mush, we combine the fruit with sugar and let it macerate to draw out the liquid. The fruit's juices can then be mixed with starch and heated to form a cohesive pie filling. The fruit is still cooked at the end to thicken the filling, but less heat overall is required, and the fruit doesn't become too soft.

Step 1: Prepare the fruit. Peel, core, remove pits, and cut the fruit into pieces if needed. It's important to follow the cutting size recommendation on each recipe. For example, in Peach Pie Filling (page 238), if the peach slices are too thin, they can fall apart after being heated, frozen, and baked. In general, bigger pieces tend to be better than small ones for this type of filling.

Step 2: Macerate the fruit. Combine the prepared fruit with the sugar and salt, along with any citrus juice, if the recipe calls for it. Refrigerate until some of the juices have been pulled out of the fruit, which usually takes about 1 hour.

Step 3: Add the starch. Pour the cold fruit and all its juices into a large pot, and stir in the starch until it is fully dissolved. Don't worry; starch stirred into cold liquid won't clump. This is also the time to add any flavorings like cinnamon or vanilla.

Step 4: Heat to thicken. Cook over medium-high heat, folding the fruit almost continuously with a silicone spatula, making sure to scrape the bottom and sides of the pot. It usually takes about 5 minutes for the filling to warm through and then thicken. It will lightly thicken at first and become more gooey as all the starch molecules bind up with the juices. It should look like a typical baked pie filling when it's done.

Step 5: Cool. Remove the pot from the heat immediately and pour the filling onto a baking pan to cool.

Thickeners for Frozen Pie Fillings

To avoid a watery fruit pie, we use thickener to help bind the juices. This is a substance that contains starch, and once heated it transforms a pie's runny juices into a filling that keeps its shape and doesn't run out when sliced. Make sure to choose a thickener that will hold up in the freezer; otherwise your pie filling can lose its gel and become watery or separated.

There are two prevailing thickeners that stand up to being cooked, frozen, and then cooked again: tapioca flour and modified cornstarch.

Tapioca flour, which comes from the cassava root, is my number one choice for precooked freezer pie fillings. It's pleasant to work with, behaving just like cornstarch. Most importantly, it makes a sensational filling! Once cooked, tapioca flour forms a clear gel, holds a pie filling together well, and doesn't have any discernable taste, thus letting the fruit shine. It can appear a bit gooey when you first make a precooked filling, but it will have a pleasant mouthfeel once baked into a pie. Tapioca flour is available online, at most large grocery stores (often in the natural foods section), and at health food stores. My preferred brand is Bob's Red Mill.

Tapioca flour and tapioca starch are the same product, and different manufacturers might call them by either name. Even though tapioca flour comes from the cassava root, it is not the same as cassava flour. Cassava flour is not suitable for these pie filling recipes. You might come across something called "modified tapioca starch," which is harder to find and isn't necessary for home freezing.

Modified cornstarch is the most common ingredient you'll find in store-bought frozen pies and store-bought or homemade canned pie filling. It has a wide variety of commercial uses because it's been physically, chemically, or enzymatically altered to stand up to different cooking conditions. Modified cornstarch is available online and often where canning supplies are sold. Regular cornstarch (the type you probably have in your pantry) will not hold up in precooked freezer pie fillings.

All-purpose flour and "cup for cup" rice-based gluten-free blends should be used with caution in freezer pie fillings. How well the flour holds up in the freezer will depend on the type and brand, and that can vary. If you want a starch that never fails in the freezer, stick with tapioca. Flour will give a more cloudy or opaque appearance to the filling, which I like for apple pie but don't prefer for fillings made with colorful berries.

Selecting Fruit for Frozen Pie Filling

You can get away with using lower quality fruit in things like sauces, but not in pie fillings. Bland, mushy, or overly soft fruit will create inferior pies. Berries should be ripe, plump, and sweet, and peaches should be tender but not mushy. For apple and pear fillings, it's important to use varieties that hold their shape when cooked, or you'll end up with a sauce pie. Pumpkin pie filling should be made with squash that has deep orange, dense flesh and not from pumpkins meant for carving, which are bland and watery.

Individual fruits can have a large variety of characteristics. Strawberries, for example, can be more acidic or sweet, more firm or soft. Peaches can be dripping down your arms with juice when you eat them, or drier inside. This is dependent on details like when they were picked, how they were stored, and the specific variety. To that end, following a recipe is a great start, but you'll also need to be an attentive cook. For example, if your filling is too tart, fold in a little more sugar; if it's not gelling strong enough, add a touch more thickener to any subsequent batches. Adjusting to the needs of the specific fruit you're working with means you'll be able to make a blue-ribbon filling every time!

Frozen pie filling looks oddly congealed when thawed, but it will turn smooth and silky again once baked.

Thawing & Baking Frozen Pie Filling

Frozen pie filling should be thawed overnight in the refrigerator or with the cold-water method (see page 21), not in the microwave. I prefer to peel away and remove the freezer bag from the block of filling while it's still frozen. I place it in a dish to thaw, and that way I don't have to deal with the bag sitting in a puddle of juice if it should happen to leak (which it often does). For one less dirty dish, I thaw it right in the baking dish when I'm planning on a crisp or crumble.

It is best to use pie filling immediately after it has thawed. Give it a gentle stir to loosen it and help redistribute any liquid that might have separated out. It's okay if the filling is still a little icy, as long as it can be broken apart and spread out in the crust or pan.

Baking with a previously frozen filling is similar to baking with a freshly made filling. Pour the thawed filling into a chilled piecrust or baking dish, add a top crust or topping, and bake as directed.

Preventing a Crisp or Crumble Topping from Sinking

One issue with crisps and crumbles made with small, juicy fruits like blueberries, strawberries, and raspberries is that they don't have enough body to hold the weight of a hefty topping; this is especially true when using frozen pie fillings. Sometimes the topping can sink into the center and bake up underneath the filling like a cookie iceberg. It still tastes good, but it's not what we're going for. Fortunately there are ways to minimize or avoid this problem. This doesn't happen with pie, as the top crust is supported by being crimped to the bottom crust along the edge.

To prevent sinking toppings entirely, bake the filling and the topping separately. I do this for a lot of my berry crisps and crumbles. It's a slightly unconventional approach that gives you the best of both worlds: a bubbly fruit filling and a topping that is golden brown and crispy crunchy.

Simply bake the filling in a dish covered with aluminum foil, and bake the topping on a parchment paper-lined sheet pan. Because it isn't on top of a fruit filling, the topping bakes up quickly, in about 15 minutes. Once baked, it looks like a big cookie and can be broken or cut into smaller pieces, or left in larger sheets. See the fruit crumble recipe on page 249 for full instructions. The fruit crisp recipe (page 248) can also be cooked using this method.

If serving the entire dish at once, place the baked topping on the fruit filling in the pan after they both cool. If serving individual portions over several days, keep the filling and topping separate, and construct the crisp or crumble as each plate is dished up; this will keep the topping supremely crunchy.

One other option that minimizes topping sinkage (though it doesn't eliminate it) is to "shingle" the topping on top of the filling. Use your hands to pick up pieces of the dough, about 1 tablespoon at a time, and form them into flat shingles ¼ inch thick. Place them on top of the filling, covering the whole surface. This distributes their weight more evenly over a wider surface. I also use this technique for chunky fillings like apple and pear. Those fruits aren't notorious sinkers, but I like the extra insurance.

Other Uses for Frozen Pie Filling

Frozen fruit pie filling can also be used for cold applications, like topping a cheesecake, filling a layer cake, or in the Blueberry Cream Cheese Pie on page 236. In general they can be used in similar ways as canned pie fillings.

Frozen pie filling will look congealed when it thaws and needs to be heated briefly to make it smooth again. To do this, heat the filling in a large pot over medium heat, stirring gently with a silicone spatula, until just warmed through and glassy. Chill the pie filling in the refrigerator again before using it in a cold dessert.

Can You Freeze Whole Unbaked Pies?

Yes, a whole unbaked fruit pie can be frozen, but as a pie connoisseur, I can't recommend this. The quality of a homemade pie will be best when the filling and crust are frozen separately. That said, there are certain situations where freezing pies could be useful—for example, if you will be traveling with the pies and won't have time or kitchen space to roll out dough.

It's easy to pack pie filling into freezer bags, remove all the air from those bags, and stack them in the freezer. Well protected from freezer burn, they will last for over a year. This is the best approach when freezing pie fillings with the goal being preservation. A whole unbaked pie is awkward, takes up more space, and is difficult to properly package, so it won't keep very long.

Baking a whole pie from frozen requires a longer cooking time, and you run the risk of burning the crust before the filling is cooked through. Thawing the pie in the refrigerator before baking will likely result in a very soggy crust—and nobody wants that. If you do want to freeze a whole unbaked pie, package it well, don't store it for too long, bake it from frozen, and use crust shields to prevent burning the crust edge.

My Flaky All-Butter Piecrust dough (page 246) freezes flawlessly, so I always keep a stash of the dough in the freezer along with my pie fillings. When wrapped in plastic wrap and sealed in a freezer bag, the discs of dough will keep up to a year. Freezing both pie elements separately will give you the best of both worlds: It's still convenient, and the pie will be most excellent!

Instead of freezing a whole unbaked pie, freeze the filling and pie dough separately. It's still convenient, and it will give you the best pie.

Apple Pie Filling

My grandma made the best apple pie with a flaky crusty, lots of warm spices, and plenty of love (the secret ingredient!). I've aspired to make pie as good as hers. My version of apple pie filling is perfectly sweet and spiced, with enough sauciness to hold the apples together without being runny. Make sure to use apples that will hold their shape when baked, such as Honeycrisp or Granny Smith, so that you don't end up with an applesauce pie!

YIELD: FILLING FOR ONE 9-INCH PIE, CRISP, CRUMBLE, OR COBBLER

Do not double. To increase yield, make consecutive batches.

- ½ cup granulated sugar
- ¼ cup firmly packed brown sugar (see Note)
- 3 tablespoons tapioca flour, all-purpose flour, or gluten-free flour blend
- 1 teaspoon ground cinnamon
- ½ teaspoon sea salt
- ¼ teaspoon ground allspice
- ¼ teaspoon grated nutmeg
- 9 cups peeled, sliced apples, ¼ to ½ inch thick (about 3½ pounds whole)
- 2 tablespoons water
- 1 teaspoon vanilla extract

1. Combine the sugars, flour, cinnamon, salt, allspice, and nutmeg in a small bowl and set the mixture aside.
2. Combine the apples and water in a large pot over medium heat. Cover and cook, gently folding the apples occasionally with a silicone spatula, until they have slightly softened and released some of their juices in the bottom of the pot, 10 to 15 minutes; replace the cover between stirrings.
3. Fold in the sugar mixture and vanilla. Continue cooking, uncovered, gently folding the apples frequently with a silicone spatula and making sure to scrape the bottom and sides of the pot, until the mixture thickens and turns slightly translucent, about 2 minutes.
4. Pour the pie filling onto a baking sheet to cool.
5. **TO FREEZE:** Cool completely before freezing. This filling packs well in a freezer bag or a rigid container. The recipe fits in a 1-quart freezer bag.
6. **TO SERVE:** Bake the thawed filling into a pie, crisp, crumble, or cobbler following the instructions on pages 247 to 251.

NOTE: *If you prefer a pie that is less sweet, omit the brown sugar.*

TIP Each variety of apple has its own flavor notes, so whatever apple recipe you're making (especially pie) will benefit from using more than one type of apple to get the most well-rounded flavor.

Blueberry Pie Filling

I never cared that much for blueberry pie until I had the real-deal homemade kind. This filling is bursting with fresh berries and has a robust flavor thanks to the butter, lemon zest, and vanilla; it has definitely won me over! While it's great in a traditional piecrust, my favorite use for this filling is as a crumble with the Almond Fruit Crumble topping on page 250.

YIELD: FILLING FOR ONE 9-INCH PIE, CRISP, CRUMBLE, OR COBBLER

Do not double. To increase yield, make consecutive batches.

- ½ cup granulated sugar
- ¼ cup firmly packed brown sugar
- ¼ cup plus 1 tablespoon tapioca flour
- ½ teaspoon finely grated lemon zest
- ¼ teaspoon sea salt
- 2 tablespoons butter
- 6 cups blueberries
- 1 tablespoon freshly squeezed lemon juice
- 1 teaspoon vanilla extract

1. Combine the sugars, tapioca flour, lemon zest, and salt in a small bowl and set the mixture aside.
2. Melt the butter in a large pot over medium heat. Add the blueberries and lemon juice. Cover and cook, gently folding the berries occasionally with a silicone spatula, until they have released some of their juices in the bottom of the pot, about 5 minutes; replace the cover between stirrings.
3. Fold in the sugar mixture and vanilla. Continue cooking, uncovered, gently folding the berries frequently with a silicone spatula and making sure to scrape the bottom and sides of the pot, until the mixture thickens and turns slightly translucent, about 3 minutes.
4. Pour the pie filling onto a baking sheet to cool.
5. **TO FREEZE:** Cool completely before freezing. This filling packs well in a freezer bag or rigid container. The recipe fits in a 1-quart freezer bag.
6. **TO SERVE:** Bake the thawed filling into a pie, crisp, crumble, or cobbler following the instructions on pages 247 to 251.

BONUS USE FOR FILLING

Blueberry Cream Cheese Pie

Precooked frozen pie filling is surprisingly versatile, and in this recipe we're using it to make a cold or "no-bake"-style pie (though I do like to bake the crust). Gently heating the filling on the stove will bring back its silky texture after being in the freezer. Once cooled, it's ready to be spooned onto a layer of creamy cheesecake in a graham cracker crust.

YIELD: 8–10 SERVINGS

- 1 recipe frozen Blueberry Pie Filling (page 235), thawed
- 1½ cups finely ground graham cracker crumbs
- 2 tablespoons granulated sugar
- 6 tablespoons butter, melted
- ⅛ teaspoon sea salt
- 8 ounces cream cheese, softened
- 1 cup confectioners' sugar
- 1 teaspoon vanilla extract

1. Place the pie filling in a large pot over medium heat. Cook, gently folding the filling frequently with a silicone spatula, making sure to scrape the bottom and sides of the pot, until the mixture melts into a uniform smooth consistency, about 8 minutes. Remove the pot from the stove and set aside to cool.
2. Preheat the oven to 350°F (180°C).
3. Stir together the graham cracker crumbs, granulated sugar, butter, and salt in a large mixing bowl. Press the mixture into the bottom and up the sides of a 9-inch pie pan. Use your hands to evenly distribute the crumbs and pack them into place, then switch to using the bottom of a drinking glass to pack them more firmly.
4. Bake for 15 minutes, then cool completely before assembling the pie.
5. Combine the cream cheese, confectioners' sugar, and vanilla in a large bowl. Using a hand mixer or stand mixer fitted with a paddle attachment, beat together on medium-high speed until light and fluffy, about 1 minute. Scrape down the sides and bottom of the bowl with a spatula as needed.
6. To assemble the pie, pour the cream cheese mixture into the bottom of the crust and spread it in an even layer. Spoon the cooled pie filling on top and spread it all the way to the edges of the pie in an even layer.
7. Chill the pie in the refrigerator for 6 hours or overnight before serving.

Mixed Berry Pie Filling

Berries are delicate and have a high water content, so a mixed berry pie is one of the trickiest to make. But when you get it right, gosh, is it a great pie! (It's especially good with a scoop of vanilla ice cream on top . . . but what pie isn't?!) This filling recipe never lets me down: It's sweet and tart, sets up nicely, and is rich with vibrant berries.

YIELD: FILLING FOR ONE 9-INCH PIE, CRISP, CRUMBLE, OR COBBLER

Do not double. To increase yield, make consecutive batches.

- 3 cups cut strawberries, halved if medium and quartered if large
- 2 cups blueberries
- 2 cups raspberries
- ¾ cup sugar
- ¼ teaspoon sea salt
- 1 tablespoon lemon juice, fresh or bottled
- ⅓ cup plus 1 tablespoon tapioca flour
- 1 teaspoon vanilla extract

1. Combine the strawberries, blueberries, raspberries, sugar, salt, and lemon juice in a bowl and fold them together until the berries are coated with the sugar. Refrigerate for 1 hour to macerate, and stir occasionally to help release the juices.
2. Pour the berry mixture and all the liquid into a large pot, and stir in the tapioca flour and vanilla. Place the pot over medium-high heat. Cook, gently folding the berries frequently with a silicone spatula and making sure to scrape the bottom and sides of the pot, until the mixture thickens and turns slightly translucent, about 4 minutes.
3. Pour the pie filling onto a baking pan to cool.
4. **TO FREEZE:** Cool completely before freezing. This filling packs well in a freezer bag or a rigid container. The recipe fits in a 1-quart freezer bag.
5. **TO SERVE:** Bake the thawed filling into a pie, crisp, crumble, or cobbler following the instructions on pages 247 to 251.

Peach Pie Filling

Peaches don't really grow where I live in the North, but you'll always find peach pie filling in my freezer. Southern orchards send peaches up our way on semitrucks, and we meet in local grocery store parking lots to buy them by the bushel! Peaches can be delicate, so for this filling I like to macerate them to extract their juices before heating them briefly to thicken.

YIELD: FILLING FOR ONE 9-INCH PIE, CRISP, CRUMBLE, OR COBBLER
Do not double. To increase yield, make consecutive batches.

- 7 cups peeled, sliced peaches (about 8 medium; see Note)
- ¼ cup firmly packed brown sugar
- ¼ cup granulated sugar
- ¼ teaspoon sea salt
- ¼ cup tapioca flour
- 1 teaspoon vanilla extract
- ¼ teaspoon ground cinnamon

1. Combine the peaches, sugars, and salt in a bowl and fold them together until the peaches are coated with the sugar. Refrigerate for 1 hour to macerate, and stir occasionally to help release the juices.
2. Pour the peach mixture and all the liquid into a large pot, and stir in the tapioca flour, vanilla, and cinnamon. Place the pot over medium-high heat and cook, gently folding the peaches frequently with a silicone spatula, making sure to scrape the bottom and sides of the pot, until the mixture thickens and turns slightly translucent, about 5 minutes.
3. Pour the pie filling onto a baking pan to cool.
4. **TO FREEZE:** Cool completely before freezing. This filling packs well in a freezer bag or a rigid container. The recipe fits in a 1-quart freezer bag.
5. **TO SERVE:** Bake the thawed filling into a pie, crisp, crumble, or cobbler following the instructions on pages 247 to 251.

NOTE: *To peel the peaches, cut a small "X" on the bottom of each and place them two or three at a time in boiling water for 30 to 60 seconds. Cool to a safe handling temperature, but work while the peaches are still warm. The peels should come off easily; if they don't, try boiling the peaches for up to 1 minute longer. Underripe peaches don't peel well, so make sure you're working with ripe, juicy ones!*

Cut peaches into big slices for this recipe: Cut each peach in half and cut each half into four even slices. If working with very large peaches, cut each half into five slices.

Pear Pie Filling

While this filling can certainly be baked into a formal pie, I think a fruit crisp suits its homey personality a bit better. There's just something about the old-fashioned nature of pears that says, "Keep it simple." And it doesn't get much easier than whipping up a crisp topping!

YIELD: FILLING FOR ONE 9-INCH PIE, CRISP, CRUMBLE, OR COBBLER
Do not double. To increase yield, make consecutive batches.

- ⅓ cup granulated sugar
- 3 tablespoons firmly packed brown sugar
- ¼ cup tapioca flour
- 1 teaspoon ground cinnamon
- ¼ teaspoon ground ginger
- ¼ teaspoon sea salt
- 8 cups peeled, chopped pears, in 1- to 2-inch pieces (about 10 medium; see Note)
- 1 tablespoon water
- 1 teaspoon vanilla extract

1. Combine the sugars, tapioca flour, cinnamon, ginger, and salt in a small bowl and set the mixture aside.
2. Combine the pears and water in a large pot over medium heat. Cover and cook, gently folding the pears occasionally with a silicone spatula, until they have slightly softened and released some of their juices in the bottom of the pot, about 5 minutes; replace the cover between stirrings.
3. Fold in the sugar mixture and vanilla. Continue cooking, uncovered, gently folding the pears frequently with a silicone spatula and making sure to scrape the bottom and sides of the pot, until the mixture thickens and turns slightly translucent, about 2 minutes.
4. Pour the pie filling onto a baking pan to cool.
5. **TO FREEZE:** Cool completely before freezing. This filling packs well in a freezer bag or rigid container. The recipe fits in a 1-quart freezer bag.
6. **TO SERVE:** Bake the thawed filling into a pie, crisp, crumble, or cobbler following the instructions on pages 247 to 251.

NOTE: *Use ripe pears, which will be just slightly soft at the top but still firm and will glisten with juice when peeled. Make sure to use varieties meant for processing, like Bartlett or Bosc, as they will hold their shape when cooked. Peel the pears and cut them into 1-inch-thick slices, then cut the slices into blocky 2-inch pieces.*

Strawberry Rhubarb Pie Filling

The arrival of tart rhubarb and sweet strawberries marks the beginning of summer here on our homestead. I prefer a traditional pie with a lattice top for this duo, as it seems to complement their cheery disposition the best. When adapting this recipe to a crumble or crisp, I like to bake the filling and topping separately, as shown in the Fruit Crumble recipe on page 249.

YIELD: FILLING FOR ONE 9-INCH PIE, CRISP, CRUMBLE, OR COBBLER

Do not double. To increase yield, make consecutive batches.

- 4 cups cut rhubarb, in 1-inch pieces
- 3 cups cut strawberries, halved if medium and quartered if large
- ¾ cup sugar
- ¼ teaspoon sea salt
- 1 tablespoon lemon juice, fresh or bottled
- ¼ cup plus 1 tablespoon tapioca flour
- 1 teaspoon vanilla extract

1. Combine the rhubarb, strawberries, sugar, salt, and lemon juice in a bowl and fold them together until the berries are coated with the sugar. Refrigerate for 1 hour to macerate, and stir occasionally to help release the juices.
2. Pour the berry mixture and all the liquid into a large pot, and stir in the tapioca flour and vanilla. Place the pot over medium-high heat. Cook, gently folding the berries frequently with a silicone spatula and making sure to scrape the bottom and sides of the pot, until the mixture thickens and turns slightly translucent, about 5 minutes.
3. Pour the pie filling onto a baking pan to cool.
4. **TO FREEZE:** Cool completely before freezing. This filling packs well in a freezer bag or a rigid container. The recipe fits in a 1-quart freezer bag.
5. **TO SERVE:** Bake the thawed filling into a pie, crisp, crumble, or cobbler following the instructions on pages 247 to 251.

Roasted Strawberry Galette

The brilliant idea of wrapping roasted strawberries in pastry comes from Erin Jeanne McDowell, author of *The Book on Pie*. Slow-roasting the berries causes them to become jammy and surrounded by a flavorful strawberry syrup. Lucky for us, they freeze beautifully in this state! My version of this sweet and tart rustic pie makes for an extraordinarily special dessert.

YIELD: FILLING FOR TWO 9-INCH GALETTES

Do not double. To increase yield, make consecutive batches.

MAKING & FREEZING THE STARTER

- 12 cups cut strawberries, halved if medium and quartered if large (about 4 pounds whole)
- ¾ cup sugar
- ¼ cup honey
- 2 teaspoons vanilla extract
- ½ teaspoon sea salt

1. Preheat the oven to 250°F (120°C).
2. Combine the strawberries, sugar, honey, vanilla, and salt in a large bowl, tossing gently to coat. Transfer the mixture to an 18- by 13-inch rimmed sheet pan and spread the berries in an even layer (do not use foil or parchment paper on the pan, and note that the pan size here is important).
3. Bake for about 3½ hours, stirring once every hour with a silicone spatula. Stir gently, and make sure that any berries that are starting to darken on top get flipped over. The strawberries will release a lot of liquid, and that liquid will reduce as the strawberries bake. The strawberries are done when they are deep red and the liquid has thickened to the consistency of maple syrup.
4. **TO FREEZE:** Cool completely before freezing. Divide into 2 portions, making sure to include an equal amount of berries and syrup in each. Because it cooks down into a relatively small amount, this starter packs best in rigid containers. Each portion fits in a 1½-cup container.

MAKING THE GALETTE

- 1 disc Flaky All-Butter Piecrust (page 246), thawed if frozen
- ½ recipe frozen Roasted Strawberry Galette starter, thawed
- 1 tablespoon heavy whipping cream
- 1 tablespoon coarse sugar or granulated sugar
- 3 tablespoons confectioners' sugar
- 1 teaspoon water

1. Preheat the oven to 425°F (220°C).
2. Unwrap the disc of dough and allow it to sit at room temperature for 10 minutes. Place the dough between two pieces of parchment paper and use a rolling pin to roll it into a large circle about 12 inches in diameter and, more importantly, about ⅛ inch thick.

3. Remove the top sheet of parchment paper and transfer the bottom piece with the dough on it to a large baking sheet.

4. Spoon the starter, including any liquid from the container, into the center of the piecrust. Spread the filling into an even, thin layer, leaving a 2-inch border of crust around the edges.

5. Gently fold the edges of the dough over the filling, overlapping them as needed. Be careful not to let any cracks form in the crust edge when folding (or repair them if they do); otherwise the liquid will leak out while baking.

6. Brush the top of the folded-over crust edge with the cream, then sprinkle evenly with the coarse sugar.

7. Bake for 20 minutes. Reduce the oven temperature to 350°F (180°C) and bake for 25 to 30 minutes longer, until the crust is golden brown but before the strawberries start to burn. Allow the galette to cool completely.

8. Stir together the confectioners' sugar and water until it forms a smooth glaze. Drizzle the glaze over the galette right before serving.

Pumpkin Pie

This pie begins with a frozen starter, which offers as much convenience as possible while still producing the best pie. Freezing the filling without the eggs and then whisking them in right before baking means you'll end up with a smooth and luscious pumpkin custard that doesn't curdle or split. I like to write a note on the freezer bag to add 3 eggs once thawed, just so I don't forget.

YIELD: ONE 9-INCH PIE

Do not double. To increase yield, make consecutive batches.

MAKING & FREEZING THE STARTER

- 2½ cups roasted pumpkin or winter squash purée (see Note)
- ⅔ cup firmly packed brown sugar or maple syrup
- ½ cup heavy whipping cream
- 1½ teaspoons pumpkin pie spice
- 1 teaspoon ground cinnamon
- ½ teaspoon sea salt
- 1 teaspoon vanilla extract

1. To make the starter, whisk together the pumpkin purée, sugar, cream, pumpkin pie spice, cinnamon, salt, and vanilla in a large mixing bowl.
2. **TO FREEZE:** This starter packs well in a freezer bag or rigid container. The recipe fits in a 1-quart freezer bag.

NOTE: *To make roasted pumpkin or winter squash purée, preheat the oven to 400°F (200°C). Cut the squash in half and place the halves cut-side down on a large sheet pan. Bake for 45 to 75 minutes (depending on size), until the squash is soft, which you can feel by poking the rind. Allow the squash to cool to a safe handling temperature, then use a spoon to scoop out and discard the seeds and guts. Scoop out the flesh and process in a food processor or blender until smooth, about 30 seconds.*

MAKING THE PIE

- 1 disc Flaky All-Butter Piecrust (page 246), thawed if frozen
- 3 eggs
- 1 recipe frozen Pumpkin Pie starter, thawed
- Whipped cream, for serving

1. Unwrap the disc of dough and allow it to sit at room temperature for 10 minutes. Place the dough between two pieces of parchment paper and use a rolling pin to roll it into a large circle about 12 inches in diameter and, more importantly, ⅛ inch thick.
2. Transfer the piecrust to a 9-inch pie pan and press it into the bottom and sides. Leave about 1 inch of dough sticking out past the pan's edge and trim off any excess. Roll the extra dough under until it's flush with the edge of the pan, and crimp it with your fingers to form a decorative crust. Use a fork to poke several holes in the bottom of the pie shell, then place it in the refrigerator while the oven heats.
3. Preheat the oven to 425°F (220°C). To blind bake the crust, nestle a piece of parchment paper into the pie shell and fill it to the top with pie weights or dried beans.

4. Bake the crust for 15 to 20 minutes, until the edges of the crust start to turn golden brown. Carefully remove the pie weights and parchment paper, and bake about 5 minutes longer, until the bottom is set and doesn't appear wet.
5. Allow the crust to cool for 10 minutes. Reset the oven to 350°F (180°C).
6. Whisk the eggs in a large mixing bowl until they are broken up and uniform, then whisk in the thawed starter until just combined. Pour the filling into the crust.
7. Bake for 45 to 50 minutes, until the custard is just set but still slightly jiggly in the very center.
8. Chill for 4 hours or overnight in the refrigerator before serving. Serve each slice with a dollop of whipped cream.

Flaky All-Butter Piecrust

There's nothing better than a buttery, flaky crust done right! The secret to a crisp and tender piecrust that holds its shape but shatters in your mouth is folding the dough over itself again and again. Laminating the dough this way is a bit more work but will result in the best piecrust you've ever had. This dough does very well in the freezer, so stash some away to go with all your frozen pie fillings.

YIELD: TWO 9-INCH PIECRUSTS
This recipe can be doubled.

- 2½ cups all-purpose flour (see Note for gluten-free)
- ½ teaspoon sea salt
- 1 cup (2 sticks) cold butter, each stick cut into 20 pieces
- ⅓ cup ice water, plus more as needed

1. Combine the flour and salt in a large mixing bowl. Add the butter and toss to coat it in the flour, then use your fingers to pinch all the pieces of butter into flat discs.
2. Add the water and use your hands to mix the dough. It will appear dry, but just keep stirring and gently kneading it against the inside of the bowl. If the dough is very dry and crumbly and not coming together after 1 minute of mixing, add 1 tablespoon of water at a time, stirring between each addition. Give it a chance to come together; using too much water will result in a tough crust. The dough is ready when it holds together after squeezing it and all the dry crumbs in the bottom of the bowl are incorporated.
3. Form the dough into a rectangle about 10 inches long by 4 inches wide. Wrap the dough in plastic wrap and refrigerate for 30 minutes.
4. Unwrap the dough and allow it to warm for 10 minutes. Place the dough between two pieces of parchment paper and use a rolling pin to flatten it to about ½ inch thick, maintaining the rectangle shape. Cut the dough in half so you have two short pieces, then stack one on top of the other. Place the dough between the parchment paper again and roll until it is a similar ½-inch-thick rectangle; the shape doesn't have to be exact. Repeat this five more times until you've cut, stacked, and rolled the dough a total of six times.
5. Cut the dough into 2 equal pieces and form each into a disc shape; the more round, the better it will roll out later. Wrap each piece in plastic wrap and refrigerate for 30 minutes. The dough can be used to make a pie now, held in the refrigerator for 2 days, or frozen for later.
6. **TO FREEZE:** This dough does best when double-wrapped, so place the plastic-wrapped discs of dough into a freezer bag for storage.
7. **TO USE:** Thaw the dough overnight in the refrigerator; do not thaw with heat.

NOTE: *For gluten-free crust, use a "cup for cup" gluten-free flour blend and add 2 teaspoons sugar and 1½ teaspoons xanthan gum to the dry ingredients in step 1.*

How to Make a Fruit Pie

Now that you have a freezer full of fruity pie fillings and a cache of piecrusts, it's time to put them together! A buttery, flaky crust combined with sweet and tender fruit is the perfect match.

YIELD: ONE 9-INCH FRUIT PIE

- 1 recipe Flaky All-Butter Piecrust (page 246)
- 1 recipe frozen fruit pie filling, thawed
- 2 tablespoons heavy whipping cream or 1 beaten egg
- 2 tablespoons coarse sugar (like turbinado)

1. If frozen, thaw the piecrust dough overnight in the refrigerator; do not thaw with heat. To bake a double-crust pie, allow the dough to sit at room temperature for 10 minutes. Place each disc of dough between two pieces of parchment paper, and use a rolling pin to roll them into large circles about 12 inches in diameter and, more importantly, ⅛ inch thick.
2. Transfer one of the piecrusts to a 9-inch pie pan and press it into the bottom and sides. Leave about 1 inch of dough sticking out past the pan's edge and trim off any excess.
3. Preheat the oven to 425°F (220°C).
4. Spoon the fruit pie filling of your choice into the crust, including any liquid from the container, and spread in an even layer.
5. Cover with the second crust and cut away any dough that hangs over the edge of the pie pan. Roll the bottom and top dough under until it's flush with the edge of the pan, and crimp it with your fingers to form a decorative crust. Cut five 2-inch slits in the top to allow steam to escape. Brush the entire top and outer lip of the crust with the cream, then sprinkle with the sugar. (Alternatively, use a lattice or crumble topping.)
6. Bake for 20 minutes. Reduce the oven temperature to 375°F (190°C) and bake for 40 to 45 minutes longer, until the filling looks bubbly and the crust is golden brown. Allow the pie to cool completely before slicing; otherwise it will be runny.

How to Make a Fruit Crisp

Is it a crisp or a crumble? It's generally agreed that a crisp topping contains oats, whereas a crumble does not. The oats make this topping distinctly hardy and well suited for cinnamon-spiced fillings like Apple Pie Filling (page 232), Pear Pie Filling (page 240), and Peach Pie Filling (page 238). I prefer a fruit crumble topping (page 249) for lighter, more summery fruits like berries, but they are interchangeable no matter which you choose.

YIELD: ONE 9-INCH FRUIT CRISP

- ¾ cup old-fashioned oats
- ¾ cup all-purpose flour or gluten-free flour blend
- ½ cup firmly packed brown sugar
- ¼ cup granulated sugar
- ¼ teaspoon sea salt
- 1 teaspoon vanilla
- ½ cup (1 stick) butter, melted
- 1 recipe frozen fruit pie filling, thawed
- Vanilla ice cream (optional)

1. Preheat the oven to 400°F (200°C).
2. Stir together the oats, flour, sugars, and salt in a large bowl. Stir the vanilla into the butter, then stir the butter into the flour mixture to form a crumbly dough.
3. Pour the pie filling into a 9-inch square (or similar) glass or ceramic baking pan. Stir it around to help break up clumps and evenly distribute any liquid.
4. Use your hands to pick up pieces of the dough, about 1 tablespoon at a time, and form them into flat shingles about ¼ inch thick. Place them on top of the fruit filling, covering the whole surface (this will help minimize the topping sinking into the filling).
5. Bake for 40 to 45 minutes, until the filling is bubbly and the topping is turning golden brown. Serve with vanilla ice cream, if desired.

How to Make a Fruit Crumble

This crumble topping is reminiscent of a sugar cookie, and it feels a bit lighter than a crisp topping. There's not a fruit filling it doesn't pair well with, but it's especially suited for dark fruits like berries. Because I use this topping for berry fillings, I prefer to bake it separately on a sheet pan instead of directly on top of the fruit. This way it doesn't sink into the berries, and it stays wonderfully crispy crunchy even days after being made.

YIELD: ONE 9-INCH FRUIT CRUMBLE

- 1 recipe frozen fruit pie filling, thawed
- ¾ cup all-purpose flour or gluten-free flour blend
- ¼ cup firmly packed brown sugar
- ¼ cup granulated sugar
- ¼ teaspoon sea salt
- 1 teaspoon vanilla
- 5 tablespoons butter, melted
- Vanilla ice cream (optional)

1. Preheat the oven to 400°F (200°C).
2. Pour the pie filling into a 9-inch square (or similar) glass or ceramic baking pan. Stir it around to help break up clumps and evenly distribute any liquid. Cover tightly with aluminum foil.
3. Bake for 45 to 50 minutes, until the filling is bubbly around the edges.
4. Line a large sheet pan with parchment paper.
5. Stir together the flour, sugars, and salt in a large bowl. Stir the vanilla into the butter, then stir the butter mixture into the flour mixture to form a crumbly dough. Pour the crumbs onto the prepared sheet pan, break them apart with your hands, and spread them in an even layer over the entire pan.
6. Bake for 10 to 15 minutes, until the crumbs turn golden brown.
7. The crumbs will bake up like a big cookie. Allow them to cool, and then break or chop into smaller pieces, or leave in larger sheets. Place them on top of the filling right before serving. Serve with vanilla ice cream, if desired.

How to Make Almond Fruit Crumble

This is my preferred recipe for using with blueberry or peach pie filling. The sliced almonds bake up all toasty in the oven, plus the almond extract gives this topping that unmistakable sweet almond scent. Baking the topping separately from the filling gives it a crispy-crunchy texture and prevents it from sinking.

YIELD: ONE 9-INCH FRUIT CRUMBLE

- 1 recipe frozen Blueberry Pie Filling (page 235) or Peach Pie Filling (page 238), thawed
- 1 cup all-purpose flour or gluten-free flour blend
- ½ cup sliced raw almonds
- ¼ cup firmly packed brown sugar
- ¼ cup granulated sugar
- ¼ teaspoon sea salt
- 1 teaspoon vanilla extract
- ½ teaspoon almond extract
- 6 tablespoons butter, melted
- Vanilla ice cream, for serving (optional)

1. Preheat the oven to 400°F (200°C).
2. Pour the pie filling into a 9-inch square (or similar) glass or ceramic baking pan. Stir it around to help break up clumps and evenly distribute any liquid. Cover tightly with aluminum foil.
3. Bake for 45 to 50 minutes, until the filling is bubbly around the edges.
4. Line a large sheet pan with parchment paper.
5. Stir together the flour, almonds, sugars, and salt in a large bowl. Stir the vanilla and almond extracts into the butter, then stir the butter mixture into the flour mixture to form a crumbly dough. Pour the crumbs onto the prepared sheet pan, break them apart with your hands, and spread them in an even layer over the entire pan.
6. Bake for 10 to 15 minutes, until the crumbs turn golden brown.
7. The crumbs will bake up like a big cookie. Allow them to cool, and then break or chop them into smaller pieces, or leave in larger sheets and place them on top of the filling right before serving. Serve with vanilla ice cream, if desired.

How to Make a Fruit Cobbler

Cobblers come in a few different forms, most commonly either a runny batter that forms a cakelike topping or a biscuit top; I actually prefer a hybrid of the two. This is a loose biscuit topping that bakes up tender and golden brown on top and dumpling-like on the bottom where it's simmering in the fruit. This recipe works particularly well with saucy fillings like Blueberry Pie Filling (page 235), Mixed Berry Pie Filling (page 237), and Peach Pie Filling (page 238).

YIELD: ONE 9-INCH FRUIT COBBLER

- 1½ cups all-purpose flour
- ⅓ cup plus 2 tablespoons sugar
- 1 teaspoon baking powder
- ¼ teaspoon baking soda
- ¼ teaspoon sea salt
- 6 tablespoons cold butter, cut into 24 pieces
- 2 teaspoons lemon juice, fresh or bottled
- ½ teaspoon vanilla extract
- ½ cup plus 2 tablespoons whole milk
- 1 recipe frozen fruit pie filling, thawed
- 1 egg, beaten

1. Preheat the oven to 375°F (190°C).
2. Stir together the flour, ⅓ cup of the sugar, baking powder, baking soda, and salt in a large mixing bowl.
3. Add the butter and stir until it is coated. Using your hands, rub the butter into the dry ingredients until it is the size of peas. Alternatively, use a pastry cutter.
4. Combine the lemon juice, vanilla, and milk in a small bowl, then immediately stir the mixture into the dry ingredients. Continue stirring until everything just comes together into a dough and there are no streaks of dry flour left; don't overmix.
5. Pour the pie filling into a 9-inch square (or similar) glass or ceramic baking pan. Stir it around to help break up clumps and evenly distribute any liquid.
6. Use a large spring-loaded scoop or a serving spoon to drop big dollops of the dough, about ¼ cup each, on top of the filling. Use a butter knife to spread the dough around so that the dough clumps are just touching each other.
7. Brush the top of the dough gently with the egg; you will only use about half of the egg. Sprinkle the remaining 2 tablespoons sugar evenly over the top.
8. Bake for 55 to 60 minutes, until the topping is golden brown and the filling is bubbling.

CHAPTER 9

FRUIT & VEGETABLE BAKED GOODS

Freezing homemade muffins, pancakes, cookies, loaf cakes, and other baked treats is a satisfying way to preserve fruits and veggies or use up something in your fridge before it goes bad. And they're a very desirable food item to have tucked away! My philosophy when making baked goods with produce is to incorporate as much produce as possible—I want it to be the star.

Which Baked Goods Freeze Best?

Most flour-based baked goods freeze well, including those made with all-purpose flour or "cup for cup" gluten-free flour blends. If the texture and flavor are good going into the freezer, they should be good once thawed. A smart rule to follow is that baked items that still have a good texture on their second day will freeze well. There's a short list of things that are great only when eaten the same day they were made, and these are not good candidates for the freezer. Scones fall into this category for me, but I've discovered it works to freeze the unbaked dough instead, like in the Sweet Cherry Almond Scone Dough on page 272.

One reason why fruit- and veggie-heavy baked goods freeze so well is because fruits and vegetables contain a lot of moisture. The freezer can be drying, so this extra moisture helps them keep beautifully. I've found that it's better for that moisture to be spread out rather than concentrated in only a few places. This means that smaller pieces of fruit and vegetables work better than larger pieces. For example, Spiced Pear Muffins (page 281) use shredded pears. The pear flavor gets infused throughout the entire muffin, and there are no big soggy pieces. Baked goods made with zucchini or carrots, like Spiced Carrot Bread (page 268), turn out best when those veggies are finely shredded, like on the small side of a box grater. Fruits and veggies with a soft texture, like bananas and cooked squash, will do very well when mashed and incorporated as a purée, like in the Pumpkin Cake Roll on page 290.

While I love the flavor that butter imparts in loaf cakes and muffins, oil gives these treats a slightly better texture. They'll be moister and bouncier after being frozen and thawed. Avocado oil is my favorite choice for baked goods because it has a neutral but slightly nutty and buttery flavor.

Be mindful when freezing baked goods that have a topping. Coarse sugar or icing on top of loaf cakes and muffins can become melty or soggy when thawed. Large pieces of nuts or streusel won't stick well, and you'll lose most of it. However, very finely chopped nuts, small crumbles of streusel, or mini chocolate chips used sparingly will freeze and thaw intact.

For baked goods destined for the freezer, shred or cut fruits and veggies into small pieces. This infuses flavor throughout the item and prevents soggy spots.

Freezing Baked Goods

Once your baked goods are out of the oven, follow these general guidelines to help ensure they freeze with great success.

Cool baked goods completely before packaging them. Otherwise condensation will form on the inside of the bag and make ice crystals. For the best results, allow the item to cool to room temperature on the counter, then package and freeze immediately. Avoid cooling baked goods in the refrigerator, which can steal their moisture.

Freeze baked goods the same day they were made. I like to think of freezing as a way to capture and hold something at its highest quality. For most baked goods, this is the day they were made.

Package carefully to avoid freezer burn. Freezer burn is of utmost concern with baked goods. This is because they are often bulky and awkwardly shaped, making them harder to package properly. Wrap them as snugly as possible, and use two layers of protection (like plastic wrap or foil plus a freezer bag) if the item will be stored for several months or more.

Prevent freezer burn by wrapping baked goods in a layer of plastic wrap or aluminum foil before putting them in a freezer bag.

FREEZING LOAF CAKES & QUICK BREADS

I prefer to freeze loaf cakes and quick breads whole or cut in half. The larger the portion, the longer it will keep with better quality. Whole loaves wrap up tightly and when stored properly can keep for 6 months. For my small household, I usually cut the loaf in half and freeze the two portions separately. Half a loaf is a nice amount for two people and is still very freezer friendly.

If you wish to freeze individual slices, be sure to consume them quickly, within 1 month. Flash freeze slices on a parchment paper-lined pan, then transfer them to a freezer bag for storage. The browned outer crust of a loaf cake seems to protect it in the freezer, and when cut into slices they lose the benefit of that. A single slice has a lot of exposed surface area and will become freezer burned much faster than whole or half loaves.

FREEZING MUFFINS

Muffins can be piled in a freezer bag without sticking together, so there's no need to flash freeze. To keep them in pristine condition (for example, if you want to gift them), place the muffins on a piece of food-safe cardboard, and then slide it into a freezer bag to give the muffins a sturdy base. Their golden crust helps protect them from freezer burn, so plan on up to 4 months of storage life. Using muffin liners or wrapping the muffins in plastic or aluminum foil before packaging in a freezer bag also increases their shelf life.

FREEZING PANCAKES & WAFFLES

Pancakes and waffles will tend to stick together, so consider separating them with sheets of parchment paper, or flash freeze them before storing. This isn't necessary if you will thaw and use the whole bag at once.

Depending on how well you're able to package them, pancakes and waffles will keep in good quality for 2 to 4 months in the freezer. Square pancakes, like Sheet Pan Blueberry Freezer Pancakes (page 264), are designed to fit snuggly in a quart freezer bag.

FREEZING COOKIES & COOKIE DOUGH

Baked cookies can be frozen in bags or rigid containers. Rigid containers take up a little more space in the freezer, but they better protect the cookies from breaking. I like a rigid container because it feels like opening a little treasure box from the freezer every time I take one out! Cookies resist freezer burn well, and most will keep in the freezer for up to 6 months.

Unbaked cookie dough, like Carrot Cake Cookie Dough (page 270), also freezes very well. Dough can be portioned with a spoon, but the best tool for this job is a spring-loaded scoop. Flash freeze individual balls of dough on a parchment paper-lined pan so they don't stick together, then transfer the balls to a freezer bag once frozen. Cookie dough can also be frozen in special puck-shaped silicone molds or wrapped in plastic wrap or parchment paper in the "slice and bake" style. Cookie dough will keep for up to 6 months.

When baking the cookies, you have the option of thawing the dough first or putting frozen pucks of dough into the oven. If the dough is in thicker scoops, the best results will come from thawing the dough first. I let the dough thaw on the pan for 10 to 15 minutes while the oven is preheating, then flatten them before baking. If the dough was frozen in flat, thinner pieces, it can usually be baked from frozen. How you

A spring-loaded scoop is the best tool for portioning and then flash freezing Carrot Cake Cookie Dough (page 270).

bake the frozen dough ultimately depends on the type of cookie, how big it is, and the finished texture you desire.

Thawing Baked Goods

Most large baked goods will thaw best in the refrigerator overnight. Thinner and smaller items like single muffins will thaw much more quickly than large items like loaf cakes. Avoid defrosting baked goods in the microwave, as they can overheat on the outside before the middle thaws. If you *need the muffin right now*, use the microwave on low power for short bursts.

Pancakes and waffles can be heated from frozen in the toaster or microwave without thawing first. Baked cookies will thaw very fast and don't need to be heated to bring them back to life . . . though I'll never pass up a warm cookie.

RESTORE THE SOFT TEXTURE OF FROZEN BAKED GOODS

Once thawed, gentle heat will soften the crumb of baked goods like muffins and slices of loaf cake. These soft and bready items can feel a bit dry and stiff after being chilled, but they will return to their freshly baked texture after just 15 to 20 seconds in the microwave (or toaster in some cases). It's best to heat smaller portions like slices, rather than a whole loaf. Even if you prefer to eat the item at room temperature, heating it briefly and then letting it cool will improve the texture.

Garlic Cheddar Zucchini Bread (page 286) slices can be warmed in a toaster instead of a microwave after thawing, which will make them soft on the inside with crispy edges on the outside.

Custard Apple Oatmeal Cups

Thanks to the cottage cheese and eggs, these baked oatmeal cups have a creamy texture and taste reminiscent of a lightly sweetened apple custard cake. They also have a decent amount of protein, which means they are a pretty filling breakfast or snack. By shredding the apples, you can pack more of them into the recipe for maximum apple flavor. These cups are best served warm, so give them a spin in the microwave or toaster oven after thawing.

YIELD: 10 CUPS

This recipe can be doubled but requires an additional pan.

- 1 cup cottage cheese
- 2 eggs
- 2 cups lightly packed shredded apples, peeled or unpeeled (about 3 medium)
- ⅓ cup firmly packed brown sugar
- 1 teaspoon vanilla extract
- 1½ cups old-fashioned oats
- 1 teaspoon baking powder
- 1 teaspoon ground cinnamon

1. Combine the cottage cheese and eggs in a blender and blend on high until smooth, about 1 minute.
2. In a large mixing bowl, stir together the cottage cheese mixture, apples, sugar, and vanilla. Stir in the oats, baking powder, and cinnamon, then let the batter sit for 15 minutes to hydrate the oats.
3. Preheat the oven to 350°F (180°C). Line a standard 12-cup muffin pan with 10 paper liners.
4. Divide the batter evenly among the muffin cups, using about ¼ cup batter for each and filling them to the top. Give the pan a light tap on the counter to help nestle the oats into the liquid.
5. Bake for 20 to 25 minutes, until just set and the tops no longer appear wet. Cool for 10 minutes in the pan, then remove them to finish cooling.
6. **TO FREEZE:** Cool completely before freezing. These cups pack best in a freezer bag.

Cinnamon Swirl Banana Bread

Just like a cinnamon roll, this banana bread has an intense swirl of buttery sweet cinnamon running through the top. It really does taste like you crossed banana bread with a cinnamon roll! Banana bread is a notoriously wonderful freezer loaf, and this one is no exception.

YIELD: ONE 9- BY 4-INCH LOAF

This recipe can be doubled to make two loaves.

FOR THE BREAD

- Cooking spray, for greasing the pan
- 1½ cups well-mashed ripe bananas (about 3 large)
- 2 eggs
- ½ cup granulated sugar
- ⅓ cup avocado oil or other neutral oil
- 1 teaspoon vanilla extract
- 1½ cups all-purpose flour or gluten-free flour blend
- 1 teaspoon baking powder
- ½ teaspoon baking soda
- ½ teaspoon sea salt

FOR THE CINNAMON SWIRL

- 2 tablespoons butter, melted
- 2 tablespoons firmly packed brown sugar
- 2 teaspoons ground cinnamon

1. To make the bread, preheat the oven to 350°F (180°C). Grease a 9- by 4-inch loaf pan with cooking spray and line the bottom with a rectangle of parchment paper (don't skip this step).
2. Combine the bananas, eggs, granulated sugar, oil, and vanilla in a large bowl. Using a hand mixer or stand mixer fitted with a paddle attachment, beat together on high speed until the mixture is light and fluffy, about 1 minute. Scrape down the sides and bottom of the bowl with a spatula as needed.
3. Stir together the flour, baking powder, baking soda, and salt in a bowl, then add it to the banana mixture and beat on low speed until just combined.
4. To make the cinnamon swirl, stir together the butter, brown sugar, and cinnamon in a small bowl.
5. Pour the batter into the prepared pan and smooth out the top. Spoon the cinnamon swirl mixture evenly over the top of the batter. Stick a butter knife into the batter halfway to the bottom of the pan and drag it around in a figure-eight swirl pattern. Repeat the swirling a few times.
6. Bake for 70 to 75 minutes, until a toothpick inserted in the center comes out clean. Cool for 15 minutes in the pan, then remove the bread to finish cooling.
7. **TO FREEZE:** Cool completely before freezing. This bread packs best as a whole or half loaf wrapped in foil or plastic wrap, then placed inside a freezer bag.

Double Chocolate Beet Cookies

For beet lovers only . . . which probably goes without saying, since putting them in your cookies would only appeal to true beet fans. The beet flavor pairs so well with earthy dark chocolate, and it's surprisingly mild for the amount of beets stuffed into these uniquely fudgy cookies.

YIELD: ABOUT 20 COOKIES
This recipe can be doubled.

- ½ cup (1 stick) butter, at room temperature
- ¾ cup sugar
- 1 egg
- 1 teaspoon vanilla extract
- 2 cups peeled, shredded raw beets
- 1½ cups all-purpose flour or gluten-free flour blend
- ½ cup Dutch process cocoa powder
- ½ teaspoon baking soda
- ½ teaspoon sea salt
- ¾ cup dark chocolate chips

1. Preheat the oven to 350°F (180°C). Line a large sheet pan with parchment paper.
2. Combine the butter and sugar in a large bowl. Using a hand mixer or stand mixer fitted with a paddle attachment, beat together on medium-high speed until combined, about 1 minute.
3. Add the egg and vanilla, and continue beating until very light and fluffy, about 2 minutes. Add the beets and continue beating until incorporated, about 15 seconds. Scrape down the sides and bottom of the bowl with a spatula as needed.
4. Stir together the flour, cocoa powder, baking soda, and salt in a bowl, then add it to the beet mixture and beat on low speed until just combined; the dough will be very thick and sticky. Add the chocolate chips and beat on low speed until just incorporated.
5. Because the dough is thick, a medium spring-loaded scoop works best for portioning the dough balls. Use about 1½ tablespoons of dough for each cookie. Arrange the dough balls 2 inches apart on the prepared pan.
6. Bake for 12 to 14 minutes, until the cookies are set in the middle. Cool for 5 minutes on the pan, and then remove them to finish cooling.
7. **TO FREEZE:** Cool completely before freezing. These cookies pack well in freezer bags or rigid containers; there is no need to flash freeze, as they won't stick together.

Sheet Pan Blueberry Freezer Pancakes

This is the very practical, utilitarian version of a blueberry pancake. Instead of making each pancake one at a time over the stove, these are baked in a large pan and cut into squares. This gets the job done quickly, fills your freezer with yummy pancakes, and helps preserve your blueberries! They become crispy on the outside and pillowy on the inside when reheated from frozen in the toaster.

YIELD: 8 LARGE PANCAKES

This recipe can be doubled but requires an additional pan.

Cooking spray, for greasing the pan
2½ cups all-purpose flour or gluten-free flour blend
2 teaspoons baking powder
½ teaspoon baking soda
½ teaspoon sea salt
2 cups whole or 2% milk
2 eggs
¼ cup avocado oil or other neutral oil
2 tablespoons maple syrup
1 tablespoon lemon juice, fresh or bottled
2 teaspoons vanilla extract
1½ cups blueberries

1. Preheat the oven to 425°F (220°C). Line the bottom of an 18- by 13-inch rimmed sheet pan with parchment paper, then grease the bottom and sides of the pan with cooking spray.
2. Stir together the flour, baking powder, baking soda, and salt in a large bowl.
3. In a separate bowl, whisk together the milk, eggs, oil, maple syrup, lemon juice, and vanilla. Pour the wet mixture into the dry ingredients and whisk until just combined; don't overmix, or the batter will be lumpy. Use a spatula to scrape the bottom and sides of the bowl as needed.
4. Pour the batter onto the prepared pan and smooth it into an even layer, making sure to get it all the way into the corners. Scatter the blueberries evenly on top, but try to avoid putting them where they touch the edges of the pan.
5. Bake for 15 to 17 minutes, until the edges are golden brown and the center is set.
6. Cool completely, then cut into 8 rectangles. You may cut them smaller, if desired, but this size fits snuggly in a 1-quart freezer bag.
7. **TO FREEZE:** Stack the pancakes together in a freezer bag in whatever quantity you'll use for a meal. If you want to take out individual pancakes, separate them with parchment paper, or flash freeze pancakes on a parchment paper-lined pan, then transfer to a freezer bag for storage. This recipe fits in a 1-gallon freezer bag or two 1-quart freezer bags.
8. **TO SERVE:** Heat the pancakes in the toaster from frozen for one or two cycles, until warm. Alternatively, heat at 50 percent power in a microwave for 30 to 60 seconds.

Blueberry & Peach Steel-Cut Oats

I'm usually drawn to old-fashioned oats because they cook much more quickly, but I love the texture and mouthfeel of the steel-cut type. Making a big batch and freezing in individual portions means I can cook once and enjoy them many times. This recipe uses blueberries and peaches, but feel free to experiment with other fruit combinations; try blackberry and nectarine, strawberry and raspberry, or cherry and plum.

YIELD: 8 CUPS

This recipe can be doubled or tripled.

- 4 cups water
- 2 cups whole milk
- 2 cups steel-cut oats
- 1 teaspoon ground cinnamon
- ½ teaspoon sea salt
- 2 cups blueberries
- 2 cups diced peaches, in ½-inch pieces
- ⅓ cup maple syrup or firmly packed brown sugar
- 2 tablespoons butter
- 1 teaspoon vanilla extract

1. Combine the water and milk in a large pot over medium heat and bring to a gentle boil. Add the oats, cinnamon, and salt. Return to a light simmer and cook, stirring frequently and making sure to scrape the bottom of the pot, until the oats are just tender, about 25 minutes.
2. Stir in the blueberries, peaches, maple syrup, butter, and vanilla. Continue cooking, stirring frequently, until the oats are fully tender and the blueberries just start to burst, about 5 minutes.
3. **TO FREEZE:** Cool completely before freezing. These oats pack best in rigid containers. Alternatively, freeze in ½-cup or 1-cup portions in a silicone mold, then transfer to a freezer bag for storage.

Spiced Carrot Bread

This humble loaf cake is lightly sweet and lightly spiced. It's simple to make but has one unconventional step: The shredded carrots are cooked before being mixed into the batter. This gives the cake a more tender texture and allows it to thrive in the freezer.

YIELD: ONE 9- BY 4-INCH LOAF

This recipe can be doubled to make two loaves.

- 2 cups lightly packed peeled and finely shredded carrots (see Note)
- 1 cup water
- Cooking spray, for greasing the pan
- ⅓ cup avocado oil or other neutral oil
- ½ cup firmly packed brown sugar
- ¼ cup granulated sugar
- 2 eggs
- 1 teaspoon vanilla extract
- 1½ cups all-purpose flour or gluten-free flour blend
- 2 teaspoons ground cinnamon
- 1 teaspoon baking powder
- ½ teaspoon baking soda
- ½ teaspoon ground ginger
- ½ teaspoon sea salt
- ¼ teaspoon grated nutmeg
- ⅓ cup finely chopped walnuts (optional)

1. Combine the carrots and water in a large pot over medium heat. Cook, stirring occasionally, until the carrots are tender, about 10 minutes; there will be a little water left in the bottom of the pot. Remove the pot from the stove and allow it to cool for 15 minutes (otherwise it can cook the eggs when added).
2. Preheat the oven to 350°F (180°C). Grease a 9- by 4-inch loaf pan with cooking spray and line the bottom with a rectangle of parchment paper (don't skip this step).
3. Working in the pot with the carrots, stir in the oil and sugars, then stir in the eggs and vanilla.
4. Stir together the flour, cinnamon, baking powder, baking soda, ginger, salt, and nutmeg in a bowl, then add to the carrot mixture and stir until just combined. Scrape down the sides of the pot with a spatula as needed.
5. Pour the batter into the prepared pan and smooth out the top. Sprinkle the walnuts evenly over the top, if desired.
6. Bake for 55 to 60 minutes, until a toothpick inserted in the center comes out clean. Cool for 15 minutes in the pan, then remove the bread to finish cooling.
7. **TO FREEZE:** Cool completely before freezing. This bread packs best as a whole or half loaf wrapped in foil or plastic wrap, then placed inside a freezer bag.

NOTE: *This bread cooks up and freezes best when the carrots are shredded finely, like on the small side of a box grater.*

Carrot Cake Cookie Dough

These hefty, bakery-style cookies are chewy in the middle, crispy around the edges, and gently spiced. They're reminiscent of carrot cake with big chunks of walnuts and white chocolate chips. When you have heaps of cookie dough in the freezer, a warm cookie is never far away. Bake up one at a time for a personal snack, or make the whole batch for unexpected company.

YIELD: 15 COOKIES

This recipe can be doubled or tripled.

MAKING & FREEZING

- 10 tablespoons (1 stick plus 2 tablespoons) butter
- ½ cup firmly packed brown sugar
- ½ cup granulated sugar
- 1 cup lightly packed peeled and finely shredded carrots (see Note)
- 1 egg
- 1 teaspoon vanilla extract
- 1½ cups all-purpose flour or gluten-free flour blend
- ½ cup old-fashioned oats
- ½ teaspoon baking soda
- ½ teaspoon ground cinnamon
- ½ teaspoon sea salt
- ¼ teaspoon grated nutmeg
- ½ cup white chocolate chips
- ½ cup chopped walnuts
- ¼ cup raisins

NOTE: *This cookie dough freezes and bakes up best when the carrots are shredded finely, like on the small side of a box grater.*

1. Brown the butter by melting it in a medium saucepan over medium heat. Cook, swirling the pan occasionally to stir, until it is golden brown and smells nutty, about 10 minutes; it will pop, crackle, and turn foamy, which is all normal. Immediately pour the browned butter into a heatproof bowl and refrigerate for 20 minutes to cool slightly.
2. Combine the browned butter and sugars in a large bowl. Using a hand mixer or stand mixer fitted with a paddle attachment, beat together on high speed until combined, about 1 minute.
3. Firmly squeeze the shredded carrots to get rid of the excess moisture (I usually do this in 3 to 4 fistfuls). Add the carrots, egg, and vanilla, and continue beating until fluffy, about 1 minute. Scrape down the sides and bottom of the bowl with a spatula as needed.
4. Stir together the flour, oats, baking soda, cinnamon, salt, and nutmeg in a bowl, then add it to the carrot mixture and beat on low speed until just combined. Add the chocolate chips, walnuts, and raisins, and beat on low speed until incorporated.
5. **TO FREEZE:** Line a large sheet pan with parchment paper. Use a large spring-loaded scoop or a measuring cup to drop the dough ¼ cup at a time on the pan. Freeze the cookie dough for 4 hours or overnight, until completely frozen. Transfer to a freezer bag for storage.

SERVING

1. Preheat the oven to 350°F (180°C). Line a large sheet pan with parchment paper.
2. Space balls of frozen dough 2 inches apart on the prepared pan. Allow the dough to thaw while the oven preheats, then flatten the dough into discs about ½ inch thick; these cookies bake up best when the dough is fully thawed before baking.
3. Bake for 14 to 16 minutes, until just starting to brown around the edges. Cool for 5 minutes on the pan, and then remove them to finish cooling.

Sweet Cherry Almond Scone Dough

There's no better time to eat a scone than freshly baked and still warm from the oven. Because of that, I prefer to freeze the unbaked dough. When plump sweet cherries are in season, this is an elegant way to put some up. Take dough out of the freezer and bake one scone at a time or the entire batch—it's up to you.

YIELD: 8 SCONES

Do not double. To increase yield, make consecutive batches.

MAKING & FREEZING

- 2 cups all-purpose flour or gluten-free flour blend
- ⅓ cup sugar
- 2 teaspoons baking powder
- ½ teaspoon sea salt
- ½ cup (1 stick) cold butter
- 1½ cups pitted, diced sweet cherries
- ¼ cup sliced almonds
- ½ cup heavy whipping cream
- 1 teaspoon almond extract
- 1 teaspoon vanilla extract

1. Whisk together the flour, sugar, baking powder, and salt in a large mixing bowl.
2. Use the large side of a box grater to grate the butter into shreds. Stir the butter into the flour mixture until all the shreds are separated and coated with flour. Add the cherries and almonds, and toss until coated with flour.
3. Combine the cream, almond extract, and vanilla in a small bowl, then immediately stir it into the dry ingredients using a fork. Scrape the sides of the bowl with a spatula as needed. Do not overmix; the dough should look a little dry and shaggy.
4. Transfer the dough to a lightly floured cutting board and knead several times until it comes together and any loose crumbs are incorporated; don't overknead. If it seems dry, let it sit for 1 minute to allow the cherries to hydrate more of the flour, then knead again. Form the dough into a circle about 8 inches wide and use a sharp knife to cut it into 8 even wedges.
5. **TO FREEZE:** Flash freeze by placing the dough in a single layer on a parchment paper-lined pan. Freeze for 4 hours or overnight, until completely frozen. Transfer to a freezer bag for storage.

SERVING

1. Preheat the oven to 425°F (220°C). Line a large sheet pan with parchment paper.
2. Space wedges of frozen dough 2 inches apart on the prepared pan (you can bake anywhere from one scone to the entire batch). Allow the dough to thaw for 15 minutes while the oven preheats.
3. Bake for 20 to 25 minutes, until the tops are golden brown.

TIP ❄ These scones are great served plain as they are, but you can dress them up a little by brushing them with cream and sprinkling with more almonds before baking. Or drizzle them with a confectioners' sugar glaze when they come out of the oven.

EKCO
1060
CHICAGO

Green Smoothie Muffins

Blueberries and spinach give these muffins a striking green color, like a deep ocean teal, or perhaps "swamp monster" green if you're feeding them to your littles. You can stuff a lot of spinach into these muffins before you start to taste it, and I love that about them!

YIELD: 12 MUFFINS

Do not double. To increase yield, make consecutive batches.

- 2 eggs
- ¼ cup honey
- ¼ cup avocado oil or other neutral oil
- 2 teaspoons lemon juice, fresh or bottled
- 1 teaspoon vanilla extract
- 1 cup blueberries, fresh or frozen and thawed
- 1 medium banana, cut into pieces
- 1½ cups firmly packed baby spinach
- 2 cups old-fashioned oats
- 1 teaspoon baking soda
- ¼ teaspoon sea salt
- ¼ cup sliced almonds or hemp seeds (optional)

1. Preheat the oven to 350°F (180°C). Line a standard 12-cup muffin pan with paper liners.
2. Place the ingredients in a high-speed blender in this order: eggs, honey, oil, lemon juice, vanilla, blueberries, banana, spinach, oats, baking soda, and salt. Blend on high until smooth, about 1 minute.
3. Divide the batter evenly among the muffin cups, filling each one about two-thirds full. Sprinkle the tops evenly with the sliced almonds, if using.
4. Bake for 15 to 20 minutes, until a toothpick inserted in the center of a muffin comes out clean. Cool for 10 minutes in the pan, then remove them to finish cooling.
5. **TO FREEZE:** Cool completely before freezing. These muffins pack best in freezer bags.

Spinach Tortillas

The vibrant green color of these tortillas comes only from spinach—there's a lot of it packed in here. Homemade tortillas are soft and pliable, and the dough is pleasant to work with once you get the hang of it. I like to make smaller taco-size tortillas, but the size is flexible. Use these wherever you would use regular flour tortillas: for quesadillas, breakfast burritos, or wrap sandwiches.

YIELD: SIXTEEN 7-INCH TORTILLAS
This recipe can be doubled or tripled.

- ¾ cup water
- 4 cups firmly packed baby spinach
- ½ cup avocado oil
- 3 cups all-purpose flour
- 1 teaspoon baking powder
- 1 teaspoon sea salt

1. Pour the water into a medium saucepan and bring it to a simmer over medium heat. Add the spinach, stirring it around continually until it is wilted into the water, about 2 minutes.
2. Transfer the spinach and all of the water to a blender. Add the oil and blend on high until puréed, about 30 seconds.
3. Whisk together the flour, baking powder, and salt in a large mixing bowl. Stir in the spinach mixture, mixing and kneading the dough until it is smooth and all the flour is incorporated. It should be nice to work with; if it's dry and crumbling, add a little more water. If it's sticky, add a little more flour.
4. Wrap the dough in plastic wrap and let it sit at room temperature for 1 hour.
5. Form the dough into a log about 12 inches long and cut it into 16 equal pieces. Take each piece of dough and form it into a smooth ball by rolling it in a circular motion between your palms.
6. Preheat a large cast-iron or nonstick pan over medium heat. While it heats, start rolling out the tortillas. Roll each ball of dough into a circle about 7 inches in diameter and less than ⅛ inch thick. The dough should stick to the counter just enough to help it keep its shape while rolling, but not enough that you can't easily remove it; if it sticks too much, very lightly flour the counter.
7. Carefully peel the dough from the counter and transfer it to the ungreased pan, taking care to lay it in the pan without creases or folds. Cook on the first side until it puffs up and light brown spots develop on the bottom, about 1 minute. Flip and cook until brown on the second side, about 30 seconds longer. Cooking them hot and fast helps keep the tortillas pliable; if they take longer than that to cook, turn up the heat.

8. Transfer the tortilla to a clean kitchen towel and cover with a second towel so that it steams. Repeat until all the tortillas are cooked, piling them up in the towel. Let all the tortillas cool to room temperature in the towel.

9. **TO FREEZE:** These tortillas pack best in freezer bags. They will fit in a 1-gallon freezer bag. There is no need to flash freeze or use parchment paper, as they won't stick together.

10. **TO SERVE:** Heat from frozen or partially thawed in a dry skillet over medium heat until warmed through and pliable, about 30 seconds on each side.

Greens & Ham Breakfast Sandwiches

Wilting the spinach before baking it into the eggs is the key to packing a lot of greens into these sandwiches. From there, feel free to customize however you like. Substitute another type of bread, like bagels or even leftover hamburger buns, use pepper jack instead of cheddar, or bacon instead of ham. These are an absolute treasure to have in the freezer!

YIELD: 6 SANDWICHES

This recipe can be doubled but requires an additional pan.

- Cooking spray, for greasing the pan
- 2 tablespoons butter
- 4 cups firmly packed chopped spinach or Swiss chard leaves (see Note)
- 10 eggs
- ⅓ cup whole or 2% milk
- ½ teaspoon sea salt
- ¼ teaspoon freshly ground black pepper
- 6 English muffins, toasted
- 6 slices medium-sharp cheddar cheese
- 12 slices deli ham

1. Preheat the oven to 350°F (180°C). Grease an 8-inch square baking pan with cooking spray.
2. Heat the butter in a large skillet over medium heat. Add the spinach and sauté until it is just wilted, about 2 minutes. Allow the spinach to cool in the pan for 5 minutes.
3. Combine the eggs, milk, salt, and pepper in a large mixing bowl and whisk until uniform in color. Stir the spinach into the eggs, then pour the mixture into the prepared pan.
4. Bake for 15 to 17 minutes, until just set in the center. Allow the eggs to cool completely and then cut into 6 evenly sized rectangles.
5. To assemble the sandwiches, place a rectangle of egg on the bottom half of an English muffin. Next, add 1 slice of cheese followed by 2 slices of ham. Top with the remaining half of the English muffin. Repeat until all the sandwiches are made.
6. **TO FREEZE:** Wrap each sandwich in plastic wrap and freeze for 4 hours or overnight, until completely frozen. Transfer to a freezer bag for storage.
7. **TO SERVE:** Thaw the sandwiches overnight in the refrigerator and then unwrap and warm in a toaster oven or microwave. If heating from frozen in a microwave, use the defrost or 50 percent power function and keep a close eye on it.

NOTE: *To prepare and measure the spinach or Swiss chard, tear the leaves from the center rib, then chop the leaves into 2- to 3-inch pieces. No need to remove the ribs if using baby greens. Pack them firmly into the measuring cup until you have 4 cups.*

Fresh Peach Streusel Bread

Ripe peaches make this cake light and summery, and it feels like freezing loaves of sunshine! Roasting the peaches in a slow oven before stirring them into the batter concentrates their flavor and makes this cake supremely peachy without being too wet and soggy.

YIELD: ONE 9- BY 4-INCH LOAF

This recipe can be doubled to make two loaves.

FOR THE BREAD

- 3 cups diced peaches, in ¼- to ½-inch pieces (about 5 medium)
- ⅓ cup granulated sugar
- ¼ cup firmly packed brown sugar
- Cooking spray, for greasing the pan
- ⅓ cup avocado oil or other neutral oil
- 2 eggs
- 2 teaspoons vanilla extract
- 1¾ cups all-purpose flour or gluten-free flour blend
- 1½ teaspoons baking powder
- ½ teaspoon baking soda
- ½ teaspoon sea salt

FOR THE STREUSEL

- 3 tablespoons all-purpose flour or gluten-free flour blend
- 2 tablespoons firmly packed brown sugar
- ¼ teaspoon ground cinnamon
- 2 tablespoons butter, melted

1. To make the bread, preheat the oven to 250°F (120°C). Combine the peaches and sugars in a 9-inch square (or similar) baking pan.
2. Bake for 1 hour, then allow the peaches to cool for 30 minutes.
3. Preheat the oven to 350°F (180°C). Grease a 9- by 4-inch loaf pan with cooking spray and line the bottom with a rectangle of parchment paper (don't skip this step).
4. Combine the oil, eggs, and vanilla in a large bowl. Using a hand mixer or stand mixer fitted with a paddle attachment, beat together on high speed until the mixture is combined, about 1 minute. Add the peaches along with all their juices and beat on low until just incorporated, about 15 seconds. Scrape down the sides and bottom of the bowl with a spatula as needed.
5. Stir together the flour, baking powder, baking soda, and salt in a small bowl, then add it to the peach mixture and beat on low speed until just combined.
6. Pour the batter into the prepared pan and smooth out the top.
7. To make the streusel, combine the flour, brown sugar, and cinnamon in a bowl, then stir in the butter; the streusel will be slightly wet. Use your hands to distribute it in small pieces evenly on top of the batter.
8. Bake for 55 to 60 minutes, until a toothpick inserted in the center comes out clean. Cool for 15 minutes in the pan, then remove the bread to finish cooling.
9. **TO FREEZE:** Cool completely before freezing. This bread packs best as a whole or half loaf wrapped in foil or plastic wrap and then placed inside a freezer bag.
10. **TO SERVE:** I like to thaw this particular bread in a bag with the top of the loaf exposed. This prevents the streusel top from getting soggy from condensation.

Spiced Pear Muffins

With all that cinnamon, ginger, and cardamom, these muffins will warm you right up! They use shredded pear instead of chunks, which helps distribute moisture throughout the entire muffin. There's a lot of flavor right underneath the skin of a pear, and the skins soften nicely in the oven, so I don't peel mine.

YIELD: 12 MUFFINS

This recipe can be doubled but requires an additional pan.

- ¼ cup avocado oil or other neutral oil
- 4 tablespoons butter, melted
- ½ cup sugar
- 2 tablespoons honey or sugar
- 2 eggs
- 1 teaspoon vanilla extract
- 3 cups unpeeled, shredded pears (about 4 medium)
- 1⅓ cups all-purpose flour or gluten-free flour blend
- 1 teaspoon baking powder
- ½ teaspoon baking soda
- 2 teaspoons ground cinnamon
- ½ teaspoon ground cardamom
- ½ teaspoon ground ginger
- ½ teaspoon sea salt
- ¼ teaspoon grated nutmeg
- ⅓ cup finely chopped walnuts (optional)

1. Preheat the oven to 350°F (180°C). Line a standard 12-cup muffin pan with paper liners.
2. Combine the oil, butter, sugar, honey, eggs, and vanilla in a large bowl. Using a hand mixer or stand mixer fitted with a paddle attachment, beat together on low speed until combined, about 1 minute. Add the pears and beat on low until just incorporated. Scrape down the sides and bottom of the bowl with a spatula as needed.
3. Stir together the flour, baking powder, baking soda, cinnamon, cardamom, ginger, salt, and nutmeg in a bowl, then add it to the pear mixture and beat on low speed until just combined.
4. Divide the batter evenly among the muffin cups, filling each one about three-quarters full. Sprinkle the tops evenly with the walnuts, if using.
5. Bake for 20 to 25 minutes, until a toothpick inserted in the center of a muffin comes out clean. Cool for 10 minutes in the pan, then remove them to finish cooling.
6. **TO FREEZE:** Cool completely before freezing. These muffins pack best in freezer bags.

Chocolate Chip Zucchini Bread

You can never have enough zucchini bread in the freezer, I always say! (That might be obvious by the plethora of zucchini bread recipes in this book—see also Lemon Poppyseed Zucchini Bread on page 284 and Garlic Cheddar Zucchini Bread on page 286.) Plain zucchini bread can be a little bland, so I use double vanilla, brown sugar, and a hint of cinnamon to enhance the flavor. I am strongly pro-chocolate chips in zucchini bread, but feel free to leave them out for a more classic loaf.

YIELD: ONE 9- BY 4-INCH LOAF

This recipe can be doubled to make two loaves.

Cooking spray, for greasing the pan

2 cups lightly packed finely shredded zucchini (see Note)

½ cup granulated sugar

¼ cup firmly packed brown sugar

⅓ cup avocado oil or other neutral oil

2 eggs

2 teaspoons vanilla extract

1¾ cups all-purpose flour or gluten-free flour blend

1 teaspoon baking powder

1 teaspoon sea salt

¾ teaspoon ground cinnamon

½ teaspoon baking soda

½ cup plus 2 tablespoons mini semisweet chocolate chips

1. Preheat the oven to 350°F (180°C). Grease a 9- by 4-inch loaf pan with cooking spray and line the bottom with a rectangle of parchment paper (don't skip this step).
2. Use a fork to stir together the zucchini, sugars, oil, eggs, and vanilla in a large mixing bowl.
3. Stir together the flour, baking powder, salt, cinnamon, and baking soda in a bowl, then add it to the zucchini mixture and stir until just combined. Scrape down the sides and bottom of the bowl with a spatula as needed. Fold in ½ cup of the chocolate chips.
4. Pour the batter into the prepared pan and smooth out the top. Sprinkle the remaining 2 tablespoons chocolate chips evenly over the top.
5. Bake for 55 to 60 minutes, until a toothpick inserted in the center comes out clean. Cool for 15 minutes in the pan, then remove the bread to finish cooling.
6. **TO FREEZE:** Cool completely and allow the chocolate chips on top to harden before freezing. This bread packs best as a whole or half loaf wrapped in foil or plastic wrap and then placed inside a freezer bag.

NOTE: *This bread cooks up and freezes best when the zucchini is shredded finely, like on the small side of a box grater. Smaller, more tender zucchini work best; if the zucchini is more than 2 inches in diameter, cut it in half and scoop out the soft, spongy center before shredding.*

Lemon Poppyseed Zucchini Bread

I try to grow enough zucchini every year so that I have plenty to eat fresh, enough to preserve, plus a few extra to leave on the neighbors' doorsteps. This bread is a staple in my freezer, and it is one of the most cheerful ways to put up zucchini. This yellow bread with vibrant green flecks and dark blue poppy seeds is a stunner!

YIELD: ONE 9- BY 4-INCH LOAF

This recipe can be doubled to make two loaves.

- Cooking spray, for greasing the pan
- 2 cups lightly packed finely shredded zucchini (see Note)
- ½ cup sugar
- ⅓ cup avocado oil or other neutral oil
- 2 tablespoons honey or sugar
- 2 eggs
- 1 tablespoon finely grated lemon zest
- 1 teaspoon freshly squeezed lemon juice
- 1 teaspoon vanilla extract
- 1¾ cups all-purpose flour or gluten-free flour blend
- 1 tablespoon poppy seeds
- 1 teaspoon baking powder
- 1 teaspoon sea salt
- ½ teaspoon baking soda

1. Preheat the oven to 375°F (190°C). Grease a 9- by 4-inch loaf pan with cooking spray and line the bottom with a rectangle of parchment paper (don't skip this step).
2. Use a fork to stir together the zucchini, sugar, oil, honey, eggs, lemon zest, lemon juice, and vanilla in a large mixing bowl.
3. Stir together the flour, poppy seeds, baking powder, salt, and baking soda in a bowl, then add it to the zucchini mixture and stir until just combined. Scrape down the sides and bottom of the bowl with a spatula as needed.
4. Pour the batter into the prepared pan and smooth out the top.
5. Bake for 55 to 60 minutes, until a toothpick inserted in the center comes out clean. Cool for 15 minutes in the pan, then remove the bread to finish cooling.
6. **TO FREEZE:** Cool completely before freezing. This bread packs best as a whole or half loaf wrapped in foil or plastic wrap and then placed inside a freezer bag.

NOTE: *This bread cooks up and freezes best when the zucchini is shredded finely, like on the small side of a box grater. Smaller, more tender zucchini work best; if the zucchini is more than 2 inches in diameter, cut it in half and scoop out the soft, spongy center before shredding.*

TIP ❄ Try this bread (or any of the zucchini bread recipes here) with yellow summer squash instead of green zucchini. It works just as well, and it gives this particular loaf more of a lemon-yellow color.

Garlic Cheddar Zucchini Bread

This savory bread is stuffed with zucchini and cheddar and brushed with garlic butter when it comes out of the oven. Once thawed, I like to cut this into thick slices and run it through the toaster until the edges turn brown and crispy. I recommend it with eggs for breakfast!

YIELD: ONE 9- BY 4-INCH LOAF

This recipe can be doubled to make two loaves.

FOR THE BREAD

- Cooking spray, for greasing the pan
- 2 cups lightly packed finely shredded zucchini (see Note)
- 1 teaspoon sea salt
- ¼ cup warm water
- 4 tablespoons butter, melted
- 1 egg
- 1 teaspoon apple cider vinegar
- 1¾ cups all-purpose flour or gluten-free flour blend
- 2 teaspoons baking powder
- ½ teaspoon baking soda
- 4 ounces sharp cheddar, shredded

FOR THE TOPPING

- 1 tablespoon butter, melted
- ¼ teaspoon granulated garlic
- ¼ teaspoon granulated onion
- ¼ teaspoon sea salt

1. Preheat the oven to 375°F (190°C). Grease a 9- by 4-inch loaf pan with cooking spray and line the bottom with a rectangle of parchment paper (don't skip this step).
2. To make the bread, stir together the zucchini and salt in a large mixing bowl and allow it to sit for 15 minutes; do not drain. Stir in the water, butter, egg, and vinegar.
3. Stir together the flour, baking powder, baking soda, and cheddar in a bowl, then add it to the zucchini mixture and stir until just combined. Scrape down the sides and bottom of the bowl with a spatula as needed.
4. Pour the batter into the prepared pan and smooth out the top.
5. Bake for 45 to 50 minutes, until a toothpick inserted in the center comes out clean.
6. Immediately make the topping by combining the butter, garlic, onion, and salt in a small bowl. Use a pastry brush to spread the butter mixture evenly on top of the loaf while it's still warm. Cool for 15 minutes in the pan, then remove the bread to finish cooling.
7. **TO FREEZE:** Cool completely before freezing. This bread packs best as a whole or half loaf wrapped in foil or plastic wrap and then placed inside a freezer bag.

NOTE: *This bread cooks up and freezes best when the zucchini is shredded finely, like on the small side of a box grater. Smaller, more tender zucchini work best; if the zucchini is more than 2 inches in diameter, cut it in half and scoop out the soft, spongy center before shredding.*

Strawberry Ricotta Muffins

With ricotta cheese and fresh strawberries, these muffins feel substantial but have a light and bouncy crumb. The ricotta keeps them ultramoist and imparts a flavor that reminds me of strawberry shortcake!

YIELD: 12 MUFFINS

This recipe can be doubled but requires an additional pan.

- 2 cups diced strawberries, in ¼-inch pieces
- ½ cup plus 2 tablespoons sugar
- 3 tablespoons butter, melted
- 2 eggs
- ¾ cup whole-milk ricotta cheese, at room temperature
- 2 teaspoons vanilla extract
- 1 cup all-purpose flour or gluten-free flour blend
- 1 teaspoon baking powder
- ½ teaspoon baking soda
- ¼ teaspoon sea salt

1. Preheat the oven to 400°F (200°C). Line a standard 12-cup muffin pan with paper liners.
2. Combine the strawberries and 2 tablespoons of the sugar in a small bowl. Let sit for 10 minutes, stirring occasionally to help release some of the juices.
3. Combine the butter and remaining ½ cup sugar in a large bowl. Using a hand mixer or stand mixer fitted with a paddle attachment, beat on high speed until combined, about 1 minute. Add the eggs one at a time, beating well after each addition. Add the ricotta and vanilla, and beat until light and creamy, about 1 minute. Finally, add the strawberries and all their juices, and beat on low until just incorporated. Scrape down the sides and bottom of the bowl with a spatula as needed.
4. Stir together the flour, baking powder, baking soda, and salt in a bowl, then add it to the strawberry mixture and beat on low speed until just combined.
5. Distribute the batter evenly among the muffin cups, filling each one just over three-quarters full.
6. Bake for 20 to 25 minutes, until a toothpick inserted in the center of a muffin comes out clean. Cool for 10 minutes in the pan, and then remove the muffins to finish cooling.
7. **TO FREEZE:** Cool completely before freezing. These muffins pack best in freezer bags.

Pumpkin Cake Roll

While I could eat cream cheese buttercream frosting with a spoon, it's even better rolled up in a soft, spongy pumpkin cake. Making a rolled cake takes a little bit of finesse, but you'll be rewarded with a dessert that comes out of the freezer ready to put on a show! Add a sprinkle of confectioners' sugar for extra flair, then slice and serve.

YIELD: 8–10 SERVINGS

This recipe can be doubled but requires an additional pan.

FOR THE CAKE

- 3 eggs
- ⅔ cup roasted pumpkin or winter squash purée (see Note)
- ½ cup granulated sugar
- ¼ cup firmly packed brown sugar
- 1 teaspoon vanilla extract
- ¾ cup all-purpose flour or gluten-free flour blend
- 1 teaspoon ground cinnamon
- 1 teaspoon pumpkin pie spice
- ½ teaspoon baking powder
- ½ teaspoon baking soda
- ¼ teaspoon sea salt

FOR THE FROSTING

- 6 tablespoons butter, at room temperature
- 4 ounces cream cheese, softened
- 1½ cups confectioners' sugar
- 1 teaspoon vanilla extract

1. To make the cake, preheat the oven to 350°F (180°C). Line a 15- by 10-inch jelly roll pan with parchment paper, leaving 2 inches sticking out on each short end (to help lift the cake once it's baked). The easiest way I've found to do this is to crumple up the paper into a ball, then uncrumple it and fit it into the pan; the batter will help hold it down.
2. Combine the eggs, pumpkin purée, sugars, and vanilla in a large bowl and whisk until uniform in color.
3. Stir together the flour, cinnamon, pumpkin pie spice, baking powder, baking soda, and salt in a small bowl, then whisk it into the pumpkin mixture until just combined. Pour the batter into the prepared pan and smooth it into an even layer that fills the entire pan, making sure to spread it all the way into the corners.
4. Bake for 14 to 16 minutes, until set in the center.
5. Immediately lift the cake out of the pan using the parchment paper and transfer it to a heatproof surface, like a wooden cutting board. While the cake is hot, begin rolling it gently and slowly, starting at one of the short ends. Roll the cake and parchment paper together into a tight spiral. The cake will be very hot, so use a towel or oven mitts to assist. Let the cake cool completely while rolled up, about 2 hours.
6. To make the frosting, combine the butter and cream cheese in a large bowl. Using a hand mixer or stand mixer fitted with a paddle attachment, beat together on high speed until smooth, about 1 minute. Add the confectioners' sugar and vanilla, and continue beating until light and fluffy, about 1 minute.

7. Gently unroll the cake, unrolling it only enough that you can spread the frosting on it; don't force the cake flat or you risk cracking it. Spread the frosting on the entire cake in an even layer. The center, tightest part of the spiral will be reluctant to unroll, so I use a butter knife to stuff the frosting in there.

8. Roll the cake back into a spiral, removing the parchment paper from the outside as you go. Take care to roll it tightly so there are no air gaps between the layers of frosting and cake.

9. **TO FREEZE:** Wrap the roll snuggly in plastic wrap, then place it into a 1-gallon freezer bag. Alternatively, cut the roll in half into two smaller rolls before freezing.

10. **TO SERVE:** Thaw the roll for several hours in the refrigerator. Cut into slices and serve.

NOTE: *To make roasted pumpkin or winter squash purée, preheat the oven to 400°F (200°C). Cut the squash in half and place the halves cut-side down on a large sheet pan. Bake for 45 to 75 minutes (depending on size), until the squash is soft, which you can feel by poking the rind. Allow the squash to cool to a safe handling temperature, then use a spoon to scoop out and discard the seeds and guts. Scoop out the flesh and process in a food processor or blender until smooth, about 30 seconds.*

CHAPTER 10

FROZEN TREATS

Stock your freezer with fruity treats for the warm summer months! A harvest of strawberries or peaches can be turned into ice cream starters, and a surplus of bananas or berries can be turned into freezer pops. My favorite thing about transforming fruit into frozen treats is just how adaptable the recipes are.

Fruit-filled ice creams will have the softest, creamiest texture when eaten immediately after being churned, though they can be frozen to a more solid state and eaten later, too.

Making Fruit-Forward Ice Cream or Frozen Custard

Most commercially made ice cream contains artificial or natural flavors, so homemade fruity ice cream will taste slightly different than store-bought. This is because ice cream with fruit is notoriously tricky to make. To get a strong fruit flavor, you need to use a lot of fruit, but since fruit has a high water content, it can cause your ice cream to have ice crystals in it.

Slowly roasting the fruit, like in Strawberry Ice Cream (page 304), helps solve this problem. The roasting process concentrates the berry flavor, allowing the ice cream to taste strongly of fresh strawberries, but it reduces the water content so there are fewer ice crystals. The result is a homemade ice cream with a ton of fruit flavor and a creamy texture.

Step 1: Make the fruit starter. Toss together diced fruit, sugar, and salt, then pour it into a baking pan. Roast the fruit at 250°F (120°C) for about 2 hours. The fruit will release its juices, and those juices will concentrate into a thick syrup (or in the case of Herbal Mint Chip Ice Cream on page 300, fresh mint leaves steep in warmed sugar syrup).

Step 2: Freeze the starter. Once the roasted fruit and its syrupy juices are cooled, this mixture can be frozen as a starter for use later (or churned into ice cream now). It will hold perfectly in the freezer for up to 1 year, and it's a wonderfully convenient way to preserve fruits like strawberries and peaches for making ice cream later.

Step 3: Churn into ice cream. Thaw the starter in the refrigerator overnight, then stir it into your favorite ice cream or frozen custard base before churning. Homemade fruit-forward ice creams will have the best texture when freshly made. There's something about that soft-serve character that is so compelling. And standing over the counter eating spoonfuls straight from the churn is one of my most cherished pastimes!

Step 4: Freeze. Any fresh ice cream leftovers can be spooned into an airtight container and frozen to enjoy later. A longer container with a wider area for scooping works best.

Making No-Churn Sorbet

Sorbet is sweetened fruit with an ice cream-like consistency. It's full-flavored, and the fruit really stands out in this light dessert. Even though it contains no dairy, sorbet is creamy thanks to either the churning and freezing process or a smart no-churn technique. The goal is to have it freeze firmly but remain scoopable, be sweet but not cloying, and have a creamy texture. There's a bit of science involved in nailing the perfect sorbet—but don't worry; we're keeping it simple here.

My favorite technique is the no-churn method. It's straightforward, and my sorbet is always delicious, even when I don't follow a proven recipe. This technique is best suited for fruits that are high in pectin or have a lot of substance, like berries, mangoes, bananas, pears, peaches, and plums. Fruits that are just liquid, like citrus juice or pomegranate, will benefit from a more technical approach.

Instead of churning puréed fresh fruit with a lot of sugar in an ice cream maker, I flash freeze the fruit and whirl it up in a high-speed blender or food processor. Some may call it a cheater method, but blending the fruit in its frozen form is the most foolproof and practical way I've found to make sorbet at home without having to do math. Every sorbet will turn out a little different, but that's the beauty of working with fresh produce.

Liquid sweetener gives no-churn sorbet its scoopable texture, and I prefer honey or agave syrup. I always have honey on hand, plus it adds a floral note that goes so well with fruit. One benefit of the no-churn style is that you don't need quite as much sugar as you would if using an ice cream maker. It can be tempting to leave out the added sugar entirely, but a better option for a no-sugar frozen treat is a homemade freezer pop, since that doesn't require scooping.

Step 1: Cut and freeze the fruit. Cut fruit into 1-inch pieces and flash freeze on a parchment paper-lined pan.

Step 2: Blend the ingredients. Blend the frozen fruit with sweetener and any flavorings, like citrus zest, fresh herbs, florals, or vanilla. For a blender carafe full of fruit, I start with ⅓ to ½ cup honey, depending on the sweetness of the fruit. It will blend up thick, and you'll need to use a tamper to push it down into the blades. It will start to blend more easily as it thaws slightly.

ICE CREAM VS. FROZEN CUSTARD

The difference between ice cream and frozen custard is that custard contains egg yolks, which give it a slightly richer flavor. Ice cream and custard can be made with raw ingredients (like in the Strawberry Ice Cream recipe on page 304) or cooked and chilled before churning for a more traditional approach (like the Peach Frozen Custard recipe on page 303). The starter recipes in this chapter can be used with many different styles of ice cream and custard bases.

Step 3: Taste. An important step in making no-churn sorbet is tasting it for sweetness. Instead of using a specific formula or a precise ratio of fruit to sugar, we're using our taste buds. It should taste very pleasantly sweet, so blend in more sweetener as needed. Sweetness is blunted in the freezer, and it will taste a little less sweet after being frozen solid than it does when freshly made, so I aim for making it a tad oversweet.

Step 4: Freeze. Pour the finished sorbet into an airtight container and freeze immediately (or enjoy it freshly made!). A longer container with a wider area for scooping works best. To serve, allow the sorbet to sit at room temperature for 5 to 10 minutes, until it softens enough to be scoopable.

Making Ice & Freezer Pops

Homemade ice pops (frozen treats on a stick) and freezer pops (frozen treats in thin plastic tubes—or "freezies," as we called them when I was little) are much more forgiving than ice cream or sorbet. Both treats have three main components: fruit, sweetener, and optional creaminess. Because they don't have to be scooped, the finished texture can be firmer and icier. These recipes are adaptable, and most can be frozen in either form, even when the recipe calls for one or the other.

Step 1: Flash freeze the fruit (optional). To create a softer, smoother texture in your ice pops, flash freeze the fruit and blend it frozen, similar to the no-churn sorbet method (see page 295). This creates a lighter consistency that is appreciated in ice pops.

Step 2: Blend the fruit. If using frozen fruit, it will blend up thick, and you'll need to use a tamper to push it down into the blades. It will start to blend more easily as it thaws slightly. I'm usually a proponent of using high-quality fruit no matter what type of preserving you're doing, but this category of recipes gives a little leeway. Ice and freezer pops are a smart place to use fruit that was picked a little underripe or is lacking in flavor. Combining it with other fruits, juice, or extra sweetener will help elevate dull fruit.

Step 3: Add dairy, sweetener, or additional nutrients. Dairy isn't necessary but will add a pleasing creaminess. It can be in the form of heavy cream, half-and-half, buttermilk, yogurt, or canned coconut milk. If the natural sugars in the fruit aren't enough, sweeten to taste with honey, maple syrup, or agave syrup. Protein powder or small amounts of veggies, like zucchini and cauliflower, are virtually undetectable in frozen treats when paired with bold fruits like berries or with chocolate.

Step 4: Freeze. Fill the ice pop molds or freezer pop wrappers and freeze. Ice pop molds are readily available and come in many shapes and sizes. I've used silicone, plastic, and metal styles, and I like them all. If you don't have an ice pop mold, use disposable paper cups. And don't forget the wooden sticks! Ice pops can be a little harder to package securely, so their shelf life is only around 3 months.

Plastic wrappers for freezer pops are available online and at specialty kitchen stores. Look for the zip-top or tie-top styles, and don't be intimidated by having to fill up such a small container—they're quick and easy to use if you have a funnel or a container with a pour spout. Freezer pops are inherently packaged tightly in their own wrappers, so they can keep for up to 1 year without getting freezer burned. Because the next batch isn't dependent on your unmolding and packaging up the previous batch, these are a good solution for stockpiling frozen treats when you need to use up a lot of fruit.

Flash freezing fruit before blending it will give frozen treats like ice pops a lighter, creamier texture.

Cherry Cheesecake Ice Cream Sandwiches

This recipe features a traditional "icebox cake" method. Sweetened whipped cream is folded together with cream cheese and cherries to create a fluffy filling that freezes like ice cream. While I don't prefer this method for an ice cream meant for scooping, it's perfectly suited for sandwiching between two graham crackers!

YIELD: 8 SANDWICHES

This recipe can be doubled or tripled.

- 8 whole graham cracker sheets
- ½ cup heavy whipping cream
- 4 ounces cream cheese, softened
- ½ cup plus 1 tablespoon confectioners' sugar
- 1 teaspoon vanilla extract
- 1 cup pitted, diced sweet cherries

1. Break the graham crackers sheets into individual squares; you should have 16 squares. Place half of the squares on a large sheet pan (these will be the bottom of the sandwiches).
2. Place the cream in a large mixing bowl. Using a hand mixer or stand mixer fitted with a whisk attachment, whisk on high speed until it is whipped into stiff peaks, about 5 minutes. Transfer the whipped cream to a small bowl and set aside.
3. In the same large mixing bowl, combine the cream cheese, sugar, and vanilla. Whisk on high speed until the mixture is light and creamy, about 1 minute. Add the cherries and whisk until they are just broken up and incorporated.
4. Gently fold one-third of the whipped cream into the cherry mixture until just combined, then fold in the remaining two-thirds.
5. Divide the cherry cream evenly among the graham crackers, using about ¼ cup for each; a spring-loaded scoop is helpful. Top each with one of the remaining graham cracker squares, pressing them down gently into the cream.
6. **TO FREEZE:** Freeze immediately for 6 hours or overnight, until completely frozen. Wrap each sandwich in plastic wrap, then place in a freezer bag for storage.

Herbal Mint Chip Ice Cream

Using fresh leaves gives this ice cream a delicate herbal mint flavor and a soft green color. It's a bit different than store-bought versions that typically use mint extract and green food coloring, but I'm certain that fresh mint fans will love it! This starter is simply a potent mint syrup that can be used fresh, or frozen for later when you want to churn ice cream. The chocolate flecks complement the mint perfectly, and melting the chocolate with coconut oil before streaming it into the ice cream ensures the flecks melt in your mouth instead of becoming hard and crunchy once frozen.

YIELD: ABOUT 3 CUPS

This recipe can be doubled or tripled to make additional batches.

MAKING & FREEZING THE STARTER

- ¾ cup sugar
- ½ cup water
- 1 cup very firmly packed fresh mint leaves (see Note)

1. Heat the sugar and water in a small saucepan over medium heat. Cook, stirring continually, until the sugar is just dissolved, about 3 minutes. Remove the pan from the heat and let cool for 10 minutes.
2. Place the mint leaves in a blender and pour the warm sugar water on top of them. Blend on medium until the leaves are broken up into small pieces, about 30 seconds. Allow the mixture to cool to room temperature and steep (I leave it right in the blender), about 30 minutes.
3. Set a fine-mesh sieve over a bowl and pour the pulverized mint mixture into the sieve. Use your fingers to press and squeeze every drop of liquid out of the mint leaves, then discard them.
4. **TO FREEZE:** Because it cooks down into a relatively small amount, this starter packs best in a rigid container. The recipe fits in a 1-cup container.

NOTE: *To measure the mint leaves, pull them from the stems and stuff them into the measuring cup. Hold them down with one hand in the cup while you keep stuffing in more!*

MAKING THE ICE CREAM

- 1 recipe frozen Herbal Mint Chip Ice Cream starter, thawed
- 2 cups heavy whipping cream
- 1 cup whole milk
- 1 teaspoon vanilla extract
- 1 (3-ounce) 70% dark chocolate bar, finely chopped
- 1 teaspoon coconut oil

1. Whisk together the starter, cream, milk, and vanilla in a large bowl. Pour into an ice cream maker and follow the manufacturer's instructions for churning.
2. Immediately combine the chocolate and coconut oil in a small glass bowl and microwave for 90 seconds, or until just melted, stopping every 15 seconds to stir. Let the mixture sit at room temperature to cool slightly while the ice cream churns.
3. During the last few minutes of churning the ice cream, slowly drizzle the chocolate into the ice cream, one spoonful at a time, as it churns. This ice cream is best eaten fresh when it's softer but can also be transferred to a container and frozen.

Bake

Peach Frozen Custard

As a lover of everything peaches and cream, I find that turning glowing, juicy, tree-ripened peaches into an ice cream starter is truly thrilling! Gently roasting the peaches captures and holds their best flavor, even for a long time in the freezer. Then spinning it into ice cream, or frozen custard in this case, is easy.

YIELD: ABOUT 4 CUPS

Do not double. To increase yield, make consecutive batches.

MAKING & FREEZING THE STARTER

- 3 cups diced peaches, in ½-inch pieces
- ⅓ cup granulated sugar
- ⅓ cup firmly packed brown sugar
- ¼ teaspoon sea salt

1. Preheat the oven to 250°F (120°C).
2. Fold together the peaches, sugars, and salt in a large mixing bowl. Transfer the mixture to a 9-inch square (or similar) glass or ceramic baking pan, and use a handheld masher to crush the peaches into smaller pieces.
3. Bake for about 2 hours, stirring with a silicone spatula at the 1-hour mark. The peaches will release a lot of liquid, and that liquid will reduce as they bake. The peaches are done when their liquid has thickened to the consistency of maple syrup.
4. **TO FREEZE:** Cool completely before freezing or churning into ice cream. Because it cooks down into a relatively small amount, this starter packs best in a rigid container; make sure to include the peaches and all their syrup. The recipe fits in a 1½-cup container.

MAKING THE FROZEN CUSTARD

- 1½ cups heavy whipping cream
- 1½ cups whole milk
- 5 egg yolks
- 1 teaspoon vanilla extract
- 1 recipe frozen Peach Frozen Custard starter, thawed

1. Whisk together the cream, milk, egg yolks, and vanilla in a medium saucepan over low heat. Cook, stirring constantly and scraping the bottom and sides of the pan with a silicone spatula, until the mixture thickens enough to coat the back of a spoon and reaches a temperature of 170°F (77°C), about 10 minutes. Do not allow the mixture to boil.
2. Allow the mixture to cool, then chill in the refrigerator for 4 hours or overnight.
3. Stir the starter into the chilled custard base. Pour into an ice cream maker and follow the manufacturer's instructions for churning. This ice cream is best eaten fresh when it's softer but can also be transferred to a container and frozen.

Strawberry Ice Cream

The secret to making strawberry ice cream that has both an abundance of strawberry flavor and a smooth texture is slowly roasting the berries. This concentrates their flavor and reduces iciness in the finished ice cream. Plus it's a great way to preserve the berry harvest and have homemade fresh strawberry ice cream at a moment's notice!

YIELD: ABOUT 4 CUPS

Do not double. To increase yield, make consecutive batches.

MAKING & FREEZING THE STARTER

- 3 cups diced strawberries, in ¼- to ½-inch pieces
- ⅔ cup sugar
- ¼ teaspoon salt

1. Preheat the oven to 250°F (120°C).
2. Combine the strawberries, sugar, and salt in a large bowl, tossing gently to coat. Transfer the mixture to a 9-inch square (or similar) glass or ceramic baking pan and spread the berries in an even layer.
3. Bake for about 2 hours, stirring with a silicone spatula at the 1-hour mark. The strawberries will release a lot of liquid, and that liquid will reduce as the strawberries bake. The strawberries are done when they are deep red and the liquid has thickened to the consistency of maple syrup.
4. **TO FREEZE:** Cool completely before freezing or churning into ice cream. Because it cooks down into a relatively small amount, this starter packs best in a rigid container; make sure to include the strawberries and all their syrup. The recipe fits in a 1½-cup container.

Strawberry Ice Cream starter ready to go into the freezer

MAKING THE ICE CREAM

- 1 recipe frozen Strawberry Ice Cream starter, thawed
- 1½ cups heavy whipping cream
- 1½ cups whole milk
- 2 tablespoons honey
- 1 teaspoon vanilla extract

Whisk together the starter, cream, milk, honey, and vanilla in a large bowl. Pour into an ice cream maker and follow the manufacturer's instructions for churning. This ice cream is best eaten fresh when it's softer but can also be transferred to a container and frozen.

Strawberry Rosé Sorbet

This dazzling combination of rosé wine and summer fruits was inspired by a sorbet from Jeni's Splendid Ice Creams. It was so refreshing and unique that I couldn't stop thinking about it for weeks! The strawberry, watermelon, and pear make a captivating trio when paired with a touch of wine and honey. This will be an instant hit at pool parties, bridal showers, and barbecues.

YIELD: 4–5 CUPS

Do not double. To increase yield, make consecutive batches.

- 4 cups cut strawberries, halved if medium and quartered if large
- 2 cups chopped seedless watermelon, in 1-inch pieces
- 1 large pear, chopped into 1-inch pieces
- 1 cup rosé wine
- ⅓ cup honey, plus more as needed

1. Line a large sheet pan with parchment paper. Place the strawberries, watermelon, and pear in a single layer on the prepared pan. Freeze for 4 hours or overnight, until completely frozen.
2. Combine the frozen fruit, wine, and honey in a high-speed blender. Blend on high until smooth, about 1 minute; the mixture will be thick, and you may need to press it down with a tamper to thoroughly blend. Taste the mixture to gauge its sweetness, and add up to ¼ cup additional honey if it is too tart.
3. **TO FREEZE:** Spoon the sorbet mixture into a storage container and freeze immediately. Freeze for 4 hours or overnight, until frozen solid.
4. **TO SERVE:** Let thaw for 5 to 10 minutes before scooping.

TIP ❄ This versatile recipe can also be frozen in the form of ice pops or freezer pops!

Creamy Lemonade Freezer Pops

A "creamy lemonade" is the ridiculously yummy combination of freshly squeezed lemon juice and sweetened condensed milk. Even more enjoyable in its frozen form, these freezer pops taste like frozen lemon meringue pie! Fresh cream or milk can curdle when combined with that much lemon juice, but thankfully the sweetened condensed milk won't.

YIELD: 8–10 POPS
This recipe can be doubled or tripled.

- 1 (14-ounce) can sweetened condensed milk
- ½ cup confectioners' sugar
- 2 teaspoons very finely grated lemon zest
- ½ teaspoon vanilla extract
- 1 cup freshly squeezed lemon juice
- 1½ cups water

1. Whisk together the milk, sugar, lemon zest, and vanilla in a pitcher with a pour spout or in a mixing bowl. Let this mixture sit for 10 minutes.
2. Whisk in the lemon juice and water until the mixture has a uniform consistency.
3. **TO FREEZE:** Pour the mixture into freezer pop bags, seal, and freeze.

Grape & Yogurt Freezer Pops

The sugary-sweet nature of grapes makes them a wonderful base for frozen treats. They add natural sweetness when blended with other fruit, or they can stand alone—like in these pops. Once the grapes are puréed, I add in a little bit of yogurt to give the pops a tangy creaminess.

YIELD: 4–6 POPS
This recipe can be doubled.

- 4 cups seedless red or purple grapes
- ½ cup plain whole-milk Greek yogurt

1. Place the grapes in a blender and blend on high until smooth, about 1 minute. Add the yogurt and blend again until just combined.
2. **TO FREEZE:** Pour the mixture into freezer pop bags, seal, and freeze.

Raspberry Fudge Ice Pops

We loved eating fudge pudding pops growing up—they fueled our summer days riding bikes and running through sprinklers. This is my homemade version with raspberries. It feels a little more grown-up and now fuels my summer days gardening and preserving.

YIELD: 4–6 POPS

This recipe can be doubled or tripled.

- 1½ cups raspberries, fresh or frozen
- ½ cup water
- ½ cup unsweetened cocoa powder
- ½ cup sugar
- ⅛ teaspoon sea salt
- 1 cup whole milk

1. Combine the raspberries and water in a medium saucepan over medium heat. Bring to a gentle simmer, stirring occasionally, until the raspberries start to break apart and release their juices, about 5 minutes (8 minutes if using frozen berries).
2. Stir together the cocoa powder, sugar, and salt in a bowl, then stir the mixture into the raspberries. Continue cooking, stirring frequently and making sure to scrape the bottom and sides of the pan, until it starts to thicken, about 3 minutes.
3. Turn off the heat and whisk in the milk.
4. **TO FREEZE:** Cool completely before freezing. Spoon into ice pop molds and freeze until firm.

TIP ❄ Instead of raspberries, try these pops with finely chopped strawberries or sweet cherries!

Triple Berry Ice Pops

Strawberries, raspberries, and blueberries are each great on their own, but when put together, they light up your taste buds with layers of sweet and tangy flavors. These pops are a simple combination of dark berries sweetened with apple juice. If your berries are tart and the juice isn't enough to pleasantly sweeten them, feel free to add honey or another liquid sweetener to taste.

YIELD: 6–8 POPS

Do not double. To increase yield, make consecutive batches.

- 2 cups whole strawberries
- 1 cup blueberries
- 1 cup raspberries
- 1½ cups apple juice or cider
- Honey or agave syrup (optional)

1. Flash freeze the strawberries, blueberries, and raspberries by placing them in a single layer on a parchment paper-lined pan. Freeze for 4 hours or overnight, until frozen solid.
2. Combine the fruit and apple juice in a blender, and blend on high until uniform and creamy. The mixture will be thick and may need tamping down as it blends but will thin out as it warms slightly.
3. Because some fruit is more tart than others, taste the mixture and sweeten to taste with honey, if desired.
4. **TO FREEZE:** Immediately pour into ice pop molds and freeze until firm.

Salty Watermelon Ice Pops

Wildly refreshing on a hot day, these ice pops have a base of watermelon with a hint of raspberry and fresh lime. A hefty pinch of sea salt enhances the flavor of the fruits and helps keep you hydrated.

YIELD: 6–8 POPS

Do not double. To increase yield, make consecutive batches.

- 3 cups chopped seedless watermelon, in 1-inch pieces
- ¼ teaspoon lime zest
- Juice from 1 small lime
- ½ cup raspberries, fresh or frozen
- 2 tablespoons honey or agave syrup
- ¼ teaspoon sea salt

1. Flash freeze the watermelon by placing it in a single layer on a parchment paper-lined pan. Freeze for 4 hours or overnight, until frozen solid.
2. Combine the lime zest, lime juice, raspberries, honey, and salt in a blender. Add the frozen watermelon and blend on high until uniform and creamy. The mixture will be thick and need tamping down as it blends but will thin out as it warms slightly.
3. **TO FREEZE:** Immediately pour into ice pop molds and freeze until firm.

Chocolate Peanut Butter Banana Ice Pops

Bananas are naturally sweet, and when whipped in a food processor, they take on a light and airy texture that freezes like ice cream—despite there being no dairy or added sugar! Peanut butter and chocolate flecks make these pops craveable to kids and adults alike, and melting the chocolate with coconut oil before freezing creates chocolate flecks that melt in your mouth.

YIELD: 6–8 POPS

Do not double. To increase yield, make consecutive batches.

- ⅓ cup semisweet chocolate chips
- 1 tablespoon coconut oil
- 4 large bananas (see Note)
- 1 teaspoon vanilla extract
- ¼ cup smooth unsweetened peanut butter

1. Place a piece of parchment paper on a large dinner plate. Combine the chocolate chips and coconut oil in a small glass bowl and microwave for 90 seconds, or until melted, stopping every 15 seconds to stir. Pour the chocolate onto the parchment paper and spread into a thin layer, about an 8-inch circle. Place in the freezer to harden for at least 1 hour.
2. Combine the bananas and vanilla in a food processor and process until they are whipped light and fluffy, about 1 minute. Add the peanut butter and pulse until just incorporated.
3. Transfer the sheet of chocolate to a cutting board and, working quickly, roughly chop it into ¼- to ½-inch pieces. Stir the chocolate pieces into the banana mixture with a spoon.
4. **TO FREEZE:** Immediately spoon into ice pop molds and freeze until firm.

NOTE: *The perfect bananas for this recipe are in the color range from yellow with a tinge of green to fully yellow with just a few brown spots. Do not use fully brown bananas for this recipe.*

INDEX

Page numbers in *italics* indicate photos.

C

D

E

F

G

P

Q

R

S

T

V

W

Y

Z